STEP UP

Texts,
Topics and
Language Activities for Advanced Learners

Edited by John Mc Clintock,
Lennart Peterson and Wolfgang Zydatiß

DIESTERWEG

ISBN 3-425-06644-7

Typographie und Herstellung: Julia Walch, Bad Soden
Satz und Druck: Appl, Wemding
Bindearbeiten: Großbuchbinderei Monheim, Monheim

CONTENTS

TO THE STUDENT

Das Vorwort richtet sich an Sie: die Schüler und Schülerinnen der Einführungsphase der Oberstufe an allgemein- und berufsbildenden Oberschulen. Sie sollten zunächst einmal einen Blick in das Inhaltsverzeichnis dieses Buches werfen. Vielleicht gibt es Themen, die Sie besonders ansprechen: sei es, weil Sie sie bereits behandelt haben und mehr darüber erfahren wollen; sei es, weil sie in Ihrem bisherigen Englischunterricht noch nicht aufgegriffen wurden. Auf jeden Fall sollten Sie mit Ihrem Englischlehrer darüber sprechen, welche Themen bzw. Texte Sie interessieren. Die Texte von STEP UP müssen nicht in der Reihenfolge durchgenommen werden, in der sie hier zusammengestellt sind. Sie sind in sechs Themenkreise gebündelt, die sich den Fragen von Heranwachsenden in der heutigen Welt stellen. Da es sich bei STEP UP um ein Englischlehrwerk handelt, werden diese Fragen natürlich vor allem durch die ‚Brille' der englischsprachigen Welt gesehen:

- Aspekte der Selbstfindung des Einzelnen als Individuum oder als Mitglied einer Gruppe,
- moralische Verantwortung gegenüber den Mitmenschen sowie der Umwelt im allgemeinen,
- aufregende und fragwürdige Entwicklungen in der Technik und den Naturwissenschaften,
- Englisch als Weltsprache, der Stellenwert des Fernsehens und die Schwierigkeiten zwischenmenschlicher Kommunikation,
- Schulwesen und Erziehung aus der Sicht der Jugendlichen und der Erwachsenen und schließlich
- die Begegnung und Auseinandersetzung mit Konfliktsituationen im Alltag.

Die 53 Texte von STEP UP sind etwa zur Hälfte Sachtexte, die anderen sind fiktionale Texte von überwiegend britischen und amerikanischen Autoren. Von 8 Texten findet sich zwar ein Titel im Inhaltsverzeichnis, aber kein Text im Schülerbuch. Bei diesen Texten handelt es sich um spezielle Hörverständnistexte (*Listening comprehension:*), die sich auf der das Schülerbuch begleitenden Kassette befinden. Zu dieser Kassette gehört ein Begleitheft, in dem die Hörtexte abgedruckt sind. Sie sollten Ihren Lehrer oder Ihre Lehrerin unbedingt auf den Einsatz der Kassette ansprechen, denn die systematische Schulung des Hörverstehens ist eine wichtige Voraussetzung für den erfolgreichen Umgang mit der Fremdsprache Englisch. Neben den ‚reinen' Hörverständnistexten finden sich auf der Kassette weitere Aufnahmen von Texten aus dem Schülerbuch ( ). Alle Texte haben einen Aufgabenapparat, der im wesentlichen nach wiederkehrenden Blöcken organisiert ist (selbst wenn die Überschriften dafür zum Teil wechseln): *Comprehension, Text analysis and appreciation, Language practice* und eine Rubrik *Make your point/Over to you*. Das notwendige Hintergrundwissen zu bestimmten Sachthemen wird in den *Info boxes* vermittelt.

Am Ende des Buches finden Sie ein Glossar, d. h. ein Verzeichnis der wichtigsten literarischen und linguistischen Fachbegriffe. Daran anschließend sind noch einmal die englischen Wörter und Wendungen zusammengestellt, die für die Textanalyse und Textinterpretation immer wieder gebraucht werden. Sie sollen Ihnen helfen, Ihren Stil und Ihr Ausdrucksvermögen im Englischen zu verbessern, gerade auch im schriftlichen Bereich. Uns, den Verfassern von STEP UP, geht es vor allem darum, Ihnen das Gefühl und die Sicherheit zu geben, daß Sie auch in sprachlicher Hinsicht im Englischunterricht der Oberstufe weiterkommen. Deshalb enthält dieses Buch Übungen zum Wortschatz, zu den Hauptproblemen der englischen Grammatik und zu ausgewählten Redeabsichten, die Sie im Klassengespräch und in der Kommunikation mit Muttersprachlern unbedingt brauchen. Um die Diskussionen im Klassenzimmer anregender, flüssiger und vielseitiger zu gestalten, sind am Ende des Buches (d. h. im letzten Teil des Anhangs) die wichtigsten und häufigsten Wendungen aufgelistet, die man zum Ausdruck einer Meinungsäußerung bzw. für das Stellen und Beantworten von Fragen braucht.
Nicht zuletzt hoffen wir, Ihnen Freude am Lesen zu bereiten. – Von nun an geht es auf englisch weiter ... *step by step*!

Lennart Peterson
John McClintock
Wolfgang Zydatiß

Lies

Y. Yevtushenko

Telling lies to the young is wrong.
Proving to them that lies are true is wrong.
Telling them that God's in his heaven
and all's well with the world is wrong.
The young know what you mean. The young are people.
Tell them the difficulties can't be counted,
and let them see not only what will be
but see with clarity these present times.
Say obstacles exist they must encounter
sorrow happens, hardship happens.
The hell with it. Who never knew
the price of happiness will not be happy.
Forgive no error you recognise,
it will repeat itself, increase,
and afterwards our pupils
will not forgive in us what we forgave.

2 *prove* [pruːv] (v) show that sth is true, 8 *clarity* ['---] (n) clearness: 'clarity of thinking' 9 *obstacle* ['---] (n) sth standing in the way and stopping progress 9 *encounter* (v) meet 10 *sorrow* unhappiness, sadness. *hardship* ['--] a difficult condition of life, eg. hunger 13 *error* mistake. *recognise* ['rekəgnaɪz] (v) know again, see clearly 14 *increase* [ɪn'kriːs] (v) become bigger

Working with the text

1. What statements are made by the author?
2. Which lines belong together?
3. Find out who is addressed by the author's imperatives (see lines 6–13). What does he expect of the people he talks to?

Make your point

1. What do *you* do or what *could* you do in order to:
   a) gain information
   b) get involved or
   c) improve things in this world?
2. Have another look at ll. 13–16. Being a pupil yourself what do you expect from your teacher?

1 IDENTITY

All our knowledge is,
ourselves to know.
Alexander Pope

Only by knowledge of that which is not Thyself,
shall thyself be learned.
Owen Meredith

Text 1.1

Mother of the Bride
Jacqueline Jules

We found my gown in an hour at the very first shop.
It took two more days and ten more stores to find a dress
For the mother of the bride.
"I need something very special,"
Mother explained,
Her round face glowing,
"My daughter is getting married to a lawyer."
"A junior partner at his firm," she informed,
Swaying her large hips girlishly from side to side
In front of three-way mirrors and tired salesladies
Who nodded wearily and agreed:
Yes, the blue one is too casual and the red one is too short.
The yellow is nice but not special enough for the occasion –
"My daughter is marrying a lawyer."
Mother clapped her hands together and squealed,
"Everything I have ever dreamed for my daughter
Is coming true!"

Two whole days this went on, in ten different stores.
And never once
Did Mother mention
That I was a lawyer too.

bride (n) a woman on her wedding day 1 *gown* [gaʊn] (n) a woman's dress worn in formal situations 2 *store* (n) *(AmE)=(BrE)* shop 6 *glow* (v) here: shine with happiness 7 *lawyer* (n) a person who advises people about laws and represents them in court 9 *sway* (v) move gently from side to side 9 *hip* G: Hüfte 9 *girlish* like a young girl 11 *nod* (v) move one's head up and down 11 *weary* ['wɪərɪ] very tired 12 *casual* ['kæʒjʊəl] (adj) informal 13 *occasion* here: special event 15 *squeal* [skwiːl] (v) make a long high sound

Understanding and interpreting the poem

1. Say in your own words what happened on the days described in the poem.
2. Give a description of the image the bride paints of her mother. What impression do we get of her? Give evidence from the text.
3. Which of the words below describe the mother's behaviour? Give reasons for your choice.
   excited rich proud fussy talkative caring naive easygoing boring conventional silly feminist snobbish childish generous romantic embarrassing superficial communicative
4. Interpret the salesladies' reaction towards the mother's way of behaving in comparison with the daughter's feelings.
5. In what way is the relation between mother and daughter reflected in the language used in this poem?
6. Explain your own reaction towards the last three lines of the poem.
7. What may have been Jaqueline Jules' intention in describing this event in this particular way?
8. Girls, what would *you* have done (if anything) if you had been the bride in this situation?

Follow-up

1. Give an account of a traditional wedding in your country:
   – Where does the wedding ceremony take place?
   – What do the bride and the groom wear?
   – Who else is at the wedding?
   – What happens at the ceremony?
   – Is there a reception or a party after the ceremony?
   – What do people eat and drink? What else happens?
   – Do the bride and groom usually go on a honeymoon?
   The following things or persons are connected with traditional English weddings: *hen party, stag party, the best man, bridesmaids, a veil, a bouquet, buttonholes, confetti, a toast.* – Do you know what they are?
2. Make a list of ten household chores (eg. washing-up, ironing etc.). Who does them in your house? Do you share jobs in a fair way in your family?

Text 1.2

The Secret Diary of Adrian Mole Aged $13\frac{3}{4}$

Sue Townsend

Thursday January 1st

BANK HOLIDAY IN ENGLAND, IRELAND, SCOTLAND AND WALES

These are my New Year's resolutions:

1. I will help the blind across the road.
2. I will hang my trousers up.
3. I will put the sleeves back on my records.
4. I will not start smoking.
5. I will stop squeezing my spots.
6. I will be kind to the dog.
7. I will help the poor and ignorant.
8. After hearing the disgusting noises from downstairs last night, I have also vowed never to drink alcohol.

My father got the dog drunk on cherry brandy at the party last night. If the RSPCA hear about it he could get done. Eight days have gone by since Christmas Day but my mother still hasn't worn the green lurex apron I bought her for Christmas! She will get bathcubes next year.

Just my luck, I've got a spot on my chin for the first day of the New Year!

Friday January 2nd

BANK HOLIDAY IN SCOTLAND. FULL MOON

I felt rotten today. It's my mother's fault for singing 'My Way' at two o'clock in the morning at the top of the stairs. Just my luck to have a mother like her. There is a chance my parents could be alcoholics. Next year I could be in a children's home.

The dog got its own back on my father. It jumped up and knocked down his model ship, then ran into the garden with the rigging tangled in its feet.

diary ['daɪərɪ] (n) a book giving a daily summary of the events in a person's life 6 *sleeve* (n) here: a stiff envelope to keep a gramophone record in 8 *squeeze one's spots* G: Pickel ausdrücken 11 *disgusting* horrible, very unpleasant 14 *RSPCA* Royal Society for the Prevention of Cruelty to Animals 15 *apron* ['eɪprən] something worn over the front part of one's clothes when cooking, washing up etc. 16 *bathcube* ['--] piece of sweet-smelling material for use in a bath 17 *chin* the part of the face below the mouth

My father kept saying, 'Three months' work down the drain', over and over again.

The spot on my chin is getting bigger. It's my mother's fault for not knowing about vitamins.

Saturday January 3rd

I shall go mad through lack of sleep! My father has banned the dog from the house so it barked outside my window all night. Just my luck! My father shouted a swear-word at it. If he's not careful he will get done by the police for obscene language.

I think the spot is a boil. Just my luck to have it where everybody can see it. I pointed out to my mother that I hadn't had any vitamin C today. She said, 'Go and buy an orange, then'. This is typical.

She still hasn't worn the lurex apron.

I will be glad to get back to school.

Sunday January 4th
SECOND AFTER CHRISTMAS

My father has got the flu. I'm not surprised with the diet we get. My mother went out in the rain to get him a vitamin C drink, but as I told her, 'It's too late now'. It's a miracle we don't get scurvy. My mother says she can't see anything on my chin, but this is guilt because of the diet.

The dog has run off because my mother didn't close the gate. I have broken the arm on the stereo. Nobody knows yet, and with a bit of luck my father will be ill for a long time. He is the only one who uses it apart from me. No sign of the apron.

Monday January 5th

The dog hasn't come back yet. It is peaceful without it. My mother rang the police and gave a description of the dog. She made it sound worse than it actually is: straggly hair over its eyes and all that. I really think the police have got better things to do than look for dogs, such as catching murderers. I told my mother this but she still rang them. Serve her right if she was murdered because of the dog.

17 *flu* (n) short form of 'influenza' 19 *scurvy* ['skɜːvɪ] (n) a disease caused by not eating fruit and vegetables; G: Skorbut 20 *guilt* here: the knowledge that one has done wrong

My father is still lazing about in bed. He is supposed to be ill, but I noticed he is still smoking!

Nigel came round today. He has got a tan from his Christmas holiday. I think Nigel will be ill soon from the shock of the cold in England. I think Nigel's parents were wrong to take him abroad.

He hasn't got a single spot yet.

Tuesday January 6th

EPIPHANY. NEW MOON

The dog is in trouble!

It knocked a meter-reader off his bike and messed all the cards up. So now we will all end up in court I expect. A policeman said we must keep the dog under control and asked how long it had been lame. My mother said it wasn't lame, and examined it. There was a tiny model pirate trapped in its left front paw.

The dog was pleased when my mother took the pirate out and it jumped up the policeman's tunic with its muddy paws. My mother fetched a cloth from the kitchen but it had strawberry jam on it where I had wiped the knife, so the tunic was worse than ever. The policeman went then. I'm sure he swore. I could report him for that.

I will look up 'Epiphany' in my new dictionary.

Wednesday January 7th

Nigel came round on his new bike this morning. It has got a water bottle, a milometer, a speedometer, a yellow saddle, and very thin racing wheels. It's wasted on Nigel. He only goes to the shops and back on it. If I had it, I would go all over the country and have an experience.

My spot or boil has reached its peak. Surely it can't get any bigger!

I found a word in my dictionary that describes my father. It is *malingerer*. He is still in bed guzzling vitamin C.

The dog is locked in the coal shed.

Epiphany is something to do with the three wise men. Big deal!

1 *be supposed to be* be believed to be 3 *tan* (n) brown colour on the skin caused by the sun 10 *meter-reader* person who reads the gas or electricity meter 10 *mess up* (v) to put into disorder 11 *in court* (n) G: vor Gericht 13 *trapped* caught 14 *paw* an animal's foot 16 *tunic* the jacket of a uniform 16 *muddy* covered with wet earth 23 *milometer* [maɪ'lɒmɪtə] instrument which tells the number of miles travelled 24 *wasted on* thrown away on 26 *has reached its peak* has got as big as it can get 27 *malingerer* (n) [mə'lɪŋgərə] person who avoids work by saying he is sick 28 *guzzle* (v) to eat or drink eagerly and greedily

Thursday January 8th

Now my mother has got the flu. This means that I have to look after them both. Just my luck!

I have been up and down the stairs all day. I cooked a big dinner for them tonight: two poached eggs with beans, and tinned semolina pudding. (It's a good job I wore the green lurex apron because the poached eggs escaped out of the pan and got all over me.) I nearly said something when I saw they hadn't eaten *any* of it. They can't be that ill. I gave it to the dog in the coal shed. My grandmother is coming tomorrow morning, so I had to clean the burnt saucepans, then take the dog for a walk. It was half-past eleven before I got to bed. No wonder I am short for my age.

I have decided against medicine for a career.

Friday January 9th

It was cough, cough, cough last night. If it wasn't one it was the other. You'd think they'd show some consideration after the hard day I'd had.

My grandma came and was disgusted with the state of the house. I showed her my room which is always neat and tidy and she gave me fifty pence. I showed her all the empty drink bottles in the dustbin and she was disgusted.

My grandma let the dog out of the coal shed. She said my mother was cruel to lock it up. The dog was sick on the kitchen floor. My grandma locked it up again.

She squeezed the spot on my chin. It has made it worse. I told grandma about the green apron and grandma said that she bought my mother a one hundred per cent acrylic cardigan every Christmas and my mother had *never ever* worn one of them!

5 *poached eggs* G: verlorene Eier 5 *tinned* in a tin or can (*tin* = Büchse) 5 *semolina* [ˌseməˈliːnə] G: Weizengries 5/6 *it's a good job (coll.)* it's lucky 8/9 *coal shed* a small building where coal is kept 14 *cough* [kɒf] (v) G: husten 15 *consideration* [-ˌ--ˈ--] (n) careful thought, thoughtful attention 16 *state* (n) condition 21 *be sick* throw up, vomit 25 *cardigan* [ˈ---] G: Strickjacke

Comprehension and appreciation

1. Adrian's diary is full of information (direct and indirect) about the boy himself and his family. What do you learn about the various members of the family? (Adrian, his father and mother, Nigel, Grandma, the dog).

   a) Collect the main information about these people (and the dog) taking down references from the text.

   b) Look at Adrian's relationship with himself, his relatives and the dog, characterizing in a few words his attitude towards them.

2. Consider the following remarks made by Adrian. What makes them funny to the reader? For example:
   a) p. 10, lines 15/16: "... my mother still hasn't worn the green lurex apron I bought her for Christmas." – Reader: 'No wonder, what a horrible present!'
   Now give your own readings of the following quotes:
   b) p. 11, ll. 21–24: "I have broken the arm of the stereo ... He is the only one who uses it apart from me."
   c) p. 11, ll. 30/31: "Serve her right if she was murdered because of the dog."
   d) p. 12, ll. 10/11: (The dog has caused trouble) "So now we will all end up in court I expect."
   e) Try to find (at least) four more examples in the text which can be considered funny.
3. Seeing the text as a whole, what makes it funny? Comment on the humour in Adrian's remarks.

Working with the language

Verbs and particles

There are several examples of verbs and particles in this text; eg. *hang up, put back, run off, come back, come round* etc.

a) Find expressions (or verbs) which mean the same:
- the dog has run off (p. 11, l. 21)
- the dog has (not) come back (p. 11, l. 26)
- Nigel came round (p. 12, l. 3)
- knock sb off a bike (p. 12, l. 10)
- end up in court (p. 12, l. 11)

b) Use the dictionary to find other meanings of the verb + particle phrase. Make up your own sentences with *come round, knock off, take out, let out, run off.*

Assorted prepositions

a) Select one of the following prepositions: *from, of, for, to, under*
- This is an extract ____ a diary.
- Dogs must be kept ____ control.
- Adrian's father is not very kind ____ the dog.
- His mother asked the police to look ____ their dog.
- There was no sign ____ his father.

b) Now make your own selections:
- Murderers usually end up ____ court.
- If you don't behave you might get ____ trouble.
- What did you buy her ____ Christmas?
- Apart ____ grandma everyone was there.
- Adrian wanted to report the policeman ____ swearing.

Used to *or* usually?

Compare these two examples:
- Adrian *used to* throw his trousers on the floor.
- Now he *usually* hangs them up in his wardrobe.

Choose *used to* or *usually* for the following sentences together with the verbs *eat, look, go, keep, squeeze, walk:*

- When Adrian was younger he ____ his spots all the time.
- Now he ____ five or six oranges a day, and his spots have disappeared.
- Nigel ____ to the shops on foot, but now he ____ on his new bike.
- The Moles ____ the dog under control but nowadays it is impossible.
- Adrian's room ____ nice and tidy, which makes his grandma happy.

Questioning techniques

Policeman: *Excuse me, I wonder if you could tell me* who owns this dog?
Adrian's mother: I've no idea.
Adrian: Certainly, officer. We do.
Adrian's mother: Adrian!

When asking questions, British people often use certain introductory expressions, as this is considered polite. This is particularly true when speaking to strangers or people you don't know very well. Here are three typical introductory phrases you should practise:

- *Excuse me, could you tell me* the way to the nearest post office, *please?*
- *Excuse me, I wonder if you could tell me* where the station is, *please?*
  (more polite, useful when asking older people)
- *Excuse me,* {*would* / *do*} *you mind telling me* how much you earn?
  (useful when asking personal questions, eg. about money, age or one's private life, or when asking a favour)

Practise using these expressions. Work in pairs asking the people specified the following questions:

People	Questions
1. a young woman you meet	What's the time?
2. a policeman	What's the way to the Grand Hotel?
3. a 19-year-old bus driver	When does the next bus leave for Oxford?
4. an elderly woman	Is there a bank around here?
5. a middle-aged businessman	Which bus goes to the Houses of Parliament?
6. a middle-aged woman you've just met at a café	Where did you buy that cardigan? It's exactly what I've been looking for.
7. the same woman you're sitting beside at the café	How much did it cost?
8. a student in a pub where you've just met	Will you buy me a drink? I'm not 18 yet.
9. a 35-year-old woman at a party	How many children have you got? I'm doing interviews for the *Guardian*.
10. a teacher you don't know very well	How much do you weigh? I have a bet with one of my classmates.

Using the language

1. Interview: You are interviewing Adrian Mole after the New Year. Work out questions and answers in pairs. You want to know:
   - what New Year's resolutions he has made,
   - what happened to the dog at the New Year's Eve party,
   - why he was disappointed with his mother,
   - what he thinks about the food he gets,
   - why he hopes his father will be ill for a long time,
   - why his mother rang the police and why a policeman came to see them,
   - what he thinks of Nigel's new bike,
   - about his experience of cooking a meal for his parents,
   - about the reasons for his decision *not* to be a doctor,
   - what happened when his grandma came to help.
2. Writing task: Think of a particularly exciting day and write a diary entry for that day.

Spot the mistake!
Owners of 15 dogs released since July were ordered by the Agriculture Ministry to be muzzled. They must be exercised only on a lead and will stay under restriction for six months. *(The Financial Times)*

Text 1.3

She's Leaving Home
The Beatles

The song is from the Beatles' 1967 LP *Sgt. Pepper's Lonely Hearts Club Band.*

Annotations

clutch (v) hold tightly
handkerchief ['hæŋkətʃɪf] piece of material with which you blow your nose
sacrifice (v) give up, usually for some good purpose
snore breathe heavily through the nose and mouth while asleep
dressing gown a long loose coat worn after getting out of bed and before dressing
treat thoughtlessly act badly towards
struggle hard (v) make great efforts
get by manage, survive
deny (v) refuse

Comprehension

1. Read these questions before listening:
   - What time of day is it at the beginning of the song?
   - What's the girl doing?
   - What does she leave behind?
   - How does her mother react?
   - Where's the girl going?
2. Try to find headings for the three verses.

Analysis and appreciation

Answer the following questions relating your observations and comments to the appropriate places in the text:

1. First verse
   a) How about the girl's feelings? What mental and emotional state is she in when she's leaving home?
   b) The girl leaves secretly. What does this tell us about her relationship with her parents and the reasons for her leaving home?
   c) What about the lines in brackets? Consider the parents' attitude towards their daughter.
2. Second verse
   a) What description is given of the girl's parents? How does her mother react?
   b) What can we sum up about their attitude towards life?
3. Third verse
   a) Here we learn something about the girl's new life. How does it differ from her old life?
   b) What can we guess about her attitude towards life now?

Discuss and write

1. Do you understand the girl? Do you think she did the right thing?
2. A few weeks later the girl returns. Take the daughter's point of view and answer her parents' question: 'What on earth did we do that was wrong?'
3. "Running away from home is a solution to family problems." Discuss (yes/no) and suggest alternative ways of reacting.
4. Choose one of the following tasks:
   a) After about a fortnight the girl writes her parents a postcard.
   b) The daughter writes a letter to her best girlfriend.
5. Write a few entries in the girl's diary after she left her parents' home.

In Mortal Danger

As soon as our eldest son was old enough to ride a motorcycle he wanted to buy one. All his friends already had bikes, he said. We lived out in the country, and he needed his own transport to travel to the technical college he was going to that autumn. He was very insistent. In the end we agreed and bought him a small bike. "You won't regret it, Dad," he said, smiling with pride. I looked at him, and then at the bike. "I hope not, Jim."

Many parents will probably recognize the pattern that followed. The bike soon seemed too small, and above all, too slow. It wasn't powerful enough for the journey to college. A larger bike would give an extra margin of safety and, as he would soon be 18, if we were unwilling to help him buy a bigger bike, then he would sign a hire purchase contract and get one anyway.

With a heavy heart we agreed and lent him the money to buy his new bike. But we were worried. As our son was quickly becoming expert at repairs and tuning, friends with motorcycles of all sizes came to our place. We heard, over the weeks, how first one, then another of his friends had minor falls or accidents.

One evening the telephone rang. Our son had crashed on the bend of a country road. The police were there and an ambulance was on its way. We drove hurriedly to the place of the accident. We were in a state of almost blind panic. When we arrived he had already been taken to hospital, unconscious. A policeman showed us his helmet and said, "Without this he would now be dead."

After a few days in hospital Jim returned home. He had a headache which kept him in some pain, and a few cuts and bruises which soon disappeared.

mortal (adj) causing death 4 *be insistent* [-'--] keep asking for something 5 *regret* [-'-] (v) feel sorry about sth you've done 7 *recognize* ['---] (v) to know again 7 *pattern* G: Muster; Schablone 9 *margin* ['--] (n) an amount which is more than is necessary 11 *hire purchase contract* ['pɜːtʃɪs] (n) G: Ratenkauf 12 *lend* (v) give something which you expect to get back again 17 *bend* (n) a curve, where the road is not straight 21 *unconsious* [ʌn'kɒnʃəs] (adj) not awake, as the result of an accident 25 *bruise* [bruːz] (n) a dark mark on the skin

I don't think he knew just how lucky he had been. He explained that he had taken the bend too quickly in the dark. He had learnt a lot from the accident and would be more careful in the future.

About a year and another motorcycle later I spoke to him about getting a cheap, second-hand car. I suggested it would give him more protection in case something happened. He thanked me warmly but said that he wasn't quite ready for a car yet.

Two days later, at 6.45 in the evening, there was a phone call from the Casualty Department of the local hospital. Could we come down at once? Our son had been hit by a car and was very poorly indeed.

When we arrived we were told that he was still alive but that he had very severe injuries to his chest and lungs. They would have to perform a major operation to see if any other vital organs had been damaged. If they didn't, it might be too late to save his life.

At 4 o'clock in the morning we were told that he had survived the operation. If he could live through the next few days, he might be all right.

On the fourth day the consultant who had operated, greeted us with a smile. Our son would survive!

It is now three years since the accident happened. Our son's been driving the second-hand car we bought him when he came out of hospital. He's 21 and lives on his own in the town. He moved out in order to try and cope on his own, he told us.

In fact, we've just found out that one of the reasons for moving was that once again he's riding motorbikes. He tells us he cares for us and that he doesn't want to upset us. But he gets depressed when he isn't able to ride a bike. It's a passion with him that he can't give up. He's not satisfied just driving a car. There's no excitement in it.

We know that it is *his* life and that we can't live it for him. Yet, every time the phone rings we imagine something has happened to him. We can no longer sleep well at night. The sound of ambulance sirens returning from an accident brings back all the horror.

There were about 12 close friends in the motorcycle group as we knew it a few years ago. Of these, two have been killed, and two others are severely handicapped. Others, who have had minor accidents, are riding again.

As parents of a youngster who is addicted to something that seems to be far more dangerous than drugs we are far from being alone.

5 *suggest* [sə'dʒest] (v) G: vorschlagen 9 *casualty department* ['kæʒjʊəltɪ] (n) place in a hospital where injured people are taken for treatment 10 *poorly* (adj) *(infml.)* seriously ill 12 *chest* the upper front part of the body 13 *vital organs* organs that are necessary for life 21 *in order to* with the purpose of 21 *cope* (v) manage 27 *excitement* G: Erregung, Aufregung 35 *be addicted to* (v) G: süchtig sein

Understanding the text

1. While reading the text take down notes on Jim's development.
2. On the basis of these notes make a summary of important events in Jim's development.
3. Comment on the parents' reaction towards their son's 'way of life'. Do you think they have spoiled him?
4. What are the reasons for Jim's decision to ride a motorbike again? Do you think the boy is dishonest or selfish in any way?

Vocabulary work

1. Find the nouns in the story that go with the following adjectives:

a) protective	b) horrible	c) exciting
d) passionate	e) proud	f) young

2. Find the adjectives in the story that are related to the following nouns:

a) care	b) satisfaction	c) depression
d) worry	e) severity	f) insistence

Grammar revision: reported speech

Compare the following sentences in *direct speech* and in *reported speech:*

Direct speech	Reported speech
"I want to buy a motorbike."	*He said he wanted* to buy a motorbike.
"Your son has crashed on his bike."	*We were told* our son *had crashed* on his bike.

Change the sentences below from direct to reported speech observing especially the change of personal pronouns and tenses plus the use of a reporting verb (*say, promise, tell* etc.):

1. "All my friends have motorbikes." – He said ...
2. "You won't regret it." – He promised I ...
3. "This bike isn't powerful enough." – He explained that the ...
4. "I'll sign a hire purchase contract." – He ...
5. "One of Jim's friends has had an accident." – We ...
6. "He's been taken to hospital." – A policeman ...
7. "I took the bend too quickly." – Jim ...
8. "I've learned a lot from the accident." – ...
9. "I'll be more careful in the future." – ...
10. "You should buy a car." – ...

Dialogues

The do-construction in questions and negatives (revision)

Pair work: Complete the following dialogue and read it out aloud afterwards. Use *do, don't, does* or *doesn't* in the appropriate space:

Sal: Hello Jim, ... tell me you've bought a new motorbike.
Jim: Yes. What's wrong? ... you like it?
Sal: No, I ... . What ... your parents say about it?
Jim: They ... know about it yet.

Sal: I . . . believe this . . . . you think they should know?
Jim: I suppose so, but my father . . . understand these things.
Sal: I suppose your mother . . . understand either.
Jim: No, she . . . . They . . . know what it means to me, having a bike.
Sal: And you . . . know what it means to them, . . . you?
Jim: They worry too much. It . . . help to worry.
Sal: It . . . matter to you if they worry or not – you . . . care at all.
Jim: O Sal, you . . . understand either!
Sal: No Jim, I . . . .

Dialogue practice: delaying tactics

Jim's father: You're not thinking of getting a more powerful bike, are you?
Jim: Er . . . that's a good question, Dad . . . mm, I thought you'd ask me that . . . er, well, the fact is . . . yes, I am thinking about it.

Sometimes we are unwilling to give a direct answer to a question. The question may be sensitive, or difficult, or even embarrassing. Consequently we often use "delaying tactics" in order to give us more time to think of a suitable answer.
The following expressions are frequently used in this context:

- *That's a good question . . .*
- *Well, let me see . . .*
- *Ah, I thought you'd ask me that . . .*
- *Well, I'll have to think about that . . .*
- *Oh dear, I haven't really thought about that . . .*

Ask each other questions:
Using the questioning techniques given on page 15 you should ask each other the questions below. The person asked should use "delaying tactics" (one or more) before trying to reply to the questions.

1. Could you lend me a hundred marks?
2. What's your worst habit?
3. Which political party do you support?
4. What do you think of the Federal Chancellor?
5. What's the meaning of life?

Refusing an answer:
Sometimes questions are too sensitive and you may wish to refuse to give an answer. Here are some useful expressions:

- *I really don't wish to discuss that.*
- *I don't think that's any of your business.*
- *I'll tell you some other time.*
- *I don't feel like talking about that just now.*

Try them out in response to the following questions:

1. Do you believe in God?
2. What do you think of Mr/Mrs X (a teacher)?
3. Who are you in love with?
4. *Your own suggestions . . .*

Interviews with a local newspaper

a) Scene-setting: A is a reporter from a local newspaper. B is Jim who is in hospital after his second accident. C is Jim's father or mother respectively.

b) Interview 1: The reporter is in hospital to interview Jim about this second accident. Jim tells him about it, his injuries and why he will continue riding his bike.
c) Interview 2: The reporter is at Jim's home to interview his father and/or mother to get the other side of the argument (the parents' fears and worries about motorbike riding).

What do you think?

1. Can you understand or share Jim's feelings? How would you act now if you were as interested as Jim in motorbikes?
2. As Jim's father or mother would you have done the same?
   What would you advise a parent to do in this kind of situation?
3. Do you know anyone who has got the same passion as Jim? What are his or her reasons for being addicted to riding a motorbike?
4. Tell your classmates about accidents, injuries or even deaths among friends and acquaintances of yours who ride motorbikes.
5. Do you agree with the father's statement that riding motorcycles is far more dangerous than drugs? Give your reasons.

Text 1.5

Feels like Spring
Milton Kaplan

I stop at the corner drugstore for a breakfast of doughnuts and coffee. I eat fast because I'm late, and then I race to the subway station to catch my usual train. I hold on to the strap and pretend I'm reading my newspaper, but I keep glancing at the people crowded in around me. They're the same ones I see every day. They know me and I know them, but we don't smile. We're strangers thrown together accidentally.

I listen to them talking about their troubles and their friends, and I wish I had someone to talk to, someone to break the monotony of the long subway ride.

1 *drugstore* ['--] *(AmE)* a shop which sells not only medicine and toilet articles, but also simple meals and drinks   1 *doughnut* ['dəʊnʌt] (n) G: Krapfen, Berliner   2 *subway* (n) ['--] *(AmE)=(BrE)* underground, *(infml.)* tube   3 *hold on to* (v) keep one's grip on; G: sich an etwas festhalten   3 *strap* a strip of leather or plastic material hanging from the roof   3 *pretend* [-'-] (v) do as if; G: vorgeben   4 *glance* (v) [glɑːns] look quickly   6 *accidentally* [ˌ--'---] (adv) by chance

As we approach the 175th Street Station, I begin to get tense again. She usually gets into the train here. She gets in quietly, not pushing like the rest, and she squeezes into a little space, holding on to an office envelope that probably contains her lunch.

There's a fresh outdoor look about her. She has a sweet face with that scrubbed look that doesn't need powder or rouge. She never wears make-up except for lipstick. And her wavy hair is natural, just a nice light brown. And her eyes are clear blue and warm.

1 *approach* [əˈprəʊtʃ] (v) come close to 1 *get tense* (v) to become nervous 3 *squeeze into* [skwiːz] (v) push oneself into a narrow gap 6 *scrubbed* (adj) cleaned by hard rubbing, G: gescheuert, geschrubbt 7 *wavy* (adj) not straight, with curves

I always like to watch her, but I have to be careful. I'm afraid she'll get sore and move away if she catches me at it, and then I won't have anyone because she's my only friend, even if she doesn't know it. I'm all alone in New York City, and I guess I'm kind of shy and don't make friends easily. The fellows in the bank are all right, but they have their own lives to lead. Besides, I can't ask anyone to come up to a furnished room; so they go their way and I go mine.

The city is too big and noisy – too many people for a fellow who's all by himself. I can't get used to it. I'm used to the quiet of a small New Hampshire farm. But there isn't any future there any more, and I suppose my job in the bank is all right – it's just that I'm kind of lonesome. Sometimes I'm tempted to smile at her, just friendly like, and say something like "Nice morning, isn't it?" But I'm scared. She might freeze up and look straight through me as if I didn't exist, and then the next morning she wouldn't be here any more and I'd have no one to think about.

I keep dreaming that maybe some day I'll get to know her. Like maybe she'd be coming through the door and someone would push her and she'd brush against me and she'd say, "Oh, I beg your pardon", and I'd lift my hat politely and answer, "That's perfectly all right," and I'd smile. Then she'd smile back and say, "Nice day, isn't it?" and I'd say, "Feels like spring." And we wouldn't say anything more, but when she'd be ready to get off at 34th Street, she'd say "Good-bye", and I'd lift my hat again.

The next morning she'd see me and say "Hello", and I'd answer and add something like "Violets ought to be coming up soon" to show her I really know a little about spring. I wouldn't want her to think that I was one of those smooth-talking guys who pick up girls in the subway.

And, after a while, we'd get a little friendlier and start talking about things like the weather or the news, and one day she'd say, "Isn't it funny? Here we are talking every day and we don't even know each other's names." And I'd say, "I'd like you to meet Mr Thomas Pearse," and she'd say very seriously, "How do you do, Mr Pearse. I want you to meet Miss Elizabeth Altemose." The other people around us would smile because people in the subway are so close to you that they can't help sharing a little of your life.

"Thomas," she'd say, as if she was trying out the sound of it.

"What?" I'd say.

"I can't possibly call you Thomas," she'd say. "It's so formal."

"My friends call me Tommy," I'd tell her.

1/2 *get sore* [sɔː] (v) *(AmE)=(BrE)* get angry 6 *furnished room* a rented room with furniture in it 12 *be tempted* (v) feel very strongly like doing something 13 *scared* (adj) frightened 13 *freeze up* (v) here: become cold, distant 18 *brush against* (v) touch lightly when passing 24 *violet* G: Veilchen 26 *smooth-talking guy* [smuːð] G: ein Mann, der andere überreden kann

"And mine call me Betty."

And that's the way it would be. Maybe after a while I'd mention the name of a good movie, and suggest if she weren't doing anything particular ... And she'd say, "Oh, I'd love it." I'd meet her where she worked, and we'd go out for dinner somewhere. I'd ask someone at the bank for the name of a good restaurant. And I would tell her about New Hampshire and maybe mention how lonesome I was, and how shy I was, and she'd be listening with shining eyes, and she'd lean over the table and she'd whisper, "I'm shy too." Then we'd both lean back and smile secretly, and we'd eat without saying much because, after all, what's there to say after that?

We'd go to the movie and we'd sit there, relaxed, enjoying ourselves. Some time during the movie, in an exciting part, maybe her hand would brush against mine and she wouldn't take it away, and I'd hold it, and there I'd be in the middle of eight million people, but I wouldn't be alone any more; I'd be out with my girl.

And afterwards I'd take her home. "I live in New Jersey," she'd say. "It's very nice of you to offer to take me home but I couldn't ask you to make a long trip like that. Don't worry, I'll be all right." But I'd take her arm and say, "Come on. I want to take you home. I like New Jersey." And we'd take the bus across the George Washington Bridge with the Hudson River flowing dark and mysterious below us, and then we'd be in New Jersey, and we'd see the lights of small homes and we'd stop in one of those little towns, and she'd invite me in but I'd say it was too late and then she'd turn to me and say, "Then you must promise to come for dinner on Sunday," and I'd promise and then ...

The train is slowing down. It's the 175th Street Station. There's a big crowd waiting to get in. I look for her, but I don't see her anywhere and my heart sinks. Just then I catch a glimpse of her, away over at the side. She's wearing a new hat with little flowers on it. The door opens and people start pushing in. She's caught in the rush and there's nothing she can do about it. She bangs into me and grabs the strap I'm holding and hangs on to it.

"I beg your pardon," she gasps.

I answer politely, "That's all right."

The doors close and the train begins to move. She has to hold on to my strap; there isn't any other place for her.

"Nice day, isn't it?" she says.

My heart is beating like mad.

"Feels like spring," I say.

2 *mention* (v) say the name of 28 *catch a glimpse of* (v) see for just a moment 31 *bang into* (v) bump into, collide with 32 *gasp* [gɑːsp] (v) say while breathing with difficulty

Comprehension

1. On the left there are some nouns used in the story. Which adjectives on the right describe these nouns? You may want to choose more than one adjective for each noun. You can also use each adjective more than once:

the young man	unfriendly
New York	young
the journey	peaceful
the subway train	crowded
his home	hurried
his breakfast	natural
his job and colleagues	boring
the girl	lonely
	quiet
	self-conscious
	romantic
	unhealthy
	shy
	attractive
	big and noisy
	nervous
	uncommunicative
	monotonous

   Compare what you have chosen with other pupils' selections. Discuss the reasons for your choices.
2. Explain the young man's reasons for coming to New York and his attitude towards living there.
3. Comment on the significance of country life and nature for the young man.
4. At the end (l. 37) the writer says "My heart is beating like mad." Comment on this expression and the particular ending the story has.
5. Find words and phrases in the story that are typical of American English.

Using the language

Contextualized grammar practice: the use of the "past perfect"

The use of the *past perfect* is the appropriate choice in narratives in which *retrospection* takes place. Both the tenses and the personal pronouns are different from the ones used for the events narrated in chronological order. The *inner monologue* is a common technique in narratives to reflect people's thoughts, impressions and associations.

Imagine Tommy's dreams *did* come true. One day he looks back on the events which *happened* exactly as he had *imagined* they would take place:

The girl *looked* exactly the way I *had imagined*. She *had* a sweet face, with that look I *had* always *dreamt* of . . . etc.

Underline all the expressions in the story indicating the narrator's hopes, wishes and fantasies as far as the girl is concerned. Then write about the girl. Add retrospective passages in which the narrator looks back on his hopes and dreams of a time *before* those events. The following verbs will help you: *hope for, dream of, desire, long for, wish/want (very much), miss, expect (to happen), lack, need, imagine, wait for.*

Communicative functions

1. Introducing oneself
   British people usually wait to be introduced to strangers by a common friend or acquaintance. If, however, there is no one there to perform this task for you, the only alternative is to take the initiative and introduce yourself. The following expressions will help you in this kind of situation:

   A: *By the way, my name is . . . .* or *I don't believe we've met (before) . . . My name is . . . .*

   B: *Pleased to meet you. I'm . . .* or *Glad to know you. I'm . . .*

   Now, working in pairs, imagine that you meet each other at a students' party in England. Try to make some initial "small talk" (eg. about the weather, the other people at the party, the food or drink) before you practise introducing yourselves. Don't forget to change roles.
2. Making and responding to an apology
   The girl in the story bumps into the boy and says:
   "I beg your pardon," (to which the boy politely answers)
   "That's all right."
   Here are some other ways of apologizing and responding which you can use in similar situations:
   (On a bus)
   A: Oh, did I stand on your foot? I'm awfully sorry.
   B: Not at all.
   (At the theatre)
   A: I'm very sorry – I seem to have taken your seat.
   B: Oh, never mind. It doesn't really matter.
   (In a shop)
   A: I beg your pardon – I didn't realize it was your turn.
   B: That's ok. I'm in no hurry.

Practise using these expressions, working in pairs. Don't forget to change roles.

Talking points

City life vs. country life

a) Loneliness is just one of the problems that people may face in big cities. Can you think of other disadvantages of city life? What are the advantages of living in a big city?

b) Make a list of arguments for and against city or country life. Where would *you* prefer to live? Explain why.

Text 1.6

The following text is an extract from Willa Appel: *Cults in America. Programmed for Paradise*. New York 1983. Study the info box before you read it.

INFO BOX

THE CHILDREN OF GOD

The cult:
- "Children of God" or "Family of Love"
- founded by David ('Moses') Berg in 1967 in California, USA,
- about 7,000 members of which 1,000 were in Germany in the mid-1970s.

Berg's vision of the world:
- essentially a fundamentalist one,
- the Bible never errs, Berg only interprets God's leadership,
- all conventional religious groups are worthless corruptions of true Christianity,
- the whole western system is corrupt and will eventually be destroyed (=the Antichrist's work),
- Christ will win the battle against the Antichrist.

Cult members:
- they refuse the corrupt values of the western system; only this exclusive elite will survive the troubles which are to come,
- they sacrifice everything to learn the ultimate truth (how to survive the 'end-time' confusion),
- they turn over all their savings and earnings to the group,
- women have the sacred obligation to use sex as a means of recruiting potential converts; prostitution in the name of Jesus turns into divine love,
- during the 1980s group members have increasingly moved to the Third World since North America and Europe are threatened by destruction in the mid-1990s (=Armageddon).

Getting Out

Willa Appel

Alison Peters was 19 years old when she became a member of the Children of God, one of the best known cults in the world.

The following is a description of what happened when, for the first time, she was allowed to leave the commune where she lived with other members of the movement.

Getting permission to visit her parents for Christmas took Alison Peters over a month. During that time she was given literature to read about deprogramming – horrific accounts of torture, of being drugged and put in a mental institution. She was coached about how to behave with her parents: "Soak 'em for all you can get."

She arrived home on Christmas Day. The following day, her parents took her shopping for a present. When they returned home, her brother was waiting with a stranger. Alison thought the man might be a friend of her parents, until he gave her the special handshake of her cult and remarked upon the necklace she was wearing, "You're a member of the Children of God."

"When he said all that, I knew immediately who he was. First I thought, 'This is my ultimate test for God. I'm either going to die or I'm going to be used on this earth in a very special way, for I'm face to face with the Devil in the flesh.'"

Alison had just met Ted Patrick. Patrick, "Black Lightning," as he is sometimes called, was the first of the deprogrammers, and the most controversial. He began his crusade against cults in the early 1970s, after his own son was nearly converted to the Children of God. Patrick investigated the group, and what he found propelled him into action. In consequence, he has been jailed and continually involved in court cases, and his methods have been attacked both by the cults and by those who oppose them. Nonetheless, he continues his campaign against what he considers to be a terrible evil.

Alison: "My initial reaction was to get out of there physically, but there was no way I could do it. The next idea was to do as I had been told – to keep chanting, praying inside, staying in the Kingdom of God – and wait until there was a moment of lax in their security and then make a run for it, conning them in the meantime if necessary. If there was no escape, it meant God wanted to use me in Heaven. And it would be much better to commit suicide than give up the Kingdom of God."

1 *permission* [-'--] (n) agreement giving a person the right to do something 3 *deprogramming* [ˌ--'--] (n) a course of treatment to help a person change his mind about certain beliefs he has; G: 'Entprogrammieren' 3 *account* (n) report, descriptive story 4 *mental institution* hospital for the mentally ill; G: Nervenklinik 4 *coach* [kəʊtʃ] (v) train 5 *soak'em (=soak them) (coll.)* ask them for a lot of money – even though you don't need it 11 *immediately* (adv) [ɪ'miːdjətlɪ] at once, instantly 12 *ultimate* ['---] (adj) greatest, happening at the end 16 *controversial* [ˌkɒntrə'vɜːʃəl] (adj) causing a lot of argument 17 *crusade* [-'-] (n) struggle for an idea or principle 18 *investigate* [-'---] (v) examine the reasons for sth 19 *propel sb into action* (v) drive sb to do something 19 *jail* (v) put in prison, imprison 21 *oppose* (v) be against, to act against 23 *initial* (adj) [ɪ'nɪʃl] first 25 *chant* (v) sing the same thing, over and over again 26 *make a run for it* (v) try to escape 27 *con* (v) *(slang)* trick, deceive 28/29 *commit suicide* (v) ['sjʊɪsaɪd] kill oneself

Most cult members who are forcibly deprogrammed react much as Alison did. Trapped, confronted by the "Devil," they initially want desperately to escape. Deprogrammers expect this. They also expect that their clients will begin to chant and meditate in order to escape internally.

"The cults," Patrick maintains, "completely destroy the mind. They destroy your ability to question things, and in destroying your ability to think, they also destroy your ability to feel. You have no desires, no emotions, you feel no pain, no joy.

"When you deprogram people, you force them to think. The only thing I do is shoot them challenging questions. I hit them with things that they haven't been programmed to respond to. I keep them off balance, and this forces them to begin questioning, to open their minds." But if necessary, Patrick also uses tactics to shock his clients into reacting. He has torn up photographs of the individual's cult leader and cut off the ritual ponytail of Hare Krishna members.

Alison: "Ted looked right at me and said, 'Moses David's real name is David Berg. He's a criminal. If I ever see that sonofabitch, I'll kill him.' And I thought, 'Oh my God, this man is the Devil!'" She rushed out of the room

1 *forcibly* ['---] (adv) by force, against one's will 2 *trapped* caught 2 *desperately* ['----] (adv) very badly, very much 5 *maintain* [-'-] (v) G: behaupten 7 *destroy* (v) ruin, spoil 10 *challenging* demanding; G: herausfordernd 14 *ponytail* (n) hair tied high at the back of the head and falling like a horse's tail 17 *sonofabitch* (n) *(taboo)* G: Scheißkerl

shouting that she'd rather kill herself than listen to Patrick. Her family tried to reason with her, to no avail. "Why are you trying to take away the only happiness I've ever found?" she screamed.

Alison's deprogramming was relatively short and easy. Within twenty minutes of her confrontation with Patrick, she felt herself starting to cry. She'd begin to cry and try to hold it back. When her mother walked over to her, weeping, Alison could no longer restrain her tears. "I remember I just looked at her and started to cry, and she came over and just hugged me, and I remember I pulled away from her, and then I said to myself, 'Okay, that's it. I believe there's a God, and if this is real, God, you're going to show me, and if it isn't, I have faith you're going to get me out of it.' "

After a while she agreed to talk with Patrick, though she continued to fear he might be the Devil. There was, as she expressed it, an internal struggle going on. Some of what Patrick said would penetrate for a moment or two, and then her mind would cloud over again. "All of a sudden I became very silent, and I began to think to myself, 'My God, he may be right, and I may not have to do all these things [for the cult] that I hate so much.' After that realization, everything changed. I looked up and I noticed the bookcases, my father's and mother's and brother's faces. The room solidified, came into focus. There was an actual visual change, and that was so overwhelming, and so profound that I was speechless. I looked up and said, 'Wow!' "

Such an experience during deprogramming, according to Ted Patrick, is not the exception but the rule. "The first time I lay eyes on a person I can tell if his mind is working or not. Then as I begin to question him, I can determine exactly how he has been programmed. From then on, it's all a matter of language. It's talking and knowing what to talk about. I start challenging every statement the person makes. I start moving his mind, slowly, pushing it with questions, and I watch every move that mind makes. I know everything it is going to do, and when I hit on that one certain point that strikes home, I push it. I stay with that question – whether it's about God, the devil, or that person's having rejected his parents. I keep pushing and pushing. Then there'll be a minute, a second, when the mind snaps, when the person realizes he's been lied to by the cult and he just snaps out of it. It's like seeing a person change from a werewolf into a man. It's a beautiful thing, the personality changes, the eyes, the voice. Where they had hate and a blank expression, you can see feeling again."

2 *reason* (v) talk sense 2 *to no avail* (adv) without success 7 *restrain* [-'-] (v) hold back 8 *hug* (v) put one's arms around and hold tightly 14 *penetrate* ['---] (v) force a way in 19 *solidify* [-'---] (v) become solid; G: sich verdichten 19/20 *come into focus* (v) become clearly seen 20 *overwhelming* (adj) powerful, very great 21 *profound* [-'-] (adj) deep; felt very strongly 31 *reject* [-'-] (v) refuse to accept, turn away 35 *blank* (adj) empty

Alison's deprogramming was not over. In fact, the hardest part was yet to come. What had occurred had taken only a few hours. Like her original conversion, her deprogramming was a "snapping" experience, a moment of dissociation in which there was a sudden break with existing reality.

After Alison's breaking moment, she, her family, and Ted Patrick continued talking. She was still disoriented. She did not fully trust Patrick, and her mind would switch back to what she had heard about him while in the cult. She began to "float".

Patrick had warned Alison and her parents about floating. He told her to expect that she would float from time to time, that she would feel she'd made a mistake and would want to go back to the group. She'd start picking up her old habits of chanting and praying. When that happens, he advised, do something, anything to get your mind off it. Hum a song, talk to your parents, but get your mind off it.

"After this rush of feelings," Alison said, "the overriding feeling became fear. I felt like a child again in a lot of ways, I had this void, I was sick and needed to be taken care of and protected. The idea that something could be so powerful to take my mind that way was incredibly frightening."

At the suggestion of Patrick, Alison slept with her parents that night. While she slept, she dreamed of being torn between her parents and the cult. In her dream, she was back with the group, having been deceived by the deprogramming and guilty of listening to the Devil. She awoke in a terrible panic, and realized that she had been chanting, or "praising" in her sleep. "That's something we used to do a lot. We were told that Jesus is watching over you every little minute, and when you wake up in the middle of the night and roll over, that's his way of letting you know he's watching over you. Therefore you should thank him and praise him even while you sleep."

Ted Patrick left the next day and was replaced by Jennifer, an ex-cult member who was to take over Alison's "rehabilitation." Jennifer would be Alison's constant companion for the next two weeks. The only rule in the rehabilitation was that Alison be responsible for all decisions.

On the day of Jennifer's arrival, she and Alison went shopping, as Alison had left the cult with only the clothes on her back. It was her first, painful lesson in decision making. "It took me two hours to decide on one blouse. It had no meaning. I would look at the blouse and think, 'Is this something

3 *snap* (v) break 6 *disoriented* [-'----] having lost one's sense of direction 10 *float* (v) G: schweben; treiben (lassen) 12 *habit* G: Gewohnheit 15 *overriding* (adj) more important than anything else 16 *void* (n) emptiness 18 *incredibly* (adv) [-'---] unbelievably, very surprisingly 21 *deceive* [-'-] (v) trick, cheat 22 *guilty* (adj) G: schuldig 29 *rehabilitation* [,----'--] programme of treatment to train a person to lead a normal life again

that I really like?' I only managed to buy one shirt that day, and I was exhausted by the end of it."

Most of the two weeks spent with Jennifer, though difficult, was a period of tremendous excitement and rediscovery. "I almost felt like I was going through my adolescence in fast pace all over again." She had to relearn how to talk to people, how to relate to her peers, and to sort out her own feelings about sexuality. The hardest time for her was when she was in the shower alone. Then she would panic: "I'd be so frightened, I'd try to sing, and I couldn't even remember the songs."

Coming home was a letdown. She became depressed and confused. She began doubting everything, questioning herself, the meaning of life, and wondering what to do with herself, how to explain to her friends what had happened. Her feelings of loss were compounded by shame and guilt. "I felt ashamed that I as a person, Alison Peters, would do something this stupid. Ed used to try to get me into this group three years ago, and here, before I had even realized it, I was – zip – right into it. Sold, one hundred percent sold."

Alison's depression lasted a month. Then she received a call from Patrick asking her if she was interested in helping him out with deprogrammings. It was a solution. Alison worked for Patrick for six months, and when she returned home this time, the worst of her ordeal was over.

4 *rediscovery* [ˌ--ˈ---] (n) the act of finding things again 5 *adolescence* [ˌædəˈlesəns] (n) period between being a child and a grown person 5 *pace* (n) speed 6 *relate to one's peers* (v) get on with people of one's own age 10 *confused* [-ˈ-] (adj) unable to think clearly 11 *doubt* [daʊt] (v) be uncertain about 13 *loss* (n) here: the pain and damage caused by losing something 13 *be compounded by* (v) be made greater by 13 *shame* (n) G: Scham(gefühl) 13/14 *feel ashamed* (v) feel shame 18 *receive* (v) get 21 *ordeal* [ɔːˈdiːl] (n) terrible experience

Comprehension

Reading for general understanding

Read the text till "... you can see feeling again" (p. 31, l. 36) and answer these questions:

1. Describe the cult's reaction to Alison's request to go home for Christmas.
2. Who did she meet at her parents' home?
3. Consider the phrase: "... what he considers to be a terrible evil" (l. 22 on p. 29). What does it refer to?
4. Name Patrick's reasons for opposing religious cults.
5. Summarize Alison's tactics when trying to resist Ted Patrick after their first meeting.
6. What is Patrick's basic idea in deprogramming people like Alison?
7. "When the mind snaps" (l. 32 on p. 31): which point in a person's development does this expression mark?

Selective reading

1. Read the text carefully again, making detailed notes of the information given in it about:
   a) the *cult,* especially the kind of instructions and programming techniques used by the sect,
   b) *Alison's fate,* especially her life with the sect including attempts and difficulties to free herself from the cult,
   c) the procedure of *deprogramming.*
2. Comment on the changes in Alison's life with regard to her identity.

Asking permission, giving or refusing permission

Alison wanted to go home for Christmas. She might have said:
"Can I go home for Christmas?" – At first the answer was: *"I'm afraid that's not possible."* But, in the end, they said, *„Yes, all right"* or *"Yes, of course."*
Study the following ways to ask for permission, and how to respond:

Asking for permission	Giving permission	Refusing permission
Can/May I come in?	Yes, of course. Yes, all right.	I'm afraid that's not possible (at the moment).
Could I borrow your pen?	Yes, certainly.	I'm sorry, but ... I need it myself.
Do you mind if I smoke?	Not at all. No, please do.	I'd rather you didn't.

Now practise asking for permission and giving or refusing it. Work in pairs and change roles alternately.

1. It's very hot in the room. You want to open a window.
2. You want to borrow your friend's motorbike.
3. You feel thirsty and want a glass of water.
4. You need an English dictionary, and your friend's got one.
5. You don't feel well and need someone to drive you home.
6. The radio is on too loud and you want to turn it down.
7. Your friend is doing some homework and you want to see a special programme on the TV.
8. Your friend has invited you to a party and you want to bring someone else with you.
9. You need to go to the toilet during the lesson. Ask the teacher.

Going beyond the text

1. Do you know of any other sects, their aims and beliefs?
2. Do you happen to know anybody who is or used to be a member of a religious sect? Have you read or heard of particular cases in which people got involved with a cult?
3. Can you imagine reasons for people to feel attracted to cults? Note down suggestions as to what parents, teachers and friends could do to prevent this.

ext 1.7

PROCLAMATION

During the 1960s a revolution was seen to have taken place in American Indian thinking. While some native Americans still took a pessimistic view of their future, others were no longer prepared to accept decisions made by the U. S. Government. They had achieved a new sense of self-awareness which resulted in actions of protest.

One such action took place in November, 1969, when 14 American Indians occupied the island of Alcatraz in San Francisco Bay. The island, which had formerly been a state prison, had been abandoned at the beginning of the 60s. For several years the island was not used. People in San Francisco began discussing what use could be made of it. Some suggested a space museum, others a park. The Indians found that they had a right to it (one treaty states that federal land which is not used can be taken over by the native Americans). They had a specific use for it and wanted to make the public aware of their situation. So they occupied the island and sent out the following Proclamation.

TO THE GREAT WHITE FATHER AND ALL HIS PEOPLE

We, the native Americans, re-claim the land known as Alcatraz Island in the name of all American Indians by right of discovery.

We wish to be fair and honorable in our dealings with the Caucasian inhabitants of this land, and hereby offer the following treaty:

We will purchase said Alcatraz Island for twenty-four dollars (24) in glass beads and red cloth, a precedent set by the white man's purchase of a similar island about 300 years ago. We know that $ 24 in trade goods for these 16 acres is more than was paid when Manhattan Island was sold, but we know that land values have risen over the years. Our offer of $ 1.24 per acre is greater than the 47 cents per acre the white men are now paying the California Indians for their land.

We will give to the inhabitants of this island a portion of the land for their own to be held in trust by the American Indian Affairs and by the bureau of Caucasian Affairs to hold in perpetuity – for as long as the sun shall rise and the rivers go down to the sea. We will further guide the inhab-

3 *achieve* (v) gain 3 *self-awareness* [ˌ--ˈ--] knowledge about oneself 5 *occupy* [ˈɒkjʊpaɪ] (v) here: take over control of 6 *abandon* (v) leave for ever 8 *space* here: G: Weltraum 9 *treaty* (n) agreement between peoples; G: Staatsvertrag 14 *by right of discovery* because we discovered it first 18 *precedent* [ˈ---] (n) G: Präzedenzfall 18 *purchase* [ˈpɜːtʃɪs] (n) *(fml.)* the act of buying 25 *hold in trust* (v) *(law)* keep and control for the advantage of someone else 26 *in perpetuity* [ˌpɜːpɪˈtjuːətɪ] (adv) *(fml.)* for all future time, forever

itants in the proper way of living. We will offer them our religion, our education, our life-ways, in order to help them achieve our level of civilization and thus raise them and all their white brothers up from their savage and unhappy state. We offer this treaty in good faith and wish to be fair and honorable in our dealings with all white men.

We feel that this so-called Alcatraz Island is more than suitable for an Indian reservation, as determined by the white man's own standards. By this we mean that this place resembles most Indian reservations in that:

1. It is isolated from modern facilities, and without adequate means of transportation.
2. It has no fresh running water.
3. It has inadequate sanitation facilities.
4. There are no oil or mineral rights.
5. There is no industry and so unemployment is very great.
6. There are no health care facilities.
7. The soil is rocky and non-productive; and the land does not support game.
8. There are no educational facilities.
9. The population has always exceeded the land base.
10. The population has always been held as prisoners and kept dependent upon others.

Further, it would be fitting and symbolic that ships from all over the world, entering the Golden Gate, would first see Indian land, and thus be reminded of the true history of this nation. This tiny island would be a symbol of the great lands once ruled by free and noble Indians.

What use will we make of this land?

1. A CENTER FOR NATIVE AMERICAN STUDIES
2. AN AMERICAN INDIAN SPIRITUAL CENTER
3. AN INDIAN CENTER OF ECOLOGY
4. A GREAT INDIAN TRAINING SCHOOL
5. AN AMERICAN INDIAN MUSEUM

which will depict our native food and other cultural contributions as well as some of the things the white man has given to the Indians in return for the

1 *proper* (adj) here: right, correct 3 *savage* ['--] (adj) uncivilised 6 *suitable* ['s(j)uːtəbəl] (adj) appropriate; G.: passend, geeignet 8 *resemble* [-'--] (v) look like, to be like 9 *facilities* [-'---] (n) means to do things 16 *soil* (n) earth 16/17 *the land does not support game* wild animals cannot live there (because there is not enough food) 17 *game* (n) wild animals and fish 19 *exceed* [-'-] (v) to be greater than 19 *land base* (n) here: the area of the island 22 *fitting* (adj) *(fml.)* suitable 23 *Golden Gate* stretch of water between San Francisco Bay and the Pacific Ocean 32 *depict* [-'-] (v) *(fml.)* describe (often through pictures) 32 *contribution* [ˌ--'--] (n) gift

land and life he took: disease, alcohol, poverty and cultural decimation (as symbolized by old tin cans, barbed wire, rubber tires, plastic containers, etc.). Part of the museum will remain a dungeon to symbolize both those Indian captives who were incarcerated for challenging white authority, and those who were imprisoned on reservations.

1 *disease* [-'-] (n) illness, sickness 1 *decimation* [ˌ--'--] (n) great destruction 2 *tin can* G: Konservenbüchse, 2 *barbed wire* G: Stacheldraht 2 *tire* (n) *(AmE)*=*(BrE)* *tyre* G: Reifen, 3 *dungeon* ['dʌndʒən] (n) dark prison, usually underground 4 *captive* (n) *(fml.)* prisoner 4 *incarcerate* [ɪn'kɑːsəreɪt] (v) *(fml.)* put in prison

Comprehension: True or false?

If the following statements are wrong, correct them:

1. In the 1960s American Indians began to protest about the way the American government was treating them.
2. The Indians' occupation of Alcatraz was against the law.
3. The Indians offered money for the island.
4. The Indians' offer was just as much as the white men's payment for land belonging to Indians.
5. They promised to treat the white inhabitants of Alcatraz as fairly as white people had treated the native Americans.
6. Alcatraz was unsuitable as an Indian reservation because facilities were inferior to reservations on the mainland.
7. The Indians wanted to create a museum to show the cultural contributions of both the native Americans and the white man.

Analysing the text

1. Consider the following dictionary definitions:
   irony: a use of words which are opposite to one's meaning, usually in order to be amusing or to irritate.
   sarcasm: a use of words which mean the opposite to what is felt, especially in order to be unkind or offensive.
   Can you find examples of these figures of speech in the text?
2. Comment on the purpose of using words and phrases whose meanings are the opposite to what the speaker actually wants to express. Why do the authors of the "Proclamation" use the verbal mask of irony and sarcasm?
3. Find examples of the stylistic devices leading to irony and sarcasm.
4. Explain why the Indians see in this island a symbol of their own life conditions.

Talking points

1. How did different tribes of native Americans use to live (life style, culture, dress etc.)?
2. What do you know about the life of American Indians today? What problems do they face?
3. Think of the way cowboy films usually portray American Indians. Do you feel they give a realistic picture?

Hispanic Americans

On the tape you will hear an interview with three Hispanic high school students in Bayonne, New Jersey. They have all lived in the U. S. for less than five years.

Annotations

adjust [-'-] (v) change oneself so as to fit in, adapt
act American behave like an American
tough [tʌf] *(coll.)* difficult
share (v) have together
prefer [-'-] (v) like one thing more than another
ingredients [-'--] (n) the parts that go together to make a meal or a cake
dish (n) a special sort of cooked food
switch (v) change
resent [rɪ'zent] (v) feel angry or bitter about
(I would) rather (I would) prefer to
date (v) meet (boy and girl) and go out together
rough hard, cruel
smack (v) hit, usually with an open hand
give in to (v) agree to what the other person wants
fault (n) (moral) mistake; G: Schuld
disobedient [ˌ--'--] (adj) not obeying; G: ungehorsam

Comprehension

PART 1

1. Find out what subjects the three high school students are talking about.
2. Listen to the tape again concentrating on the details. Take down notes on your worksheet about what is said about Victor, Beatriz and Carlos.

PART 2

1. Look at the statements below. As you listen, decide who is making the statements – Victor, Beatriz or Carlos?
   a) American girls have too much feedom.
   b) Spanish girls are more interested in serious things than American girls.
   c) American boys take marriage more seriously than Spanish boys.
   d) American teachers are friendly and helpful.
   e) Children should be smacked if they are disobedient.
   f) To be accepted, an immigrant kid has to work twice as hard as American kids.
2. What are the differences of opinion between the three students?
   Do they share basically the same conflict and attitude?

Over to you

1. Find out about the experiences of those amongst you whose parents were not born in Germany.
2. To what extent are they (or do they feel) integrated into your class and school?
3. How could the integration of children and adolescents of nationalities other than German be made easier?

A West Ham Football Fan

Mike is nineteen and lives on a council estate on the northern outskirts of London. The low-rise blocks are a constant target for vandals, who leave behind them smashed windows, broken lifts and graffiti-covered walls. Mike shares a small council flat with his father – his parents are separated. He's been out of work for three months.

1 *council estate* (n) district of houses all built by a town or county 1 *outskirts* ['--] (n) the outer parts of a town or city 2 *target* ['--] (n) any object aimed at; G: Zielscheibe

It's lunchtime on Friday and Mike's still not sure if he's going to the match tomorrow. It depends whether he can find a buyer for the cassette recorder he's carrying around in a plastic bag. It "fell off the back of a lorry", as did the leather jacket he's wearing.

At the moment he's only got 58p in his pocket. The 300 pounds he received when he was made redundant shortly before Christmas vanished long ago and most of his 40 pounds a week dole money goes on rent and food. He owes money too: gambling debts of over 100 pounds (he used to play poker), 75 pounds that his father lent him for his holiday in Spain last year, various loans from friends adding up to about 60 pounds. And, of course, the 50 pound fine imposed a month earlier. He's supposed to pay it off at 5 pounds a week but he's already let himself get behind.

"Soccer madness ... The travelling louts of football." That was the newspaper headline. Mike had gone to Birmingham to watch the game. His team had lost and after the match the furious fans had attacked Birmingham supporters outside the stadium. He spent the weekend in a Birmingham police station. ("Fifteen to a cell – a good laugh it was.") It was the second time he had been arrested.

West Ham – that's his team. All his spare cash goes on following "the Hammers" up and down the country. He and his mates have made the headlines many times: "thugs", "maniacs", "hooligans" – that's what the papers call them. Mike used to cut out the articles and keep them in a handsome wallet ("Twenty-four quid new, real leather.") that he'd "pinched" from a department store and which was, in turn, lifted from his back pocket during a match.

Mike started early: even at primary school he had a reputation as a troublemaker. ("I was definitely a bit naughty, yeah.") He was smoking heavily by the time he was twelve and going with his parents across to the pub. At secondary school he got three O-levels out of six, including a grade A in English Literature. The book he remembers especially is "The Destructors" by Graham Greene. ("You know, the one about these kids an' this old geezer, an' when he goes on holiday, they pull the house apart. Great book.")

6 *be made redundant* [-'--] (v) be told that you are no longer needed in your job 6 *vanish* (v) disappear 7 *dole money (coll.)* money paid by the state to people who have no jobs 8 *owe* (v) G: schulden 8 *gamble* (v) play games of chance for money 8 *debt* [det] (n) a sum of money you owe to someone 10 *loan* [ləʊn] (n) a sum of money which is lent to someone 11 *fine* (n) a sum of money paid as a punishment for breaking the law 11 *impose* [-'-] (v) G: auferlegen 13 *lout* [laʊt] (n) a man or boy with bad manners 19 *spare cash* money that is left 21 *thug* (n) a violent criminal 21 *maniac* ['meɪnɪæk] (n) a mad person 21 *hooligan* (n) a noisy person who makes trouble by fighting and breaking things 22 *handsome* ['--] (adj) attractive, good-looking 23 *quid* [kwɪd] (n) *(BrE) (coll.)* £ 1 23 *pinch* (v) *(coll.)* steal 24 *lift* (v) *(coll.)* steal 26 *have a reputation as* [,--'--] be widely known as 27 *naughty* ['nɔːtɪ] badly behaved, as of children 32 *geezer* (n) *(sl.)* old person, often eccentric

He left school at sixteen and got a job as a clerk. He found the work so boring that he soon left to take up an electrical apprenticeship. That lasted a few months until he was fired for being rude to the foreman. He eventually became an apprentice machine fitter but was made redundant last November.

He lost his job and at the same time lost his girlfriend. Also, that November, his father was forced out of work through ill health. Forced to stay together in the flat all day, they really got on each other's nerves. Mike's father, who did not like him bringing his friends ("those animals") home, finally put him out on the street. The result of all this was a two-week stay in what Mike's friends still do not realise was a psychiatric hospital. He had been about to throw himself under a lorry.

"That'll remain with me for the rest of my life, I reckon," he says. "It's the worst sort of feeling I've ever had. I just didn't care about anything. And being in hospital with a load of geriatrics ... There was one woman in there, she wouldn't eat or speak. She looked so cut up inside, I don't know why. But the others were just sort of simple. A bit slow, nothing to worry about, know what I mean?"

Mike talks to you this way if he's on his own but in the pub next door to West Ham's ground at Upton Park he's no different from the rest. Nazi emblems, Nazi salutes, copies of the National Front magazine "Bulldog" and English rose tattoos have become part of football machismo in recent years. They talk of "niggers", "Pakis", "Yids" and "wogs". There is hatred and mistrust of "foreign" lifestyles and languages. There is anger that "foreigners" have jobs while so many "British" are unemployed.

Part of the ground at Upton Park is reserved for the supporters of visiting teams. That's where Mike and his mates want to be, especially if West Ham are playing another London club. "You've got to get in there. It's prestige. You can't let other supporters walk all over you." The police try to stop them but with little success.

There's never any question of *if* it will happen, only *when*. And when it does, it happens fast, even before the game has started. As violence erupts in one part of the ground, supporters in other parts of the stadium join in. Their weapons are beer cans, bottles, sharpened coins. Immediately blood starts to spring out of mouths, noses and eyes. From all parts of the ground the cry goes up, "Kill, kill, kill."

1 *clerk* [klɑːk] (n) a person who works in an office doing written work 2 *apprenticeship* [-ˈ---] (n) period of training to learn a job 3 *rude* (adj) impolite 14 *a load of (coll.)* a lot of 14 *geriatric* [ˌdʒerɪˈætrɪk] (n) *(derog.)* an elderly person 21 *tattoo* (n) G: Tätowierung 21 *machismo* [məˈtʃɪzməʊ] (n) strong or exaggerated masculinity 21 *recent* (adj) belonging to a short time ago 22 "*Pakis*" *(derog.)* Pakistanis 22 "*Yids*" *(taboo)* Jews 22 *wogs* (n) *(taboo)* foreigners, usually with dark skin 26 *mate* (n) *(coll.)* friend 31 *erupt* [-ˈ-] (v) explode 32 *join in* (v) take part in 33 *weapon* [ˈwepən] (n) an instrument used to hurt people

Mike and his mates escape the police by running on to the pitch and over to another part of the ground, ready to start battle again. "We know what we're doing. It's just like organised crime."

A few weeks later, at home, Mike's eating breakfast cereal out of a plastic bowl that has touched something hot in the past and partly melted. There are a couple of dozen empty beer cans under the table and the sink is full of dirty dishes. It's 7.20 a.m. and Mike is about to leave for work.

He has managed to get the job of assistant caretaker in a local school. He was chosen out of several dozen applicants. "They reckon the unemployment problem round here is the worst since the Depression in the Thirties. So I'm lucky. It's probably the best job I've had. Dead easy really. The only hard bit is cleaning out the toilets at the end of the day. The kids are really good down there as well. Smashing kids. Got a bit of respect for you, know what I mean?"

His job is not well paid but he goes to the pub regularly and sometimes to a night club, or to a party. Most nights, though, he sits in his room listening to the music he used to listen to with Sharon, the girl he met last year on holiday in Spain. He is planning his revenge on her for leaving him – holding an unloaded pistol to her head is the latest idea. "She doesn't know the pain she inflicted on me mentally," he says.

But there's football every Saturday, of course, so he doesn't really complain.

"When you're a kid, you've got wild dreams that you think are going to come true. But once you leave school, you realise – unless you win the pools – that you're never going to do anything special. You're just going to be Mr Ordinary."

1 *pitch* (n) football ground 4 *breakfast cereal* ['sɪərɪəl] (n) G: Getreideflocken, z.B. Cornflakes 5 *melt* (v) become liquid; G: schmelzen 8 *caretaker* ['---] (n) person who looks after a building 9 *applicant* ['---] person who asks for a job 9 *reckon* (v) think 11 *dead easy (coll.)* extremely easy 13 *smashing* (adj.) *(BrE. infml.)* wonderful 18 *revenge* [-'-] (n) G: Rache 19 *latest* (adj) most recent 20 *inflict on* (v) force on; G: zufügen 21/22 *complain* (v) express feelings of annoyance and dissatisfaction; G: sich beschweren 24 *the (football) pools* G: Fußballtoto

Comprehension

Let us assume that certain people mentioned in this text are complaining about other characters from the story. Look at the following complaints and decide who is complaining about what:

1. 'These friends of yours are nothing but animals.'
2. 'It's a miserable place to live. There's nothing for young people except the pub.'
3. 'I don't know why they put me in there, with all those old people. It was really awful.'
4. 'All he ever talked about was football, even on holiday. He was dead boring.'

5. 'He got on my nerves, that's why I threw him out. Nothing but trouble ...'
6. 'He was a bright boy but always causing trouble. A real problem.'
7. 'They're nothing but hooligans. We do our best to control them but they're worse than wild animals, most of them.'
8. 'Why don't you clear this mess up instead of sitting around listening to that rubbish?'
9. 'He's a real misery. Always grumbling at me and criticising.'

Talking about the text

1. What do we learn about Mike's childhood and family life?
2. Consider how far the social conditions he grew up in have led to his present life-style. Are his problems of his own making?
3. Which of the following adjectives would you use to describe Mike? Be prepared to give reasons. Compare your choices with those of other students:

violent	*rebellious*	*soft-hearted*	*misunderstood*	*aggressive*
racist	*irresponsible*	*sensitive*	*dishonest*	*ordinary*
dangerous	*intelligent*	*hard-working*	*stupid*	*special*

   Add any other adjectives which you think can be used to characterize Mike.
4. Consider whether there is a turning point in Mike's biography. Is he all bad, or are there also positive aspects concerning his character and future development?
5. Find differences between the way Mike talks and behaves when he is alone and when he is with his 'mates'. Is this common amongst teenagers? Comment on the importance of the peer group for an adolescent.
6. State some of the examples and causes of football hooliganism as presented in this text.
7. In your opinion, can people like Mike have a feeling of identity without the total identification with their team and/or fan club?

Variety of language use

Accent and dialect

When listening to the tape you will notice that Mike speaks with a particular London accent called *cockney*. Listen to his pronunciation:
– of [t] and [d] after a vowel or
– of the [h] at the beginning of a word.
Identify more examples of this dialect in Mike's speech.

Levels of formality

Mike also uses slang and colloquialisms (as well as phrases which should or must normally *not* be used in everyday language: taboo expressions). Find the informal or colloquial equivalents for the following neutral expressions:

a) to be unemployed/out of work
b) £ 1
c) to steal
d) a friend
e) a wonderful child
f) extremely easy
g) old person

Form your own opinion

1. Is football hooliganism as serious a problem in Germany as in Britain? Describe some incidents you have seen or heard about, and try to explain why they happened.
2. Should the police try to stop rival groups of supporters from fighting, or should they just let them get on with it? Give reasons for your point of view.
3. What do *you* think could be done to cut down violence and vandalism by football hooligans?
4. Suggest suitable punishments for football hooligans.

Text 1.10

Tuning in

1. Make a list of things you think of in connection with football hooliganism.
2. Read the poem now and see how many of your suggestions are in the poem. Is there anything in it that you didn't have on your list?

Hooliganism

Peter Kett

Ten little football fans
Making rude signs,
One swore at a policeman
Then there were nine.

Nine little football fans
Stirring up some hate,
One got bottled
And then there were eight.

Eight little football fans
The youngest was eleven,
He smashed up a buffet
And then there were seven.

3 *swear at* [sweə] (v) to say vulgar words to 6 *stir up* (v) to excite 7 *get bottled* (v) *(slang)* to get drunk 11 *smash up* (v) to break to pieces, to destroy

Seven little football fans
Hitting people with sticks,
One tried to fight alone
Then there were six.

Six little football fans
Playing with a knife,
One got stabbed
And then there were five.

Five little football fans
One fell on the floor,
He got crushed
And then there were four.

Four little football fans
Just like you and me,
One threw a penny at the goalie
Then there were three.

Three little football fans
The other team did boo,
But the fans outnumbered them
Then there were two.

Two little football fans
After all was done
One ran on the football pitch
Then there was one.

One little football fan
Glad his team had won,
Argued with some other fans
Then there was none.

19 *get stabbed* (v) to be struck with a knife 23 *get crushed* (v) G: zerquetscht werden 27 *goalie (infml. BrE) = goalkeeper;* G: Torwart 30 *boo* (v) to express disapproval

Comprehension

Take a closer look at where the ten hooligans have all 'gone' to, either momentarily or forever. Some of these events are not expressed directly (you must read between the lines). Make your own judgements.

2 MORAL RESPONSIBILITY

Morality, said Jesus, is kindness to the weak; morality, said Nietzsche, is the bravery of the strong; morality, said Plato, is the effective harmony of the whole. Probably all three doctrines must be combined to find a perfect ethic; but can we doubt which of the elements is fundamental?
Will Durant: The Story of Philosophy

The Door

Miroslav Holub

Go and open the door.
Maybe outside there's
a tree, or a wood,
a garden,
or a magic city.

Go and open the door.
Maybe a dog's rummaging.
Maybe you'll see a face,
or an eye,
or the picture
of a picture.

Go and open the door.
If there's a fog
it will clear.

Go and open the door.
Even if there's only
the darkness ticking,
even if there's only
the hollow wind,
even if
nothing
is there,
go and open the door.

At least
there'll be
a draught.

7 *rummage* (v) turn things over when looking for sth; G: herumstöbern 13 *fog* (n) a very thick mist; G: dichter Nebel 19 *hollow* (adj) not solid, empty inside 26 *draught* [drɑːft] (n) a current of air in a room

Working on the imagery of the poem

1. Make suggestions as to what "the door" might stand for.
2. What does the poet want the reader to do when he says "*Go and open the door*"?
3. Find out how the poem is structured: stanzas, rhymes, repetitions etc.
4. If you agree that the nouns *tree, wood, garden* and *magic city* in ll. 3–5 are images, what figurative meanings would *you* attach to them in the context of this poem?
5. Try to explain what *rummaging dog, face* and *eye* in ll. 7–9 symbolize.
6. Does the image the *picture of a picture* signify anything for you (ll. 10/11)?
7. Comment on the relationship between the conditional sentence of ll. 13/14 "If there's a fog it will clear" and the imperative "Go and open the door."
8. What if someone opens the door and is confronted with "darkness ticking" (l. 17), a "hollow wind" (l. 19) or even "nothing" (l. 21)?
   Try to identify the common element of the three images expressed by these nouns.
9. Looking at the last three lines of the poem, what advice does the author give to his reader?
10. Miroslav Holub is a Czech poet writing under the repressive conditions of Communist rule in his country. Try to interpret the poem in relation to Czechoslovakia's recent history.

The Peanuts

Comprehension

Put the sentences below into the correct speech bubbles:

a) 'You could never be a doctor! You know why?'
b) 'I love mankind – it's people I can't stand!!'
c) 'You a doctor! Ha! That's a big laugh!'
d) 'Because you don't love mankind, that's why!'

Text analysis

1. What makes the cartoon funny?
2. Would the 'text' work as a funny story, without the pictures? If not, what do the pictures add to the words?
3. Why has the artist chosen to let the girl give us the information in the first picture, rather than the boy? Why doesn't the boy say anything until the last picture?

Joan Baez (*1941) has been at the forefront of American folk singing since 1959. She is not just an entertainer but wholeheartedly involved in fighting pollution, discrimination, violence and war. The following extract from her autobiography *Daybreak* goes back to studies of non-violence at the school she has established at her home in California.

What Would You Do If?

Joan Baez

"OK. You're a pacifist. What would you do if someone were, say, attacking your grandmother?"

"Attacking my poor old grandmother?"

"Yeah. You're in a room with your grandmother and there's this guy about to attack her and you're standing there. What would you do?"

"I'd yell, 'Three cheers for Grandma!' and leave the room."

"No, seriously. Say he had a gun and he was about to shoot her. Would you shoot him first?"

"Do I have a gun?"

"Yes."

"No. I'm a pacifist, I don't have a gun."

"Well, say you do."

"All right. Am I a good shot?"

"Yes."

"I'd shoot the gun out of his hand."

"No, then you're not a good shot."

"I'd be afraid to shoot. Might kill Grandma."

"You haven't answered my question. You're just trying to get out of it . . ."

"I'm really trying to say a couple of things. One is that no one knows what he'll do in a moment of crisis. And that hypothetical questions get hypothetical answers. I'm also hinting that you have made it impossible for me to come out of the situation without having killed one or more people. Then you can say 'Pacifism is a nice idea, but it won't work.' But that's not what bothers me."

5 *be about to* (v) be just going to 6 *yell* (v) shout in a high voice 6 *three cheers* G: ein dreifaches Hurra 13 *be a good shot* (v) be good at shooting a gun 22 *hint* (v) suggest indirectly 25 *bother* (v) annoy or trouble

"What bothers you?"

"Well, you may not like it because it's not hypothetical. It's real. And it makes the assault on Grandma look like a garden party."

"What's that?"

"I'm thinking about how we put people through a training process so they'll find out the really good, efficient ways of killing. You know, how to growl and yell, kill and crawl and jump out of airplanes ... Real organized stuff. Hell, you have to be able to run a bayonet through Grandma's middle."

"That's something entirely different."

"Sure. And don't you see that it's so much harder to look at, because it's real, and it's going on right now? Look. A general sticks a pin into a map. A week later a bunch of young boys are sweating it out in a jungle somewhere, shooting each other's arms and legs off, crying and praying and losing control of their bowels ... Doesn't it seem stupid to you?"

"Well, you're talking about war."

"Yes, I know. Doesn't it seem stupid?"

"What do you do instead, then? Turn the other cheek, I suppose."

"No. Love thine enemy but confront his evil. Love thine enemy. Thou shalt not kill."

"Yeah and look what happened to Him?"

"He grew up."

"They hung him on a damn cross is what happened to him. I don't want to get hung on a damn cross."

"You won't."

"Huh?"

"I said you don't get to choose how you're going to die. Or when. You can only decide how you're going to live. Now."

"Well, I'm not going to go letting everybody step all over me, that's for sure."

"Jesus said, 'Resist not evil'. The pacifist says just the opposite. He says to resist evil with all your heart and with all your mind and body until it has been overcome."

"I don't get it."

3 *assault* [-'-] (n) attack 6 *efficient* [ɪ'fɪʃənt] (adj) working well 7 *growl* [graʊl] (v) make a deep sound in the throat to show anger 7 *crawl* [krɔːl] (v) move slowly on one's hands and knees 8 *stuff* (n) *(infml.)* G: Zeug 8 *bayonet* ['beɪənət] a long knife fixed to the end of a soldier's gun 12 *stick* (v) here: push in 12 *pin* G: Stecknadel 13 *bunch* (n) *(coll.)* group 13 *sweat it out (coll.)* suffer unpleasantness until it ends 15 *bowels* ['baʊlz] (n) G: Eingeweide 18 *turn the other cheek* not react to an insult or attack (biblical reference) 19 *thine* [ðaɪn] *(bibl.)* your; cf. G: dein 29 *step all over* (v) *(coll.)* take advantage of, treat badly 31 *resist* (v) fight against 33 *overcome* (v) defeat

"Organized non-violent resistance. Gandhi. He organized the Indians for non-violent resistance and waged non-violent war against the British until he'd freed India from the British Empire. Not bad for a first try, don't you think?"

"Yeah, fine, but he was dealing with the British, a civilized people. We're not."

"Not a civilized people?"

"Not dealing with a civilized people. You just try some of that stuff on the Russians."

"You mean the Chinese, don't you?"

"Yeah, the Chinese. Try it on the Chinese."

"Oh dear. War was going on long before anybody dreamed up Communism. It's just the latest justification for self-righteousness. The problem isn't Communism. The problem is consensus. There's a consensus that it's OK to kill when your government decides who to kill. If you kill inside the country you get in trouble. If you kill outside the country, right time, right season, latest enemy, you get a medal. There are about one hundred and thirty nation-states, and each of them thinks it's a swell idea to bump off all the rest because he is more important. The pacifist thinks there is only one tribe. Four billion members. They come first. We think killing any member of the family is a dumb idea. We think there are more decent and intelligent ways of settling differences. And man had better start investigating these other possibilities because if he doesn't, then by mistake or by design, he will probably kill off the whole damn race."

"It's human nature to kill."

"Is it?"

"It's natural. Something you can't change."

"If it's natural to kill, why do men have to go into training to learn how? There's violence in human nature, but there's also decency, love, kindness. Man organizes, buys, sells, pushes violence. The non-violenter wants to organize the opposite side. That's all non-violence is – organized love."

"You're crazy."

"No doubt. Would you care to tell me the rest of the world is sane? Tell me that violence has been a great success for the past five thousand years,

1 *resistance* [-'--] (n) opposition, fighting against 2 *wage* (v) conduct, carry on 13 *justification* [ˌ---'--] (n) good reason for doing something 13 *self-righteousness* ['raɪtʃəsnɪs] (n) proud certainty of one's own rightness or goodness 14 *consensus* [-'--] (n) a general agreement 18 *swell* (adj) *(infml. AmE)* great, wonderful 18 *bump off* (v) *(slang)* kill, murder 19 *tribe* (n) racial group with the same language and customs; G: Stamm 21 *dumb* [dʌm] (adj) *(infml. AmE)* stupid 21 *decent* (adj) proper; socially acceptable 22 *settle* (v) bring to an agreement 23 *by design* according to plan 30 *non-violenter* (n) person who does not believe in using violence to solve problems 33 *sane* (adj) not crazy

that the world is in fine shape, that wars have brought peace, understanding, brotherhood, democracy, and freedom to mankind and that killing each other has created an atmosphere of trust and hope. That it's grand for one billion people to live off the other three billion, or that even if it hasn't been smooth going all along, we are now at last beginning to see our way through to a better world for all, as soon as we get a few minor wars out of the way."

"I'm doing OK."

"Consider it a lucky accident."

"I believe I should defend America and all that she stands for. Don't you believe in self-defense?"

"No, that's how the Mafia got started. A little band of people who got together to protect peasants. I'll take Gandhi's non-violent resistance."

"It sounds real nice, but I just don't think it can work."

"You are probably right. We probably don't have enough time. So far we've been a glorious flop. The only thing that's been a worse flop than the organization of non-violence has been the organization of violence."

1 *in fine shape* in good condition 5 *smooth* [smuːð] here: without difficulties 5 *going* (condition of) travel 6 *minor* unimportant, small 9 *consider* (v) think of, regard; G: halten für, erwägen 10 *America and all that she ...* countries are often referred to as if they were female 13 *peasant* ['peznt] (n) poor farmer 16 *glorious* ['---] wonderful, marvellous 16 *flop* (n) failure

Comprehension

General understanding

How is the text structured? Find a heading for each of the paragraphs you have identified.

Detailed understanding

1. How does the pacifist avoid the problem of defending his (or her) grandmother?
2. What situation is the pacifist thinking of that makes "the assault on Grandma look like a garden party" (p. 50, l. 3)?
3. What does "Yeah and look what happened to Him" (p. 50, l. 21) refer to?
4. Why is Gandhi mentioned on page 51, l. 1?
5. What does the pacifist mean by saying that "the problem is consensus" (p. 51, l. 14)?
6. What is the pacifist's argument against the statement "It's human nature to kill" (p. 51, l. 25)?
7. "Man organizes, buys, sells, pushes violence" (p. 51, l. 30). Give examples of how this is done (if you accept the truth of this statement).
8. In what ways do "one billion people live off the other three billion" (p. 52, ll. 3/4)?
9. Does the author end on an optimistic rather than a pessimistic note?
   – Can you draw parallels to the last three lines of the poem "The Door"?

The writer's craft: argumentation

1. List the main arguments given here for and against pacifism.
2. In what ways does the author's line of argument change as the dialogue develops?
3. How does the author try (and manage?) to incorporate Christianity into her arguing strategy?
4. Make up your own mind on how convincing you find the arguments stated here for or against the acceptance of violence in people's behaviour. Give reasons for your opinion.

Grammar practice: imagined conditions

Consider the following question from the text:

A: 'What *would* you *do* if someone *attacked* your grandmother?'

The person asked could possibly answer:

B: { 'If somebody *attacked* my granny, / 'If my granny *were/was attacked,* } { I *would* probably *fight* the aggressor.' / I *might shoot* the fellow.' }

Now say what *you* would do if the following things happened to you. Use active or passive voice in the conditional clause:

1. if someone threatened you with a knife,
2. if you were arrested in a peaceful demonstration,
3. if a cyclist knocked you over as a pedestrian,
4. if a bunch of skinheads insulted a foreigner in the street,
5. if your opponent cheated in a tennis match (or fouled you at football),
6. if some thugs hit your little brother or insulted your sister,
7. if you were called up to do your military service.

Expressing an opinion: agreeing, disagreeing and half-agreeing

You've heard your classmates' arguments about their behaviour in imagined situations. Do you agree or disagree with them?

a) Here are some expressions which you can use when you want to *agree* with someone:

Neutral style	Informal style
Yes, you're quite right.	That's for sure.
Yes, that's very true.	
That's quite right.	
Yes, I (quite) agree.	Yes, I'll buy that.
Quite/exactly/absolutely (right).	You can say that again.
That's exactly my opinion.	
Just what I was thinking.	
I'd go along with you there.	
That's how/what I feel too.	
I think so too.	

b) To *disagree* with someone the following expressions are useful:

Neutral style	Informal style
I'm not so sure about that.	You can't mean that.
You haven't answered my question.	Surely that's not the point.
I'm afraid I can't agree with you there.	You can't be serious.
I don't think so.	No, seriously. Say ...
I don't think you're quite right here.	You must be joking.
I don't think that's right.	You're kidding.
No, that's just not true.	Come off it!
No, I completely disagree.	Nonsense/Rubbish!
No, that's absolutely wrong.	You're just trying to ...
No, I disagree with you entirely.	
I'm afraid you're wrong there.	

c) Sometimes you may wish to *agree less strongly* or *disagree politely* with an opinion:

Half-agreeing	Disagreeing politely
Yes, perhaps/in a way.	I'm not so sure (really).
Well, yes.	Well, it depends.
Mmm, possibly.	Yes, but on the other hand ...
Yes, I suppose so.	I'm not really sure you're right here.
Yes/Well, I agree (up) to a point but ...	Do you really think so?
	I see your point but (on the other hand) ...

Class Discussion

Discuss the following line of argument after having made notes for and against this position:
"Pacifism is impracticable because it is in human nature to defend oneself which may mean killing other people. As it is therefore necessary to train people to kill others, differences of opinion between nations can and must eventually be settled successfully by war."

Written work

Make up statements which you consider controversial and sketch out your own line of argument to back up your opinion.

xt 2.3

Killing an Enemy

Willis Hall

Willis Hall (*1929) is the author of a very large number of radio, television and film scripts. However, the play *The Long and the Short and the Tall* (1958), from which our extract is taken, is probably the most highly praised of his works.

The play is set in the jungles of Malaysia during the Second World War. On one of their raids, a British patrol have taken a Japanese soldier prisoner. Enemy forces have, however, managed to cut them off from their base; they will now have to attempt to slip through the Japanese lines. The problem is what to do with the prisoner – take him along with them, or . . .?

Cast: Mitchem ('Mitch'), sergeant, leader of the patrol
Johnstone ('Johnno'), corporal
Bamforth ('Bammo'), Macleish, Evans, Smith, Whitaker – British soldiers
A Japanese prisoner ('the Nip[po]')

PART 1

Annotations

sort out (v)	put right, to put into order
bloke (n) *(coll.)*	man, fellow
spare (v)	give away (as not necessarily needed)
circumstances (n)	facts, conditions, events
as far as I'm concerned	G: was mich betrifft
mess about (v)	act or speak stupidly

Comprehension I

Give a summary of the events in part 1. Concentrate on the setting and on the three main characters' opinions (Johnstone, Bamforth, Macleish).

PART 2

Annotations

guts (n) *coll.*	courage
plod on (v)	work steadily, without much interest, here: continue to walk slowly and with difficulty
make a stand (v)	here: make a decision to resist (instead of running away)

overpower (v)	subdue, get the better of
bullet ['bʊlɪt] (n)	a type of shot fired from a gun, G: Kugel
trigger (n)	the piece of metal you press to fire a gun
bury ['berɪ] (v)	here: hide
make a mess of (v)	ruin
corpse [kɔːps] (n)	a dead body
equipment	G: Ausrüstung

While listening to part 2 take notes on the other soldiers' reactions.

Comprehension II

Summarize the other soldiers' behaviour before and after the killing.

Your verdict on moral dilemmas

1. What do you think of the soldiers' behaviour?
   a) Is Bamforth's attitude realistic?
   b) To what extent must you put your own interests first at the cost of human, brotherly feelings?
2. The men in this play are all soldiers, and as such they take part in "organised killing". –
   Compare their situation with the one that is talked about in the second paragraph of the Joan Baez text "What would you do if?".
   What do you think of the execution?
3. Sergeant Mitchem made the decisions in the group. Should soldiers obey and 'plod on' (like Smith), or should they be guided by their own feelings and reasoning powers?

Text 2.4

Services for Peace

Aktion Sühnezeichen/Friedensdienste *is an organization giving young Germans the chance to go to countries victimized by Nazi Germany in order to do practical work in social projects "as a sign of reconciliation".*

Stefan Stuckert is a West German volunteer worker from Damme in Lower Saxony. He is twenty-five years old and has spent the last two years of his life working to help the homeless in New York. Stuckert belongs to a group

Services for Peace G: Friedensdienste 2 *victimize* ['vɪktɪmaɪz] (v) cause someone to suffer unfairly 3 *reconciliation* [ˌ----'--] (n) G: Aussöhnung, Versöhnung 4 *volunteer* (n) person who offers to do something, often without payment or reward 4/5 *Lower Saxony* G: Niedersachsen of twenty-two young West Germans who have been sent to the United States by *Action Reconciliation – Services for Peace.*

A. R. S. P. is an organization started by Protestants in West Berlin in 1958 to work for international peace and reconciliation. Today there are over 150 men and women working for A. R. S. P. in countries like Israel, France, Belgium, the Netherlands, Britain, Poland, Norway and the United States. The kind of work they do varies, but it is essentially practical. Some help handicapped people living in Israel; others help peace groups in France to arrange seminars; and a few – like Stefan Stuckert – help the poor people of New York to find homes. In an interview with *Time* Stuckert explained why he became a volunteer with A. R. S. P.: "We in our twenties are the last people now directly connected to the Holocaust. We are the children of soldiers. By working with minority groups and underprivileged people, you take one important step in understanding how such a thing as the Holocaust could happen."

Another A. R. S. P. volunteer is 21-year-old Reinhild Steingröver. She works – and lives – in a home for battered women in Harlem. "I've lived here for almost a year," she said, "and I'm surprised at the intensity of racial feeling in the United States. Working here makes me more sensitive to the problems of race in Germany."

Peter Hofmann, twenty-three years old, is another volunteer working in New York. He works as a general handyman at Emmaus House, a hostel for the poor and homeless in Spanish Harlem. Hofmann is shocked at the lack of government action to help the many homeless in New York City. "The problem is much worse than in West Germany," he said. "The churches can hardly deal with it, and the American Government just doesn't feel responsible."

A. R. S. P. volunteers in the United States receive at present (1991) $ 120 a month in spending money, plus room and board. It's not exactly a fortune but they don't complain. As one of them explained: "It's enough to live on. No one does A. R. S. P. work for the money."

After their work abroad, the volunteers visit West German schools and tell pupils about their experiences. They feel it is important to guide the idealism of youth into practical action. Consequently, some of the young people they

2 *Action Reconciliation* G: Aktion Sühnezeichen 7 *essential* (adj) basic, in essence 9 *arrange* (v) organise 12 *connect* [-'-] (v) link, join together 12 *the Holocaust* ['hɒləkɔːst] (n) the killing of Jews in Nazi Germany in the 1930s and 1940s 13 *minority* [maɪ'nɒrətɪ] (n) small group of people who are different in race, religion, etc., from the others in a country 17 *battered women* beaten (by their husbands) 19 *sensitive (to)* (adj) G: empfindsam, feinfühlig 22 *handyman* (n) person who does repairs and practical jobs 22 *hostel* (n) building where certain types of people can live and eat cheaply 30 *complain* [-'-] (v) G: sich beklagen 33 *guide* (v) steer, lead

meet will themselves become A. R. S. P. volunteers in the years to come. While talking to a class of 17-year-olds in Mönchengladbach, one volunteer was asked if he thought it was really worthwhile to spend two years of his life doing that kind of work. By way of reply he wrote up on the blackboard a saying he had learnt during his stay in the States:

Doing what you like is freedom;
Liking what you do is happiness.

3 *worthwhile* [ˌ-ˈ-] (adj) worth doing, worth the trouble taken 4 *by way of reply* in order to give an answer 5 *saying* (n) G: Redensart

Comprehension

1. Summarize the aim and origin of this volunteer organization.
2. What kind of work is available for the volunteers?
3. Comment on the volunteers' motives for doing this type of work.
4. What did the three volunteers in this text get out of their work, materially and mentally?
5. What value have the later visits to schools in West Germany?
6. Apart from the more idealistic justification for this kind of work, what practical reasons could there be for joining this organization? Would work for A. R. S. P. appeal to you?
7. Comment on the saying quoted at the end of the article. Can you see dangers in doing 'only' what you like? What principles guide *your* doings and actions?

Grammar: conditions which have not been fulfilled

a) Study this example:
If Peter *(stay)* in Germany, he *(go)* straight to university.
If Peter *had stayed* in Germany, he *would have gone* straight to university.
Now make similar sentences using the information given below:

1. If Peter *(be)* in New York before, he *(know)* the situation for homeless people there.
2. If Stefan *(not become)* a volunteer, he *(never work)* with minority groups.
3. If Reinhild *(not live)* for a year in Harlem, she *(not understand)* the intensity of racial feeling there.
4. If Petra *(not think)* it important, she *(not visit)* German schools to talk to pupils.
5. If she *(believe)* the pupils weren't interested, she *(not tell)* them about her experiences as a volunteer.

b) Study this example:
As I didn't go to school that day, I didn't meet the A. R. S. P. volunteer.
If I had gone to school that day, I *would have met* the A. R. S. P. volunteer.
Now make sentences according to this pattern based on the following information:

6. As Dennis didn't read that book, he didn't know what we were talking about.
7. Since they didn't tell us their address, we didn't know how to reach them.

8. Since Diana didn't give me her phone number, I didn't ring her up.
9. They didn't work hard enough for the exam, so they didn't pass.
10. Since Jenny didn't know he was married, she agreed to go out with him.

Discuss these statements

1. "Children should not be held responsible for the sins of their fathers." –
   – What are the main social or ecological problems in your country?
   – Should children try to solve the problems caused by their forefathers?
2. "It is unfair to expect students to do anything worthwhile in sensitive social areas such as drug rehabilitation, women's shelters, the homeless and disabled etc. The basic idea of the whole programme is wrong!"
   – Students have too little experience of the world.
   – Students have seldom any practical skills.
3. "It should be obligatory for all 18–20-year-olds to do social work before they start on a career." –
   Give arguments for and against this opinion.

ext 2.5

Friends of the Earth

The following is an extract from a pamphlet issued by "Friends of the Earth", a well-known British environmental pressure group.

What's happening in the world today?

The population is exploding ...
The countryside is getting smaller ...
We are using up our natural resources too fast ...
And we're killing ourselves by slow poisoning ...

We cannot continue to disregard the limits of our planet's resources. We must learn to live within its limits: limits to the number of people it can support, limits to the amount of pollution it can absorb, limits to the availability of raw materials.
Who would have forecast a few years ago how quickly environmental problems would become critical?

environmental [ˌ---'--] (adj) concerning the natural conditions (air, land, water) in which we live *resources* [rɪ'sɔːsɪs] (n) possessions, particularly of a country, like water, timber, minerals *poisoning* (n) G: Vergiftung *disregard* [ˌ--'-] (v) pay no attention to, ignore *within ... limits* up to a reasonable point or amount *amount* (n) quantity *availability* [-ˌ--'---] (n) G: Verfügbarkeit *forecast* ['--] (v) say, often with special knowledge, what is going to happen at a future time

If we are to create a secure and sustainable future we must act - and act soon.
We cannot persuade developing nations to avoid our mistakes by words alone.
We must tackle and solve the problems of energy, transport and wildlife protection, of agriculture and living conditions.
We must act as individuals and within the communities, institutions and organizations to which we belong.
We must act at a national and international level. Friends of the Earth are trying to do this, but we need your help, and the Earth needs a friend.
Quite soon it may be too late.

So what are we going to do about these problems?

It would be easy to simply think, 'What can poor little me do against the big polluters of the world?', and leave it all to someone else to sort out. But if you want to help, why don't you join *Friends of the Earth?*

sustainable [-'---] (adj) able to be maintained *persuade* [pə'sweɪd] (v) G: überreden *avoid* (v) G: vermeiden *tackle* (v) deal with *level* (n) G: Niveau *sort out* (v) put right; put in order *join* (v) become a member of (an organization)

What is Friends of the Earth?

A well-organised non party-political, national pressure group. Part of an international network covering 28 different countries. Our campaigners seek to make people aware of the key issues and publicise the environmental case on T.V., Radio and in the press. We lobby politicians and government bodies. We press for changes in the law and in policies decided by the Town Hall or Whitehall.

For example, our Natural Heritage Bill aims to protect special nature sites. We fought plans to build a nuclear reprocessing plant at Windscale. We attend public inquiries and provide evidence for Parliamentary Committees. We publish books and a wide variety of information materials. We have 20,000 supporters and 250 action groups who campaign at a local level.

Together we are a highly effective force for conservation, public safety and a clean, lasting environment.

covering which is spread over *seek* (v) try, attempt *aware* (adj) having knowledge or realization *key issues* ['ɪʃu:z] or ['ɪsju:z] most important questions, matters *lobby* (v) (try to) influence *Town Hall* G: Rathaus *Whitehall* street in London near which British government offices stand; the British government itself (particularly departments) *Natural Heritage Bill* a plan for a law to protect the countryside which will be passed on to our children *aim* (v) have as a goal or objective *site* (n) location, place *nuclear reprocessing plant* a factory for the treatment of atomic waste *attend* [-'-] (v) be present at *public inquiries* (n) G: Sitzungen eines öffentlichen Untersuchungsausschusses *provide evidence* supply words and/or objects which prove a statement, support a belief etc. *variety* [-'---] (n) a group containing different sorts of the same thing *lasting* (adj) continuing for a long time; unending

Why Friends of the Earth?

Why not? It's the only one we've got. And it has enemies. Ordinary people mostly, some of them short-sighted, more of them simply caught in a web of circumstances they did not choose and do not know how to change.

The Earth is both beautiful and useful. But with our insatiable appetite for energy, our extravagant use of resources and our failure to protect essential natural habitats, we are threatening to destroy both its beauty and its utility.

short-sighted (adj) unable to see very far *web* (n) a net of thin threads made by a spider *circumstances* conditions which affect a person and his actions *insatiable* (adj) [ɪn'seɪʃəbl] that cannot be satisfied *failure* ['feɪljə] (n) the opposite of "success" *habitat* ['hæbɪtæt] (n) the natural home of a plant or animal *destroy* [-'-] (v) ruin, put an end to the existence of something *utility* [-'---] (n) the degree of usefulness

How you can help our work.

- All the campaigns are run on a shoestring budget. We urgently need your donation and/or membership to carry on the fight.
- Persuade your friends to join FoE – the more supporters we have, the more work we can do.
- Join a local FoE Group – there will be one not far from you – or form a new one. We have staff and materials to help you.
- Many FoE Groups and supporters devise and run job creation schemes such as home insulation, bottle recovery, wastepaper collections and cycle route building.

FoE wants to save Public Transport in the town and country, and promote safe cheap travel

run (v) organize, control and carry out *shoestring budget (infml.)* a very small amount of money *urgently* ['ɜːdʒəntlɪ] (adv) G: dringend *donation* (n) a sum of money given freely, especially for a good purpose *carry on* (v) continue *staff* (n) personnel, group of workers who do the work of an organization *devise* [dɪ'vaɪz] (v) invent, create *recovery* (n) here: the business of getting back (bottles for recycling) *cycle route* special path for bicycles only

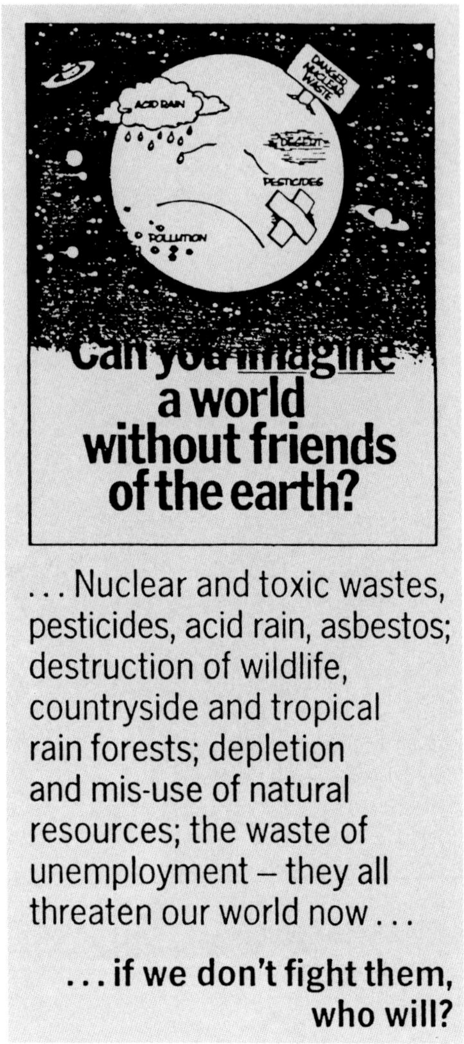

toxic ['--] (adj) poisonous, related to poisonous substances *depletion* [dɪ'pliːʃn] (n) drop in quantity

Comprehension

1. Outline briefly the need for a group such as *Friends of the Earth.*
2. State the main reason for an individual to join *Friends of the Earth.*
3. The organization identifies two main groups of "enemies" to the Earth. What are they?
4. Name the primary causes of the environmental problems which threaten this planet.
5. *Friends of the Earth* suggest a number of actions which must be taken soon. Make a list of the problems and their solutions (as advocated by this organization).

Aspects of style

Now look at the use of language in the text:
1. Name the authors' main aims and the effect of the language used on the reader.
2. List the stylistic devices by which these effects are realized.
3. What does the pamphlet try to get the reader to do?
4. Does it appeal to you? Will *you* do something now?

Communication practice: giving advice

Grammar in review: modal auxiliaries

1. Encouraging and advising: the use of *should* and *ought to*
   Look at the following dialogue in which A is asking for advice and B is giving advice (or encouragement):
   A: How can I help to make the air cleaner?
   You *should* stop smoking as soon as possible.
   B: You *ought to* leave your car at home ... cycle instead.
   You *shouldn't* burn coal in your open fire.
   Now work in pairs. A asks the question, B answers using *should* or *ought to* as well as the information given. Change roles after you have tried out the following three items and do the exercise again.
   A: How can I help to make the water cleaner?
   B: – not throw rubbish into rivers or the sea
   – wash your car at a garage, not at home in the street
   – protest about farmers who use fertilisers near lakes and rivers
   – *your own suggestion*
   A: How can I help to conserve the countryside?
   B: – not throw rubbish away on picnics or walks
   – control the use of fertilisers and pesticides in your own garden
   – work for the restriction of chemicals used in farming
   – *your own suggestion*
   A: How can I help to save energy?
   B: – insulate your home better
   – use lights and heating only when you need them
   – use your bicycle or public transport instead of the car
   – *your own suggestion*
2. Demanding and forbidding: the use of *must* and *mustn't*
   Study the following mini-dialogue:
   A: What can be done to make the air cleaner?
   B: You *must* stop smoking as soon as possible.
   People *mustn't* burn coal in their open fires.
   Speaker B expresses strong advice or a demand. Note that in forbidding something (G: *nicht dürfen*) you must say *mustn't* ['mʌsnt]. Using the same information as above, practise the use of *must* and *mustn't*.

Speech intention: giving, accepting and rejecting advice

Here are some useful expressions when *giving advice* to someone:
If I were you, I'd (I wouldn't) ...
In my opinion you should (shouldn't) ...

I think you must . . .
If you want my advice, you should . . .
Have you ever thought of . . .?
Why don't you . . .?

If you *accept the advice* you can say:
That's a good/not a bad idea . . .
Yes, I suppose you're right . . .
You've got a point there . . .
I hadn't thought of that – yes, why not? . . .
Yes, I'll think about it . . .

If you *reject the advice,* you can say:
That's easy for you to say, but . . .
When I want your advice, I'll ask for it . . . (fairly impolite)
Why don't you mind your own business . . . (impolite)
Why can't I/shouldn't I . . .?
I don't think that would help at all . . .

Work in pairs. A makes the following statements and B gives advice on what to do. Then A accepts or rejects the advice using the expressions above:
1. I've got this terrible cough – I just can't get rid of it.
2. This friend of mine wants me to join a Friends of the Earth group. I don't see the point, really.
3. The water tastes funny, but when I rang up about it they told me not to worry. Still, it does taste funny.
4. It's awful. The fish in the river have all died and they say at the factory that it's nothing to do with them. I suppose there's nothing we can do.
5. I just can't stand my job, but the pay's good and it's near home, so I suppose I'll just have to grin and bear it.
6. There's a plan to build an incineration plant (G: Müllverbrennungsanlage) just outside our village, and the politicians have all agreed on it. What are we going to do? I feel so helpless.

Comments on the Third World

INFO BOX

FACTS ON STARVATION
Grown-ups can recover after they have been near starvation, children cannot. At least 80% of the development of the human brain has taken place by the age of two. If a baby gets too little food or not enough of the right kind, he will remain retarded for the rest of his life – will never be able to develop into a normal human being. This is the fate of millions of children in the Third World today:
– 15 to 20 million children die every year,
– 40,000 children die each day, about 28 every minute, one every two seconds.

starvation (n) suffering or death from lack of food *recover* [-'--] (v) get back to good health *retarded* (adj) slower in development than other children

priority (n) something that needs attention before others *extinct* [-'-] (adj) (of a kind of animal) no longer existing *gluttony* ['---] (n) the habit of eating too much *run* (v) here: organise

Over to you

Make comments on graffiti 1–10. What is most important for the Third World?

Text 2.6

Some of the poems by Edwin Brock (*1927) have become classics in modern English poetry because of their clarity, seriousness and intensity.

Song of the Battery Hen

Edwin Brock

We can't grumble about accommodation:
We have a new concrete floor that's
always dry, four walls that are
Painted white, and a sheet-iron roof
The rain drums on. A fan blows warm air
Beneath our feet to disperse the smell
of chicken-shit and, on dull days,
Fluorescent lighting sees us.

You can tell me: if you come by
The North door, I am in the twelfth pen
On the left-hand side of the third row
From the floor; and in that pen
I am usually the middle one of three.
But, even without directions, you'd
Discover me. I have the same orange-
red comb, yellow beak and auburn
Feathers, but as the door opens and you
Hear above the electric fan a kind of
One-word wail, I am the one
who sounds loudest in my head.

Listen. Outside the house there's an
Orchard with small moss-green apple
Trees; beyond that, two fields of
Cabbages; then, on the far side of
The road, a broiler house. Listen:
One cockerel grows out of there, as
Tall and proud as the first hour of the sun.
Sometimes I stop calling with the others
To listen, and wonder if he hears me.

The next time you come here, look for me.
Notice the way I sound inside my head.
God made us all quite differently.
And blessed us with this expensive home.

battery hen (n) one of many hens kept in a line of small boxes to grow fast and lay eggs often 1 *grumble* (v) complain 1 *accommodation* (n) a place to live 2 *concrete* ['--] (n) building material made by mixing sand, small stones, cement and water 5 *fan* (n) G: Ventilator 6 *disperse* (v) spread in different directions 7 *dull* (adj) here: dark, sunless 9 *you can tell me* you can tell which one is me (=recognize me) 10 *pen* here: G: Hühnerstall 15 *discover* (v) find 16 *comb* [kəʊm] (n) G: Kamm 16 *beak* [biːk] the mouth of a hen or other bird 16 *auburn* (adj) reddish-brown 19 *wail* (n) a long cry (often of pain) 22 *orchard* ['ɔːtʃəd] (n) piece of land where fruit trees grow 22 *moss* (n) G: Moos 24 *cabbage* ['kæbɪdʒ] (n) G: Kohl 25 *broiler* (n) small young chicken raised for grilling (=broiling) 26 *cockerel* ['kɒkrəl] (n) a young cock (=young male chicken) 33 *bless* (v) wish happiness or favour to sb

Analysis and appreciation

1. Find a heading for each verse.
2. What is the difference between *accommodation* and *home* (cf. l. 1 & l. 33)?
3. Give a description of the hens' home in the first verse.
4. Interpret l. 8: "fluorescent lighting sees us".
5. What does the description in ll. 9–12 remind you of? What is indicated by "the middle one of three" (l. 13)?
6. Why does l. 14 open with a "but"? Try to identify the contrast expressed in the second verse.
7. Comment on the function of the alliterations and the use of the verb *wail* in l. 19.
8. Say what kind of impression you get from the description in ll. 21–25.

9. Comment on the description of the cockerel (ll. 26/27).
10. Give an interpretation of the last two lines of the poem.
11. Find those words and phrases in the poem which name contrasts and contradiction and thereby express an ironical attitude towards the battery hen's situation.
12. The battery hen's outlook on life can best be described as:
    – utter resignation,
    – naive contentment, or
    – unrealistic egocentricity.
13. What does the battery hen's existence stand for?

For and against

Draw up two lists of arguments:
a) for keeping animals in battery-type conditions,
b) against such means of food production.

Text 2.7

In the following article, a journalist of a national Sunday newspaper describes what happened to him one evening on his way home on the London underground.

Incident on the Underground

D. Bolton

It was about eleven o'clock on a hot, sweaty evening in late August. I was on my way home to one of the suburbs on the Metropolitan Line after working late. I had to finish a report on a football match played that evening. As I stood on the underground station platform, I had no warning of what was going to happen.

The silver six-carriage train opened its doors, and while a handful of people tried to get out, I and about a hundred other people tried to push and squeeze our way on before the doors closed. That late in the evening it could be a quarter of an hour before the next train came. Of course I wish now that I'd been more patient and waited for the next train.

A few lucky people got seats. The rest of us just had to stand, packed in like vertical sardines. The smell of sweat was almost overpowering.

incident ['---] (n) an event (which often includes violence) 2 *suburb* ['--] (n) outer district of a town or city 6 *carriage* ['kærɪdʒ] a railway passenger vehicle; G: Waggon 11 *packed in* pushed together 12 *overpowering* (adj) overwhelming; G: überwältigend

Soon after the train left the light of the station and entered the darkness of the tunnel, I noticed a group of youths near me. There were six of them altogether, all in their late teens or early twenties, they were quite smartly dressed, with brightly coloured T-shirts cut off high at their shoulders.

Suddenly I noticed one of them was talking to a young American couple a few metres away from me. As he talked, he and his friends were slowly pushing their way towards the couple until they surrounded them on all sides.

Then, to my great surprise, I saw a hand shoot out and grab the expensive-looking camera which was hanging round the American boy's neck. At the same time another hand, with a short, nasty-looking flick-knife in it, cut the neck-strap. The American started to protest but immediately shut up when the boy with the knife waved it threateningly in front of his face. The group of youths then turned to his girlfriend who by this time was crying and white with fear. Her handbag was cut from her shoulder. Her boyfriend put his arms around her, and she sobbed quietly.

A woman next to me screamed but nobody else in the carriage seemed to take much notice.

"Someone who has just been to the pub and had one too many," they probably thought.

Now it was the turn of the couple in front of me. In exactly the same way as before, the youths surrounded them and quickly 'removed' the woman's handbag and silver necklace, and the man's wallet and gold watch.

I thought about pulling the emergency brake. But if I did, we'd be trapped with the gang in a tunnel, between stations. I looked round at the other passengers. They had either not noticed what had happened, or they were trying hard to ignore it. So what could I do, on my own? I didn't have long to decide. I could see I was going to be their next victim. I stared straight in front of me, hoping that somehow they wouldn't notice me. But it was no good.

"You're next," the leader said as he came and stood right in front of me. I could smell his after-shave and I noticed a small scar under his right eye. I tried to avoid eye contact but he was so close it was impossible.

"Give me your money," he whispered in a low, threatening voice.

"I haven't got any," I lied.

3 *smartly* elegantly, fashionably 11 *flick-knife* (n) G: Springmesser 13 *threateningly* (adv) giving warning (of something bad) 16 *sob* (v) draw in breath sharply when crying 24 *emergency brake* (n) G: Notbremse 24 *be trapped* (v) be caught with no escape possible 28 *victim* (n) G: Opfer 31 *scar* (n) a mark on the skin after a wound or cut

Then, with a nasty smile, he waved his knife under my nose, as one of his friends went through my pockets.

While they were still searching me, the train came into Kilburn Station and the doors behind me opened. I saw my chance – I jumped on to the platform and ran for the nearest exit. Luckily they didn't follow me, but why should they? They didn't need to because they'd got what they wanted – my wallet with £39 in it, plus two credit cards.

I told the police of course, but they said there was very little they could do, because the gang, their victims and any witnesses were now spread out all over north London.

Many people have since asked me. "But why didn't you *do* something?" All I can say in reply is, "Well, what would *you* have done?"

BARRY FANTONI

'The mugger handed back my pension – said he couldn't live on it'

1 *nasty* (adj) unpleasant 3 *search* (v) here: look carefully through someone's pockets 12 *witness* (n) a person who sees a crime happen 16 *in reply* as an answer

Check your understanding

1. Why does the author say (p. 68, ll. 4/5): "I had no warning of what was going to happen"?
2. On page 68, ll. 9/10 the writer expresses regret about a certain decision that night. Why does he feel like this now?
3. In what way is the descriptive phrase "packed in like vertical sardines" (p. 68, ll.11/12) important for the future development of the story?
4. Summarize people's reactions when the youths attack and rob the passengers.
5. Describe how the journalist got out of this situation.

Grammar in review: *simple past* and *past progressive* in texts

Revise the differences between the simple past and the past progressive, eg. I *was going* home when they *robbed* me.
Describe what happened, using the following words and choosing between the simple past and the past progressive:

1. A journalist – travel – home – underground/when – he – notice – group of youths – near him – carriage.

2. All at once – one of them – start talking – young American couple/who – stand – a few metres away – journalist.
3. While – journalist – watch/the boys – surround – couple – on all sides.
4. The train – travel – between two stations/when – one of the boys – suddenly – grab – the American's camera.
5. Then – he – cut – strap/which – hang – American boy's neck.
6. The journalist – look round at – other passengers/they – try hard – ignore – what – happen.
7. Woman – next to – journalist – scream/when – she – see – what – boys – do.
8. The gang – still – search – journalist/when – train – come into Kilburn Station.

Talking about the text

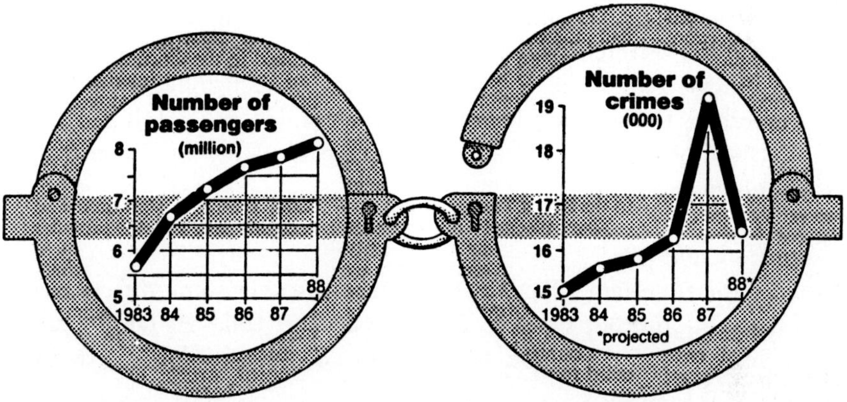

Danger ahead: the figures for passengers and crime on the London Underground since 1983

What is the diagram about, and what kind of information do you get?

'What would *you* have done?'

1. What could the passengers have done in this situation? Explain what might have happened.
2. How could the police have been more helpful to the victim and more effective in attempting to catch the criminals?
3. Consider the following facts about crime in Britain and suggest ways of preventing it:
   a) Of all crimes (in Britain about 4 million per year) 94 per cent are against property, and 6 per cent are against persons. Of all crimes against persons (about 220,000 in the UK) 90 per cent involve violence.
   b) According to a poll in February 1987 one in three Londoners thought crime and the threat of violence were the worst aspects of living in London.
   c) One in four women aged 16–24 years old said they wouldn't go out on their own (day or night) for fear of being attacked.

Text 2.8

The Untouchable

William March

A traveler, after losing his way in the mountain, took refuge for the night in a cave. He saw at once that another had preceded him and was now warming himself before a fire of sticks and leaves. When the traveler entered, the other man said, "I'm an untouchable. Be careful not to stumble and fall against me."

The traveler sat on the other side of the fire watching his companion. He wondered what differences made one of them an honorable man and the other an outcast. Not seeing any great physical difference between them, he thought perhaps the solution lay in another field. He said, "Tell me, do you feel hate and joy and love, as I do? Are you capable of feeling hope and jealousy and regret?"

"Yes," said the untouchable. "I feel all those things. I also feel shame, envy, sorrow and pity."

And so the two men talked. They tried to discover some differences between them but did not succeed. Then the traveler said, "As far as I can see, we are very much alike," and added, "Do you know why you're an untouchable and I am not?"

"No," said the other, "I only know I was born an untouchable of parents who were like myself."

There was a long silence while the two men examined each other across the fire. Finally the traveler said, "I wonder what would happen if I touched you?"

The eyes of the traveler widened at his own audacity, and he said, "You know – I'm going to touch you and find out." The outcast drew back against the wall and covered his eyes. The traveler stretched out his arms and

untouchable (n) person of the lowest social group, especially in the Hindu caste system, whose touch is considered as destroying the purity of a person belonging to a higher class 1 *traveler (AmE* for *Br. E "traveller")* 1 *take refuge* ['refju:dʒ] (v) find shelter 2 *cave* a deep natural hollow place; G: Höhle 2 *precede* [-'-] (v) go before 4 *stumble* (v) catch one's foot on the ground and start to fall 7 *honorable* (*AmE* for *BrE "honourable"*) worthy of honour or respect 8 *outcast* ['--] (n) person without friends (forced from his home) 9 *solution* (n) answer (to a problem) 10 *be capable of* (v) be able to, have the ability to 10/11 *jealousy* ['dʒeləsɪ] G: Eifersucht 11 *regret* (n) a feeling of sorrow or unhappiness for something you have done 12 *shame* (n) G: Schande 13 *envy* (n) G: Neid 13 *sorrow* (n) a feeling of sadness 13 *pity* (n) G: Mitleid, Erbarmen 15 *succeed* (v) gain a purpose or reach an aim 20 *examine* (v) look at sth very carefully 23 *audacity* [ɔ:'dæsətɪ] (n) daring, boldness touched the untouchable. After a time the outcast asked in a frightened voice, "Did the mountain totter? Did the river dry up? Did the moon fall out of the sky?"

The traveler said in astonishment, "Nothing at all happened. Everything's precisely as it was before."

2 *totter* (v) move from side to side, as if about to fall 4 *astonishment* (n) great surprise

General comprehension: True or false?

Correct the statements you consider wrong.
1. The traveller came into the cave because he needed shelter.
2. The traveller and the man in the cave sat next to each other by the fire.
3. The traveller and the untouchable discovered nothing but differences between themselves.

Essential language

1. List the words in the story that describe the kind of feelings the untouchable was capable of.
2. Make a list of all those expressions in the last two paragraphs that describe how the traveller and the untouchable acted and felt.
3. Try to classify most of the information in the story according to the following three categories:

Actions	Descriptions	Concepts/Ideas
take refuge etc.	the fire etc.	an untouchable etc.

Interpretation

1. Sum up the development of the traveller and the untouchable in the story.
2. How do the two men feel about the concept "untouchable" at the beginning and at the end of the story? In what ways is this reflected in their behaviour? Quote the appropriate expressions from the text.
3. What is the message of this parable? Does its moral teach you (the reader) anything?
4. What makes the untouchable an untouchable? How do you feel about 'labels' or social concepts suchs as *untouchable, outcast, master, upper/lower class, scapegoat* or *outsider*? Do you think they are necessary for society?
5. Why do people give labels of the above sort to each other? Do you use some yourself? Give examples. Draw parallels between this narrative and other situations in everyday life. Who – do you think – are the 'outcasts' of our time?
6. What difference (if any) would it make if the untouchable were a women instead of a man?

Text 2.9

Toeckey Jones was born and grew up in South Africa, but in 1971 moved to London where he now lives and works as a full-time writer. His first novel, *Go Well, Stay Well,* was published in 1979, and was welcomed as one of the few novels for young readers to describe what it is like to grow up in a racially segregated society.

The Meeting

Toeckey Jones

Candice is a 17-year-old white South African girl from Johannesburg. One day, while walking in the city, she trips and twists her ankle.

Almost immediately she felt a gentle touch on her arm. She opened her eyes to see a young African girl standing in front of her. Instinctively, Candy's grip on her bag tightened. The girl could be after her money. Candy knew how clever the young black pickpockets in the city were said to be. She was always being warned to keep a close hold on her purse.

"You OK?" Without waiting for an answer, the girl bent down to inspect Candy's ankle. "Tch . . . tch . . . shame." Shaking her head she straightened up.

"That's no good to walk on," she said. "You can sit down in the park. It's not far. Come, I must help you."

The girl took hold of Candy's free arm and after a moment's hesitation. Candy allowed herself to be supported as they began to move slowly along the pavement.

"Too many drinks, hey?" the girl teased.

Candy laughed, then felt herself blushing as she became aware of the curious stares they were attracting. She tried to move faster, leaning as little as possible on the supporting arm beside her. She still wasn't sure she could trust the girl. It would have been so much simpler if it had been a white person who had offered help. She didn't know why the girl was doing it. Should she offer to pay her? It was all rather embarrassing.

2 *trip* (v) stumble, catch one's foot on the ground 2 *twist* (v) hurt by turning sharply 2 *ankle* (n) part of the leg directly above the foot 3 *immediately* [-'---] (adv) at once 5 *grip* (n) act of holding on to sth 5 *tighten* (v) become harder, tighter 6 *pickpocket* ['-,--] (n) person who steals things from people's pockets, often in a crowd 8 *bend down* (v) lean forward and down 12 *hesitation* [,--'--] (n) act of pausing before doing something 14 *pavement* (n) path at the side of a street for people to walk on 15 *tease* [ti:z] make fun of in a playful way 16 *blush* (v) become red in the face with embarrassment 17 *curious* ['kjʊərɪəs] inquisitive; G: neugierig 17 *stare* (n) long look 21 *rather* quite 21 *embarrassing* [-'---] (adj) causing to feel ashamed or socially uncomfortable

The park was only two blocks away, but it seemed an age before they got there. As the girl helped her down into a sitting position on the grass, Candy was aware of her bag slipping off her shoulder and the girl stretching out to catch it as it fell. Candy held her breath, her heart beating fast. But the girl didn't run off. Instead, she waited until Candy was sitting comfortably, and then handed the bag to her.

"Better now?" she asked.

While the girl bent down to take a closer look at the injured ankle, Candy studied her thoughtfully. She was really rather pretty, Candy discovered to her surprise, for she had never thought of African features as being attractive before. But this girl's features were all in perfect proportion to each other, giving her face as a whole an open, sunny expression.

Candy didn't want her to go. She had never met an African girl of her own age before – at least not to speak to. And she was already beginning to like this girl who seemed undecided about her next move and was playing nervously with the worn collar of her blouse, trying to do up a button that wasn't there.

"Are you in hurry?" Candy asked.

"No, Why? Can I give you a lift home? My Mercedes is just round the corner."

Candy laughed and the girl sat down on the grass beside her.

"What's your name?" she asked.

"Candice. But everyone calls me Candy. And yours?"

"Rebecca. But everyone calls me Becky." And then they both laughed.

"Tell you what." Candy said. "I'm thirsty. How about you?"

"Sure. What would you like? I'll go and get it. Beer?"

"I think I'd better have a Coke. But let's go and sit down somewhere, and perhaps have something to eat as well. So long as I don't have to walk too far, my ankle should be all right."

"You know a place we can go?" Becky asked.

Candy's face slowly reddened with embarrassment. For a moment she had completely forgotten. There wasn't anywhere they could go together. Within ten minutes' walk of where they were sitting, there were at least three restaurants or coffee bars. But Becky couldn't go into them – they were all exclusively for whites. Further away there were a few cafés for African workers travelling daily into Johannesburg from the black township of Soweto. But even if Candy could have walked that far with her bad ankle, she would be stopped from going into any of them with Becky.

"Do you want us to get arrested?" Becky teased.

10 *feature* (n) any of the parts of the face 15 *undecided* [,--'--] unsure, uncertain 16 *worn* used a lot, hence in poor condition 16 *collar* (n) here: the part of the blouse around the neck

The two girls continue to talk for some time and agree to meet again. Candy then telephones her father and asks him to come and fetch her.

Candy caught sight of a blue Cortina and identified her father at the wheel.

"My dad's here," she said unnecessarily, for Becky had already got to her feet and was quickly brushing the grass off her skirt.

"I must go," she told Candy.

"Wait ... Hold on, we haven't settled anything. We don't even know how to get in touch with each other."

Candy wasn't really surprised that Becky wanted to get away before her father arrived, but she wanted the two of them to meet. It would make it easier to talk about Becky to her father later.

Suddenly Candy's father came up behind them.

"What have you done to yourself?" he called out to Candy.

Becky turned round and immediately stepped aside, separating herself from the other two.

"Hello, Dad," Candy said. "Dad, this is Becky," she went on quickly. "She's been helping me and looking after me."

"Oh." He turned and glanced at Becky, who bowed her head shyly.

"Good afternoon, sir," she said politely.

"Uh ... hello." He was already bending down to look at Candy's ankle.

"Is it very painful?" he asked.

Candy shook her head impatiently. She was aware that Becky had moved a little further away and was fidgeting nervously.

"Dad!" Candy said firmly. "Becky has been absolutely marvellous. I don't know what I would have done without her."

"Oh." He smiled briefly in Becky's direction. "That was very kind of her. Now, do you think you'll be able to walk as far as the car?"

Candy was disappointed. He could at least show some interest in Becky, and talk to her directly. She pulled a face at him, and glanced at Becky.

"What? ... Oh, yes, of course."

Too late. Candy realised that he had misunderstood her. Putting his hand into his pocket, he said:

"Here, this is for being so kind and looking after my daughter until I got here," and he held a one rand note out to her.

Helplessly, Candy stared at them both, red with shame. Anything she said now could only make the situation worse. She felt furious with her father,

3 *catch sight of* (v) see for a moment 7 *settle* (v) here: decide 14 *step aside* (v) go to one side 18 *glance at* (v) look quickly at 23 *fidget* ['--] (v) move one's body around restlessly 28 *at least* G: mindestens 34 *rand* (n) the standard money in South Africa (1 rand = DM 0,70) 34 *note* (n) piece of paper money

but she knew she couldn't really blame him for misunderstanding her. One glance at Becky was enough to see how poor she was. And normally white people automatically tipped Africans for any help they gave. But after everything that had passed between her and Becky, offering Becky money could only seem an insult.

Candy couldn't bear to watch but she had to. She saw Becky look up and slowly begin to shake her head.

3 *tip* (v) give a small sum of money for a small service 5 *insult* ['--] (n) G: Beleidigung

Comprehension

The main information

Collect the main information about the time, place and people as well as the action.

Check the details

1. Why did Candy hesitate before accepting Becky's help?
2. In what way did Becky demonstrate that she felt no racial dislike for Candy?
3. Describe the conflicting emotions felt by Candy.
4. What is the significance of the description of Becky's features (p. 75 ll.9–12)?
5. "Candy didn't want her to go" (p. 75, l.13). Explain Candy's feelings, and describe what happened.
6. Find indications of Becky's discomfort with the situation.
7. Why was a simple act like having something to eat and drink a problem for the two girls?
8. Characterize Becky's reaction after Candy's father had arrived.
9. What do we learn about Candy from the use of adverbs like *impatiently* and *firmly* (p. 76, ll. 22 & 24)?
10. Point out those aspects of Candy's father's behaviour that reveal his insensitivity to the situation.

Intensive reading: interpreting people's behaviour

Making notes

What do we learn about the emotions and the resulting behaviour of the three characters? Choose one of the three characters and try to find appropriate terms for these feelings and types of (mis)behaviour:

Candy	Becky	Father
grip on her bag	gentle touch	glancing at Becky
holding her purse	inspecting the ankle	his greeting
accepting help: hesitation	making a joke	smiling briefly
blushing	handing the bag back	in B's direction
etc.	etc.	etc.

Summing up

- Summarize the difficulties of a friendship between a white and a black girl in South Africa by presenting a suitable interpretation of the person's behaviour you have chosen.
- Comment on the reasons for their reactions and feelings.
- Identify the source of the misunderstanding between Candy and her father.
- Do you think she could have behaved differently and prevented the misunderstanding?

Grammar practice: the "direct object+infinitive" construction

Study this example:
The African girl thought *Candy should sit down* in the park. What did the African girl want? – The African girl *wanted Candy to sit down* in the park.
Complete the following sentences using the above pattern:

1. In the beginning Candy thought *the African girl would steal* her bag. – Candy expected ...
2. At first she thought it best if the African girl left her alone. – She wanted ...
3. The African girl thought Candy should lean against her. – The African girl wanted ...
4. Candy thought: 'How awful if my father saw this.' – Candy thought: 'I'd hate ...'
5. But, after a while, Candy hoped the African girl wouldn't leave her. – Candy didn't want ...
6. 'It would be nice if you stayed,' she said. – 'I'd like ...'
7. 'My name's Candice, but will you please call me Candy?' – 'My name's Candice, but I prefer ...'
8. At first Candy thought that they could go and get a drink. – At first Candy wanted ...
9. Then she thought they could have something together at a restaurant. – Then she wanted ...
10. 'We'll get arrested,' said Becky. 'Do you want that?' – Becky said to Candy: 'Do you want ...?'

Apologising and expressing sympathy

Study the following imagined pieces of dialogue, first between Candy and her father:
Candy: Offering Becky money was an insult.
Father: Oh, *I'm very sorry to hear that.*
Second, between Candy and a waiter:
Waiter: You're in the wrong restaurant.
Candy: *I'm very sorry. I didn't realize* (it was only for whites).
In the first conversation the father *expresses sympathy* whereas in the second one Candy expresses an *apology.*
Apologies can also be realized by way of the following expressions:

I'm ever so sorry. –
Oh, do forgive me (please). –
Oh dear, I'm (most) awfully sorry. –
I can't tell you how sorry I am. –
I just don't know what to say: I'm terribly sorry.

Now practise expressing sympathy or an apology.

1. You're sitting on my seat. (apologise)
2. I've just failed my exam. (express sympathy)
3. Peter's parents are getting divorced. (express sympathy)
4. You're standing on my foot! (apologise)
5. You haven't paid me back the £10 I lent you. (apologise)
6. I crashed my father's car last week. (express sympathy)
7. There's a scratch on this record I lent you. (apologise)
8. Diana's mother is seriously ill. (express sympathy)
9. I can't play on Saturday – I've twisted my ankle. (express sympathy)
10. *Your own suggestion*

Writing task

Take the role of Candy and write a letter to Becky in which you describe the feelings you had when your father arrived on the scene and behaved in the way shown in the story. Try to express sympathy and/or apology.

ext 2.10

The Turtle

George Vukelich

They were driving up to fish the White Creek and the false dawn was purpling the Wisconsin countryside when they spotted a huge hump-backed object in the middle of the sandroad and Jimmy brought the station wagon to a stop.

"Pa," he said. "Turtle. Lousy snapper."

Old Tony sat up.

"Is he dead?"

"Not yet," Jimmy said. "Not yet he isn't." He shifted into neutral and pulled on the handbrake. The snapper lay large and dark-green in the headlight

turtle ['tɜːtl] (n) G: Wasserschildkröte   1 *creek* (n) (*AmE*) a small narrow stream   1 *false* (adj) not genuine; G: falsch   1 *dawn* (n) time of day when light first appears   2 *purpling* making a purple colour   2 *spot* (v) catch sight of, see all at once   2 *hump-backed* with a rounded back   3 *station wagon* (*AmE*) = (*BrE*) "estate car"; G: Kombi   5 *snapper* (n) a turtle which snaps or bites   8 *shift* (v) here: move the gear stick   8 *neutral* the position in which none of the gears is engaged beams, and they got and went round to look at it closely. The turtle moved a little and left razorlike clawmarks in the wet sand, and it waited.

"Probably heading for the creek," Jimmy said. "They kill trout like crazy."

They stood staring down.

"I'd run the wagon over him," Jimmy said. "Only he's too big."

He looked around and walked to the ditch, and came back with a long finger-thick pine branch. He jabbed it into the turtle's face and the snakehead lashed out and struck like springsteel and the branch snapped like a stick of macaroni, and it all happened as fast as a matchflare.

"Look at that!" Tony whistled.

"You bet, Pa. I bet he weighs sixty pounds. Seventy maybe."

The turtle was darting its head around now in long stretching movements.

"I think he got some branch stuck in his craw," Jimmy said. He got out a cigaret and lighted it, and threw the match at the rockgreen shell.

"I wish now I'd brought the twenty-two," he said. "The pistol."

"You going to kill him?"

"Why not?" Jimmy asked. "They kill trout, don't they?"

They stood there smoking and not talking, and looking down at the unmoving shell.

"I could use the lug wrench on him," Jimmy said. "Only I don't think it's long enough. I don't want my hands near him."

Tony didn't say anything.

"You watch him," Jimmy said. "I'll go find something in the wagon."

Slowly Tony squatted down and smoked and stared at the turtle. Poor Old One, he thought. You had the misfortune to be caught in the middle of a sandroad, and you are very vulnerable on the sandroads, and now you are going to get the holy life beaten out of you.

The turtle stopped its stretching movements and was still. Tony looked at the full webbed feet and the powerful claws and he knew the truth.

"It would be different in the water, turtle," he said. "In the water you could cut down anybody."

He thought about this snapper in the water and how it would move like a

1 *(headlight) beams* [bi:mz] the lines of light sent out by the car's headlights 2 *razorlike* ['---] like a razor, ie. very sharp and thin 2 *clawmarks* the turtle's claws, the sharp nails on its toes 2 *claw* [klɔ:] the sharp nail on the toe of an animal 3 *head for* go towards 3 *trout* [traʊt] G: Forelle 6 *ditch* (n) G: Graben 7 *pine* (n) G: Fichte 7 *jab* (v) here: G: stochern 8 *lash out* (v) strike out (as with a whip) 8 *strike* (v) hit 8 *springsteel* (n) G: Federstahl 9 *as fast as a matchflare* in the time it takes for a match to light 12 *dart* (v) move suddenly and quickly 13 *craw* (n) throat of an animal 14 *shell* (n) the hard covering of some animals living in the sea 20 *lug wrench* [rentʃ] (n) *(AmE)* = *(BrE)* "spanner" G: Schraubenschlüssel 24 *squat down* [skwɒt] (v) sit down without a chair, balancing on one's feet 25 *misfortune* [-'--] (n) bad luck 26 *vulnerable* ['----] (adj) not well protected, easily attacked 28 *be still* (v) not move, be motionless 29 *webbed feet* G: Schwimmfüße

torpedo and bring down trout, and nobody would monkey with it in the water – and here it was in the middle of a sandroad, vulnerable as a baby and waiting to get its brains beaten out.

He finished his cigaret and got to his feet and walked to the wagon and reached into the glove compartment for the thermos of coffee. What was he getting all worked up about a turtle for? He was an old man and he was acting like a kid, and they were going up to the White Creek, and he was getting worked up about a God-forsaken turtle in the middle of a God-forsaken sandroad. *God-forsaken.* He walked back to the turtle and squatted down and sipped at the strong black coffee and watched the old snapper watching him.

Jimmy came up to him holding the jack.

"I want to play it safe," he said. "I don't think the lug wrench is long enough." He squatted beside Tony. "What do you think?"

"He waits," Tony said. "What difference does it make what I think?"

Jimmy stared at him.

"I can tell something's eating you. What are you thinking, Pa?"

"I am thinking this is not a brave thing."

"What?"

"This turtle – he does not have a chance."

Jimmy lit a cigaret and lifted the jack. The turtle moved ever so slightly.

"You talk like an old woman. An old tired women."

"I can understand this turtle's position."

"He doesn't have a chance?"

"That's right."

"And that bothers you?"

Tony looked into Jimmy's face.

"That is right," he said. "That bothers me."

"Well of all the dumb stupid things," Jimmy said. "What do you want me to do? Get down on all fours and fight with him?"

"No," Tony said. "Not on all fours. Not on all fours." He looked at Jimmy. "In the water. Fight this turtle in the water. That would be a brave thing, my son."

Jimmy put down the jack and reached for the thermos and didn't say anything. He drank his coffee and smoked his cigaret, and he stared at the turtle and didn't say anything.

1 *bring down* (v) kill or wound 1 *monkey with* (v) (*coll.*) play around with 5 *glove compartment* [glʌv] (n) small enclosed space in a car in front of the passenger seat, where small articles can be kept 6 *get all worked up* (v) become very upset, agitated 8 *God-forsaken (derog.)* G: gottverlassen, elend 10 *sip at* (v) take very small drinks of 12 *jack* (n) instrument for lifting a car off the ground 17 *something's eating you (coll.)* something is troubling you 18 *brave* courageous, fearless 21 *ever so slightly* just a little 26 *bother* (v) trouble, worry

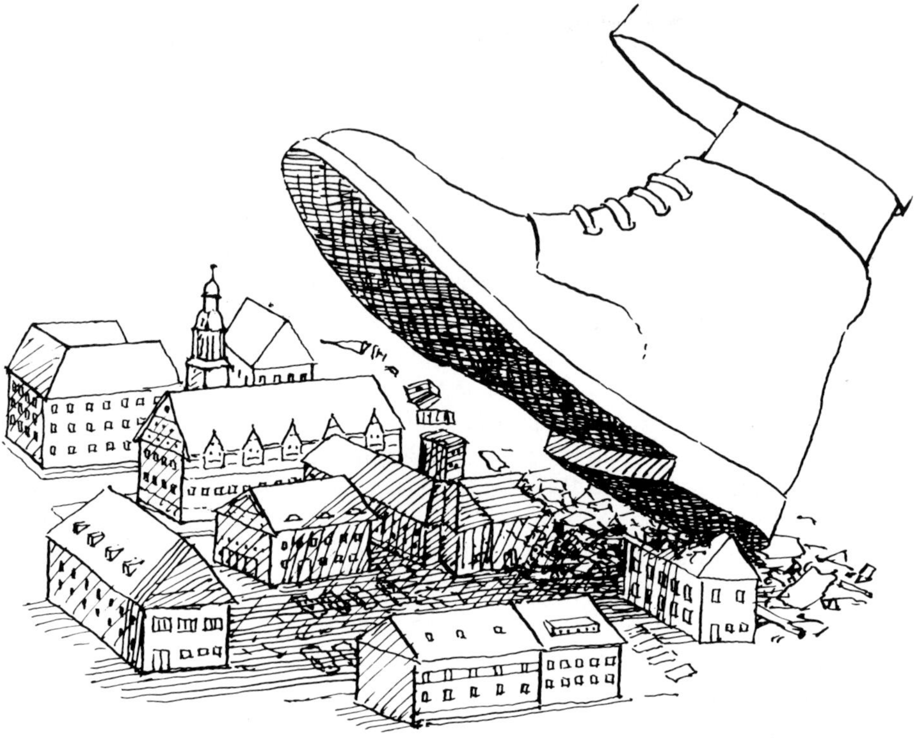

"You're crazy," he said finally.

"It is a thought, my son. A thought. This helpless old one is like a little baby in this sandroad, eh? But in the water, his home . . ." Tony snapped his fingers with the suddenness of a switch blade. "In the water he could cut down anyone, anything . . . any man. Fight him in the water, Jimmy. Use your jack in the water . . ."

"I think you're nuts," Jimmy said. "I think you're honest to goodness nuts."

Tony shrugged. "This does not seem fair for you, eh? To be in the water with this one." He motioned at the turtle. "This seems nuts to you. Crazy to you. Because in the water he could cripple you. Drown you. Because in the water you are not a match."

4 *suddenness* (n) unexpected speed 4 *switch blade* (*AmE*) = (*BrE*) *flick-knife* G: Springmesser 7 *nuts* (v) (*coll.*) crazy 7 *honest to goodness* here: really 9 *shrug* (v) raise one's shoulders in an expression of doubt or lack of interest 10 *motion at* (v) signal with a movement (usually with the hand) 11 *drown* (v) [draʊn] kill by holding under water for a long time 12 *you are not a match* you are not equal, you are not as good as he is

"What are you trying to prove, Pa?"

"Jimmy. This turtle is putting up his life. In the road here you are putting up nothing. You have nothing to lose at all. Not a finger or a hand or your life. Nothing. You smash him with a long steel jack and he cannot get to you. He has as much chance as a ripe watermelon."

"So?"

"So I want you to put up something also. You should have something to lose or it is no match."

Jimmy looked at the old man and then at the turtle.

"Any fool can smash a watermelon," Tony said. "It does not take a brave man."

"Pa. It's only a turtle. You're making a federal case."

Old Tony looked at his son. "All right," he said. "Finish your coffee now and do what you are going to do. I say nothing more. Only for the next five minutes put yourself into this turtle's place. Put yourself into his shell and watch through his eyes. And try to think what he is thinking when he sees a coward coming to kill him with a long steel jack."

Jimmy got to his feet and put out his cigaret.

"All right, Pa, he said. "All right. You win."

Tony rose slowly.

"No," he said. "Not me. You. You win."

"But Pa, they do kill trout."

"So," Tony said. "They kill trout. Nature put them here, and they kill trout. To survive. The trout are not extinct, eh? We kill trout also, we men. To survive? No, for sport. This old one, he takes what he needs. I do not kill him for being in nature's plan. I do not play God."

Jimmy walked to the back of the wagon then and flung down the jack and closed up the door and came back.

"Pa," he said. "Honest to goodness you got the nuttiest ideas I ever heard."

Old Tony walked around behind the snapper and gently prodded it with his boot toe, and the turtle went waddling forward across the road and toppled over the sand shoulder and disappeared in the brush of the creek bank.

1 *prove* (v) show that something is true 2 *put up* (v) here: G: aufs Spiel setzen 4 *smash* (v) break into many small pieces, destroy 5 *ripe* fully grown and ready to be eaten 12 *you're making a federal case* you're making a big thing (out of sth small and unimportant) 17 *coward* ['kaʊəd] (n) (*derog.*) person who cannot face danger because he lacks courage 24 *extinct* [-'-] (adj.) (of animals) no longer in existence 27 *fling down* (v) throw down (carelessly) 31 *prod* (v) push sth (with a pointed object) 32 *boot toe* the front part of the boot 32 *waddle* (v) walk from side to side, like a duck 32/33 *topple over* (v) become unsteady and fall over 33 *brush* (n) small bushes; G: Unterholz

Tony and his son climbed into the wagon and sat looking at each other. The sun was coming up strong now and the sky was cracking open like a shell and spilling reds and golds and blues, and Jimmy started the engine.

Tony put the thermos away and got out his cigarets and stuck one in his son's mouth.

"So?" he said.

They sat smoking for a full minute watching each other, and then Jimmy released the handbrake and they rolled slowly along the drying sandroad and down past the huge cleansing dawn coming, and the pine forests growing tall in the rising mists, and the quickly quiet waters of the eternal creek.

2 *crack* (v) break 3 *spill* (v) pour out accidentally 8 *release* [-ˈ-] (v) press (a handle) so as to let something go 9 *cleansing* [ˈklenzɪŋ] making clean 10 *mist* (n) thin fog 10 *eternal* [-ˈ--] without beginning or end, everlasting

Comprehension

1. What does Jimmy mean when he says "Not yet he isn't" (p. 79, l.8)?
2. Describe in your own words the turtle's reaction when Jimmy jabbed at it with the branch (p. 80, ll. 7 ff).
3. Why should Jimmy want to kill the turtle, but not with the lug wrench?
4. Tony is said 'to know the truth' (p. 80, ll.28/29). What truth?
5. Explain the expressions "What was he getting all worked up about a turtle for?" (p. 81, ll.5/6) and "I can tell something is eating you" (p. 81, l.17), with regard to Tony's feelings about the turtle's chances.
6. Summarize Tony's idea of a fair fight for the turtle, and comment on Jimmy's argument: "It's only a turtle" (p. 83, l.12).
7. What's the difference between men (as hunters) and wild animals that kill?
8. Jimmy says: "I do not play God" (p. 83, l.26). Consider the attitude towards wildlife and conservation that is reflected in this statement.

Stylistic aspects of description

1. Comment on the description of the scenery at the beginning and in the last paragraph of the story, especially the contrast between "the false" and "the cleansing dawn".
2. Find words and phrases used to describe the turtle.
3. Although the turtle is rather helpless on this sandroad it is quite capable of very quick movements (as Jimmy discovers: cf. p. 80, ll.7 ff). Pick out those verbs from the story which indicate momentary actions, eg. *to snap*.
4. Now consider phrases like the following:
   - p. 80, l.8: "the head struck *like* springsteel".
   - p. 80, l.9: "it all happened *as fast as* a matchflare".

   Write down at least five more examples of this kind. What would you call this stylistic device (a very common element of *imagery* used in fictional texts)?

Grammar practice: compounds of *some* and *any*

Study the following sentences from the text:
- p. 81, l.17: I can tell *something* is eating you.
- p. 83, ll.2/3: You are not putting up *anything*.
- p. 82, ll.4/5: In the water he could cut down *anyone, anything, any* man.

Now use the following compounds in the appropriate place in the text below:

someone	*something*	*somewhere*
anyone	*anything*	*anywhere*

Old Tony and his two sons were driving out to the White Creek when they spotted (1) ____ in the middle of the sandroad. The boys had never seen (2) ____ like it. It was a huge turtle. They stopped and got out. (3) ____ whistled. "Have you ever seen (4) ____ like that?" Jimmy asked. "Yeah," said Old Tony. "He's really (5) ____, isn't he?" "He could have picked (6) ____ else to rest," Joe suggested. "I'll move him," Jimmy said. "Wait and I'll go find (7) ____ in the wagon."
Old Tony and Joe didn't say (8) ____ . They looked at the turtle in the sand. He wasn't going (9) ____ . Then Jimmy called from the wagon. "Has (10) ____ seen the wrench? I know I put it (11) ____ in the back here. Now I can't find it (12) ____ . (13) ____ must have taken it. Do you know (14) ____ about it, Pa?" Old Tony got up and went back to the wagon without saying (15) ____ .

Make your point

1. "The needs of man are greater than the needs of the animal world." –
   Do you believe this is a reasonable view?
2. "Culling is a necessary act by man." –
   Note: *cull* [kʌl] (v) kill the weakest or unwanted members of a group of eg. seals; G: erschlagen, um den Bestand zu reduzieren (= aussortierendes Abschlachten bestimmter Tiere).
   - Which animals around the world are culled?
   - Why are they culled (eg. seals)?
   - Is culling necessary or unnecessary?

Writing task

"Put yourself into his shell" (ie. the turtle's). –
Discuss the value of this statement as a philosophy to be followed in all spheres of life. To what extent could this point of view influence *your* attitude towards (killing) animals?

3 TECHNOLOGY AND SCIENCE (FICTION)

The real danger of our technological age is not so much
that machines will begin to think like men,
but that men will begin to think like machines.

Sydney L. Harris

Text 3.1

Computers of the '90s

Education:
- Desk top computers will replace pens and paper
- Voice simulation will make it possible to learn foreign languages from mechanical tutors
- 'Libraries' full of books will be stored on optical disks
- Flexible software will make it easy for students to create their own computer programs

Children of the next decade will be baffled and amused by the mute, colorless, passive objects that today pass for personal computers. The computers on their desk tops and laps will talk and listen: they will display full-color, lifelike pictures which look just like photographs. Those computers will guide you through vast storehouses of information – from great books to daily newspapers, to films, music and art. Sounds of instruments will be a

4 tutor ['tjuːtə] (n) a teacher who gives private lessons to a single pupil or very small class 5 *store* (v) keep in a special place 5 *disk* (*AmE*) = (*BrE*) "disc"; a round and flat object (to store information for use by a computer) 6 *software* (n) the set of systems which control the operations of a computer 8 *decade* ['dekeɪd] period of ten years 8 *baffled* very confused or puzzled 8 *mute* silent, unable to speak 10 *lap* (n) G: Schoß 10 *display* (v) show 12 *guide* [gaɪd] (v) lead 12 *vast* huge, enormous 12 *storehouse* (n) *(fig.)* a place (or person) full of information natural part of those computers. And none of this is speculation: while the exact details are not known, the computer of the '90s is already taking shape in research centers around the US.

'There is no doubt,' says an IBM vice-president, 'that the computers of the future will be more user-friendly. In fact, as much as 50 per cent of the added power of tomorrow's computers will go to make the machines easier to use.'

Symbols such as a trash-can for the command 'delete' will become a standard feature, and the 'mouse' will help you navigate across the computer screen. But along with these visual cues, computers almost certainly will develop their own voices. With their new power, they can already produce very pleasing human voices. Future computer programs will probably help new users by talking them through complicated procedures: 'To erase that word, hit the backspace key. No, not that one, the one next to it.' Travelers may be able to dial their computers from the road and hear the day's electronic mail read aloud by a computer voice.

Computers will begin to understand speech as well, although this is far more difficult than imitating a regional accent. One speech-recognition system can now understand about 1,000 words of English spoken by anyone. Computers that have been 'trained' to understand only one voice can manage a much wider vocabulary – although most experts agree that the dictation-taking computer is still a decade away. One expert thinks that, to ensure security and privacy, future computers will turn on only when they hear the sound of their 'master's voice'.

Talking computers may find their warmest welcome in university language labs where, for example, they can be used to teach grammar. But that's just a start. There are already programs in which computer-controlled film clips are shown of French or Russian speakers shopping, apartment-hunting, etc.; the on-screen speakers regularly pause to ask questions. The student responds by typing an answer that the computer either accepts or corrects. However, once computers can speak fluently, they – rather than the taped humans – will interact with the student. Language teachers expect to have

2 *take shape* (v) take form 3 *research* ['--] or [-'-] (n) advanced study of a subject to learn new facts 8 *trash-can* (*AmE*) = (*BrE*) "dustbin"; container for holding rubbish 8 *delete* [dɪ'liːt] take away (sth that has been written) 9 *feature* (n) characteristic, typical quality 10 *cue* [kjuː] (n) a signal telling you how to act 12 *pleasing* attractive 13 *procedure* [-'--] (n) a set of actions necessary for doing sth 13 *erase* [-'-] (v) take away, remove, destroy 14 *backspace key* (n) G: Leertaste 15 *dial* ['daɪəl] (v) call (on a telephone) 16 *mail* (n) letters sent or received by post 18 *speech-recognition* the understanding of spoken language 23 *ensure* (v) make (something) certain (to happen) 27/28 *film clip* a section of film 30 *type* [taɪp] (v) write on a printer or typewriter 31 *fluently* ['---] without difficulty, without pause

computers that will read, with correct pronunciation, each sentence a student types – even using Chinese or Russian characters.

Simpler, 'friendlier' computers will transform schools as well. Both teachers and kids can begin to use them as daily tools rather than special-purpose drill-and-practice machines. In one research project, computers are placed under the desks but are visible through transparent desktops – out of the way, yet always accessible. In 1988, 300 kids – some as young as five – learned a program called 'Hypercard'. They use it to do their homework, take class notes, make drawings, even create data bases, on easy-to-use software. 'Children are very good at computers,' says the project leader, 'and computers make the kids look and feel smarter.'

2 *character* (n) written symbol 4 *tool* (n) G: Werkzeug 4 *special-purpose* having a special goal or intention 5 *drill-and-practice* train by repeating (*AmE* practice (v); *BrE* practise (v)) 6 *visible* (adj) able to be seen 7 *accessible* [ək'sesəbl] (adj) easy to get at, easy to reach 9 *data base* (n) bank of information 11 *smart* (esp. *AmE*) intelligent

Close reading

1. In what ways will future computers become "more user-friendly" (p. 87, l.5)?
2. What will be the advantages of 'talking' computers?
3. What will be the consequences of the "speech recognition systems" referred to in p. 87, l.18?
4. To what degree will security be a concern to the designers?
5. How will 'talking' computers be used as an aid to foreign language learning?
6. What is said in the text about the transformation of schools by 'friendlier' computers?

Language Work

Describing things and asking for more information

Suppose that you have to describe a piece of equipment, like a computer, to someone who knows nothing about it. You will have to be able to answer all sorts of questions, eg.:

What size is it?	It's ... centimetres/metres wide. It's about ... high/long/deep.
What shape is it?	It's round/square/rectangular/... It's the shape of a ...
What's it made of?	It's made of metal/rubber/plastic/wood/steel/stone/ ...
What colour is it?	It's ...
What does it look like?	It looks like ...
What are its main parts?	It consists of A, B and C ... Its main parts are ... The two/three etc. main parts are .../form Z A, B and C make up Z.

What do you use it for? — You use it . . ./It's used for . . .
The main function of it is to . . .
One function is to . . .

If the other person does not understand you, he or she can use some of the phrases below to get more information:

Sorry?/Pardon?/I beg your pardon? Sorry, I didn't quite catch that. What does that really mean? Could you say that again, please? Could you explain that in more detail please? Could you repeat that, please? Would you mind repeating that, please?

Ask another pupil to describe one of the following objects:

1. a television set
2. a tape/video recorder
3. a bicycle/moped
4. a stereo set

Giving instructions

Imagine that you have to explain to someone how to work a computer. What can you say? These expressions will help you:

First you . . . First of all you . . . The first thing you do is . . .
After that you . . . When you've done that you . . . The next thing you do is . . .
Don't forget to . . . It's very important to . . . Make sure (that) you . . .

Now explain how you work a personal computer. Others in the class should ask questions if they're not sure what you mean.

Focus on grammar: the *will*-future of the passive

Compare these two sentences:

Desktop computers will replace pens and paper.
Pens and paper *will be replaced* by desktop computers.

Change the following sentences into the future passive by beginning with the words in italics.

1. Today's personal computers will baffle *children of the next decade.*
2. The desktop computers of the future will display *pictures which look like colour photographs.*
3. Computer operators will store *'libraries' full of books* on optical discs.
4. These computers will guide *people* through vast storehouses of information.
5. Scientists will almost certainly develop *special computer voices.*
6. Computers will soon understand *our speech* as well.
7. Future computer programmes which talk will probably help *new users* through complicated procedures.
8. University students will also use *talking computers* to learn the grammar of foreign languages.
9. Language teachers will expect *these computers* to read out the sentences typed by students.

Class discussion

1. If parents do not learn about computer technology, they will be 'left behind' by their children. Do you agree?
2. How do you think computers will change the way we live in the future (eg. at school, work, in traffic etc.)?

Text 3.2

Autoguide

INFO BOX

THE BIG SQUEEZE

The 6.7 million Londoners own about 2.2 million cars. All in all drivers in the capital cover about 10,000 million miles on the city's main roads alone in one year. In the course of *one* day cars cross into and out of the central area about 1.6 million times. Altogether car drivers in London make about 8 million trips by car every day. Every year there are some 50,000 cars more on the roads in Greater London which means more driving and more pressure on the roads.

The following table summarizes the changes in traffic speeds (miles per hour = mph) in the central urban areas of some British cities during the past 20-odd years and the predictions for the late 1990s:

City \ Peak hour speeds	1967	1985	late 1990s
London	9.5	12.2	9
Liverpool	10.4	12	11
Manchester	9.1	11.7	10
Glasgow	13.5	8.6	8

While big investments are being planned for the railways in the south-east region of England no comparable developments are planned for London's roads.

Tasks

1. Can you work out the average yearly mileage of a London car?
2. How many trips do London car drivers make in a week?
3. Explain why pressure on the roads of London increases with every year that passes.
4. Describe the change in peak hour speeds in Glasgow between 1967 and 1985, comparing it with the other cities in the table.
5. What characterizes all the speed predictions for these cities in the late 90s?

Margaret Benson is a traffic expert at the European Commission in Brussels. On the tape you will hear an interview with her, in which she explains how computers will be used on European roads in the near future.

Annotations

average ['ævrɪdʒ] (adj) G: durchschnittlich
drop (v) fall
improve [-'-] (v) make better
huge (adj) enormous
research ['--] or [-'-] (n) G: Forschung
last (v) go on, continue
advanced (adj) the opposite of "basic"
achieve (v) get something done (successfully)
traffic jam (n) lots of cars, lorries, etc., crowded together, so that movement is very difficult
handy (adj) useful and simple to use
dashboard (n) the instrument board in a car
My guess is . . . I consider it likely . . .
at least G: mindestens
be wired with be connected up with wires
monitor (v) record, take note of
creep (v) here: move very slowly
beam [bi:m] (v) send out (in a certain direction)
punch (v) hit with the fist (closed hand)
destination [ˌ--'--] (n) the place you travel to
instrument panel a board with various controls or instruments
common (adj) usual
space (n) G: Raum, Platz
increase [ɪn'kri:s] (v) make larger, greater
efficiency [-'---] (n) the state of working well and without waste
capacity [-'---] (n) the amount that something can hold

Selective listening comprehension

Tuning in

Before you listen to the interview, go through these questions:

1. What is the main traffic problem in Europe as Ms Benson sees it?
2. What does she compare "Prometheus" to?
3. What does Ms Benson say about the development of the new warning system as far as time is concerned?
4. What is "Autoguide"?
5. Why would it be useful for drivers to be able to communicate with each other by computer?

Listen to the tape, and then write down your answers to the questions above.

True or false?

Read the following statements in advance, then listen to the interview again, and mark them true or false:

According to Ms Benson . . .

1. Traffic in Europe has doubled in the last 50 years.
2. In the year 2000, it will take at least twice as long to get somewhere as it does now.

3. “Prometheus” is a research project paid for by the European Community.
4. The new traffic control system for cars will be introduced in 1993.
5. The new computer warning system is already being tried out.
6. All the streets in large cities will eventually be wired with computers and sensors.
7. The computer will tell you the fastest way to get to Traffic Control.
8. There is little space for new roads and motorways in Europe.
9. “Prometheus” was produced by “Autoguide”.
10. You will be able to start your “Autoguide” by pressing a button on your car stereo.

Discussion

1. What is the traffic situation like in your home town? Can it cope with the problem of increasing traffic?
2. Can you suggest different approaches to reduce traffic jams in the big cities (apart from automated route-finding technology)?

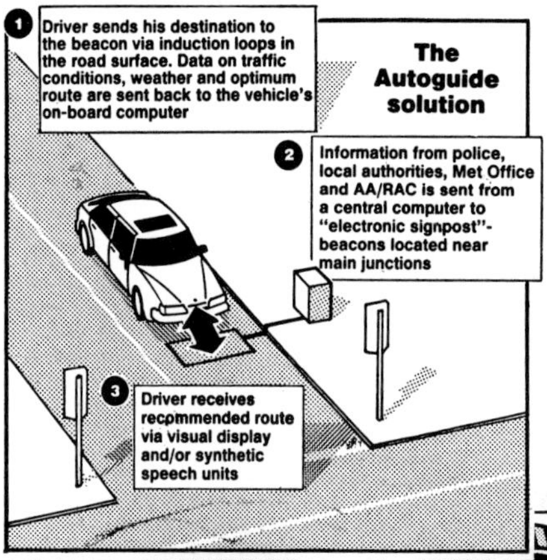

destination (n) G: das Ziel
beacon ['bi:kən] (n) a guiding or warning signal, here: G: Leitsignal
via ['vaɪə] (prep) using, by means of
loop (n) G: Schleife
surface (n) G: Oberfläche
Met Office G: Wetteramt
AA Automobile Association
RAC Royal Automobile Corps
junction (n) a place where roads come together; G: Kreuzung
display (n) G: Anzeige
screen (n) G: Bildschirm

Hello, This Is Your Future Calling

Joe X lies in bed and telephones his girlfriend in America. How wonderful to see her as well as talk to her. After that he has a friendly chat with the computer at the bank. It understands every word he says and replies in such a nice human voice. Joe should get up but first a quick look at today's news on the videoscreen on the wall . . .

Is this a scene from a science-fiction film? Not at all. By the year 2000 this could be happening in your home – provided, of course, that you have a telephone.

In the USA there are already three phones for every four people. Britain has one telephone for every two people and 55 million phone calls are made every working hour. As telephone systems expand, they become increasingly automated. Thanks to this and to other technological developments, a revolution will very soon take place in communications.

Homes of the future will be linked to the outside world by viewphones, videoscreens and talking computers. This means that there will be a vast increase in traffic over the lines and messages will have to be sent more quick-

2 *chat* (n) informal talk   3 *reply* (v) answer   7 *provided that* on condition that   11 *expand* [-'-] (v) become bigger   11 *increasingly* [ɪn'kriːsɪŋlɪ] more and more   14 *be linked to* (v) be connected to   15 *vast* enormous, huge   15/16 *increase* ['--] (n) a rise in amount

ly and accurately. Two recent developments will make this possible: digital transmission and optical fibres.

Conventional telephone messages are communicated in the form of varying electrical waves. Digital messages take the form of rapid bursts or pulses of electricity or light. By using digital messages speech, text, data and pictures can all be sent simultaneously down the same line without interfering with each other in any way. It also means that other services such as videoconferencing can be introduced. This means that businessmen in several different towns can see and speak to each other without leaving their offices.

The second new development is a remarkable new form of telephone line: the optical fibre. Words and pictures can be transmitted in digital form by laser beams down thin threads of glass covered with plastic – no thicker than the nylon thread in a string of beads. These optical fibres can carry 100,000 conversations and 200 television channels at once.

Other developments are also taking place in the field of communications. If we are going to talk to computers, they must be able to recognize the human voice and then reply just as in a normal human conversation. Scientists in America and Britain have already developed speech recognition systems, and the Japanese have produced television sets which can be turned on and off by vocal commands. Certainly it will not be long before such systems are more widely used. The same is true of voice synthesizers. At present the 'voice' they produce is rather artificial, like a machine. But it will not be long before machines can 'speak' in a more natural way.

Technological developments such as these will be of enormous benefit both in the home and at work. Information of all kinds in the form of speech, text or pictures will be transmitted more quickly and efficiently. Think of the advantages to the disabled, the sick, the old. Think of the benefits to businessmen or, indeed, to anyone who leads a busy life. And think how these developments could help people who live in isolated places where, for example, there may by poor educational facilities or little entertainment. Certainly, in ten or fifteen years' time, making a phone call will be a more interesting experience than now.

1 *recent* (adj) having happened only a short time ago 2 *fibre* (n) a type of thread made chemically 4 *burst* (n) a sudden concentration of energy 6 *simultaneous* [ˌsɪməl'teɪnjəs] at the same time 6/7 *interfere with* (v) get in the way of 8 *be introduced* (v) be brought in, presented 10 *remarkable* extraordinary, outstanding 12 *laser beam* ['leɪzə] G: Laserstrahl 12 *thread* [θred] (n) G: Faden 13 *string of beads* G: Perlenschnur 16 *recognize* (v) here: know the sound of 20 *vocal command* (n) an order given by a human voice 21 *voice synthesizer* ['sɪnθəsaɪzə] a machine which combines different sounds to become like a human voice 22 *artificial* [ˌɑːtɪ'fɪʃəl] (adj) not real, false 24 *benefit* ['---] (n) advantage 27 *disabled* (adj) handicapped 30 *facilities* (n) possibilities (to do things)

Comprehension

The main idea

Which sentence best describes the main idea of the text?
Give reasons for not choosing the other two sentences.

1. The number of telephones is going to increase enormously in the next few years.
2. Technological developments will soon revolutionize our communications.
3. Computers will soon be able to recognize speech patterns and also reply in a convincing way.

Check the details

Say whether the following sentences are true or false. If they are wrong, correct them:

1. Homes will have video screens and viewphones by the end of the century.
2. More and more machines are replacing people in the running of telephone systems.
3. Fewer telephone calls will be made in the future.
4. In years to come, telephone messages will be sent by electrical waves.
5. Laser beams will send messages down optical fibres.
6. Machines have been developed which can recognize and respond to human sound.
7. It will forever be impossible for a machine to produce a natural-sounding 'voice'.
8. The telephone system of the future will be more efficient, because it will transmit speech, text and pictures.

Technical Vocabulary

Here are some technical terms from the text. Find their correct definitions.

1. viewphone
2. optical fibres
3. speech recognition system
4. digital transmission
5. laser beam
6. voice synthesiser

a) a very bright, powerful light
b) a machine which allows you to speak to other people and see them at the same time
c) a machine which can produce a human-sounding voice
d) the system by which information is sent in the form of quick bursts of light
e) the system by which machines can 'understand' spoken commands
f) long, fine threads of very clear glass along which messages can be sent

Talking points

1. See p. 93, l. 9: "In the USA there are already three phones for every four people". Look at the table below which gives the number of *main* installations in various countries* (1987):

Country*	S	CH	DK	USA	N	D	F	GB	A	I	DDR	SU	IND
No. of phones (per 100 people)	64	52	51	51	44	44	43	39	37	32	10	9	0.5

* Nationality plates on cars

a) In which countries are the most and the fewest telephones installed?
b) Are there any figures which surprise you?

2. According to a survey published in December 1988 Britons usually have a specific reason to make a telephone call, whereas twice as many Americans like to phone just for a chat.
   - How important is a telephone for you?
   - Could you manage without it?
   - How would you interpret someone's frequent use of the telephone?
3. "The telephone calls and everybody obeys" – Is it occasionally a tyrant?
4. "People without a phone are weird and exotic." – Do you agree or disagree?
5. What do you think of the idea of viewphones?
   - Would you like to have one in your home? Why (not)?
   - Think of situations in which a viewphone would be an advantage or a disadvantage.
6. Explain how the technological developments mentioned in the text would benefit the old, sick and disabled, and why they could also be of use to people living in isolated areas.

Text 3.4

The Medical Consequences of Nuclear Weapons

Dr Patricia Gawthorpe is one of 1,500 doctors and health care workers who have signed an "Open Letter" to the British Prime Minister about the medical consequences of nuclear weapons. This Open Letter is the first national statement of an organization called the Medical Campaign against Nuclear Weapons (MCANW). In an interview, Dr Gawthorpe gave the following report of MCANW and its aims:

Dr Gawthorpe, what exactly do you say in your Open Letter?

Dr Gawthorpe: Well, first we point out that any nuclear war involving this country would result in death, injury and disease such as we have never known before.

How can you be so sure of this?

Dr Gawthorpe: If you look carefully at the medical and scientific evidence there is no other conclusion you can draw.

What about civil defence?

weapon ['wepən] (n) an instrument for killing or harming in defence or attack 5 *aim* (n) goal, objective 7 *involving* including 8 *disease* (n) illness, sickness 11 *evidence* (n) G: Zeugnis, Beweisstück 12 *draw a conclusion* (v) come to a decision 13 *civil defence* ['sɪvl dɪ'fens] G: Zivilschutz

Dr Gawthorpe: The civil defence measures which have been planned would be practically useless. The blast and heat of a nuclear explosion would kill or injure even those people who had managed to get into shelters. Please remember that these shelters are all in the cities, and it is the cities which would be the first target. In the country, radiation would kill people and animals out in the open. It would be dangerous to leave your home. Then there is the fact that radioactive fall-out would mean we couldn't use large areas of land for months, maybe years.

Is there no effective medical planning for such a disaster?

Dr Gawthorpe: No, it's an impossible task. If you remember that almost all likely targets are in or near the centres of population, then you must also realize that most hospitals are within ten miles of city centres and therefore would probably be destroyed in a nuclear explosion together with most of the medical and nursing personnel. This would also mean that medical supplies would be unavailable or inadequate and the injured would be left to look after themselves. Obviously many of them would die a painful, lingering death.

You don't paint a very bright picture, do you?

Dr Gawthorpe: If you are realistic, the picture is black. Nothing justifies the use of nuclear weapons. Nothing. And yet we go on producing them. It's insane, isn't it? We must get rid of them before it is too late. That is our most important aim. The only hope for us all is prevention, and that's the real message of the

1 *measure* ['meʒə] (n) G: Maßnahme 3 *blast* (n) explosion 5 *shelter* (n) here: a place specially built for protection 7 *target* ['tɑːgɪt] (n) something fired at 11 *fall-out* ['fɔːlaʊt] (n) the radiation in an area after a nuclear explosion 15 *disaster* (n) catastrophe 21 *destroy* (v) ruin 24 *supplies* (n) necessary materials for daily life 24 *unavailable* [ˌʌnə'veɪləbl] unable to be got 27 *lingering* ['lɪŋgərɪŋ] slow to end 32 *insane* crazy, mad

Open Letter to the Prime Minister. We, all the members of MCANW, are convinced that the only way to protect people from the medical consequences of nuclear war is to prevent nuclear war itself. And to achieve that, we must abolish nuclear weapons entirely from the face of the earth.

2 *be convinced* (v) be certain 3 *prevent* (v) stop something (before it starts) 3 *achieve* (v) be successful in 4 *abolish* (v) bring to an end, get rid of 4 *entirely* completely

INFO BOX

4 TONS OF TNT FOR EVERY MAN, WOMAN OR CHILD

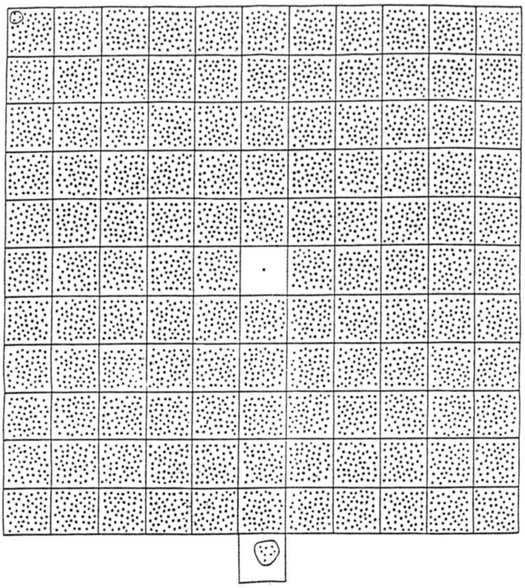

An average-sized nuclear weapon these days is a one-megaton bomb. It has the explosive power of 50 Hiroshima bombs and equals a freight train filled with TNT which is 320 km long. The dot in the centre square represents all of the firepower exploded in World War II (=3 megatons of TNT). – All the other dots represent the firepower of all existing nuclear weapons (=18,000 megatons). – These dots represent the firepower of 6000 World War II's or nearly one million Hiroshima bombs or 4 tons of TNT for every human being on earth.

Annotations

TNT = trinitrotoluene: a powerful explosive
average (adj) ['ævrɪdʒ] of the usual or standard kind; G: durchschnittlich
dot (n) a small round mark
mega ['megə] = 1,000,000
megaton = the force of an explosion equal to 1 million tons of TNT (1 billion kilograms)

Tasks

1. How is the power of a one-megaton bomb characterized here?
2. Explain the meaning of the dot in the middle of the diagram.
3. Compare this dot with all the others by referring to Hiroshima.

Comprehension

1. What is the main message of the open letter to the British Prime Minister, as explained by Dr Gawthorpe in this interview?
2. Explain how useful nuclear shelters would be in a nuclear war.
3. How would life in the country be affected by a nuclear war?
4. Explain why hospitals would be ineffectual, both for those who needed one and those involved in medical care?
5. Comment on the use of the word *lingering* in l. 27 on p. 97.
6. "It's insane" (l. 32 on p. 97). How does Dr Gawthorpe support this statement?
7. What is the key line of argument in the last paragraph expressing Dr Gawthorpe's opinion of nuclear weapons?

Grammar revision: the use of question tags

Add the appropriate question tag (the equivalent German sentence would end in ... *nicht wahr?*):

1. Patricia Gawthorpe is a doctor, ____?
2. She's signed an "Open Letter" to the prime minister, ____?
3. She gave an interview to the press a few days ago, ____?
4. Nuclear war would result in enormous loss of life, ____?
5. There's no other conclusion one can draw, ____?
6. The cities would be the first target, ____?
7. You haven't forgotten that nuclear shelters are all in the cities, ____?
8. Nothing justifies the use of nuclear weapons, ____?

Dialogue practice

Find yourself a partner and sketch out one of the two dialogue situations. Act it out afterwards:

1. A is a city businessman (or a wealthy farmer) with a nuclear shelter in his garden, where he considers himself to be safe from nuclear war. B is trying to convince him that he will have no chance of a decent life after a nuclear attack.

2. A is a top military or political leader who can be sure of a place in a nuclear shelter. Confront him with the questions and arguments of an ordinary citizen for whom no such plans exist.

Your verdict

To what extent do you agree with either of the two statements below? Support your opinion by giving reasons:
1. "Nuclear weapons have made this planet more secure."
2. "Nuclear weapons are a new and terrible form of tyranny."

Text 3.5

A New Life

The first thing you notice about Elizabeth West is that she speaks very quickly. She opens her mouth and the words simply rush out. Then she pauses to get her breath back before beginning the next sentence.

"I was a couple of years old when they first found out there was something wrong with me. I had a hole in my heart, and it was too late to operate."

The second thing you notice about Elizabeth West is her spirit. It shows itself at once in her sense of humour.

"Other kids were happy enough to have the mumps or the measles, but I'll do anything to be different. I suppose I'm just an exhibitionist at heart."

She laughs briefly at the pun before continuing.

"I led a pretty normal life anyway as a kid, though I didn't do gym or play games at school. Then one day, when I was eleven, I came home from school and Mum noticed that my hands were all blue and I was having trouble with my breathing."

"That's what first attracted me to Liz," says Bob, when she pauses to get her breath back. "Blue's my favourite colour."

2 *rush out* (v) run out very quickly 7 *spirit* (n) G: Mut, Charakter 9 *measles* ['mi:zlz] (n) G: Masern 10 *at heart* (adv) basically, essentially 11 *brief* lasting only a short time 11 *pun* (n) humorous use of words, G: Wortspiel 12 *gym* [dʒɪm] short form of "gymnastics" 12/13 *play games* (v) do sports

Elizabeth throws something at him and pretends to be angry. Bob and Elizabeth have been going steady for two years. She is now eighteen and works as a clerk in a travel agency. Throughout her teens her health has been getting steadily worse. Her only hope is a heart-lung transplant; she is waiting for a donor.

"It's awful, really," she says, "because you're waiting for someone to die, though I try not to think of it like that. The thought of the operation scares me stiff, but I've no choice; I've got to have it done."

Elizabeth pauses again and suddenly smiles.

"When Bob heard that *The Sunday Telegraph* was going to photograph the operation, he said: 'You'll have no clothes on, so they'll have to put you on the pin-up page.'"

Elizabeth says her mum doesn't understand her boyfriend's sense of humour. "I'm not sure that I do either," she adds with a mysterious grin.

"Cheeky beast," Bob snorts indignantly.

On a warm evening in July the phone rings. A woman of 24 has had a brain haemorrhage. Her blood group, heart and lungs are a perfect match for Elizabeth, she is carrying a donor card, and she is in South London. Elizabeth and her mother live in Newcastle. Her parents are divorced and her father has emigrated to Australia. Elizabeth and her mother are very close.

"I've got to do it," says Elizabeth. "It might be my only chance." She rings Bob, who is in the shower. He jumps into his car, still wet, and arrives at Elizabeth's house looking like a drowned rat. "Thank God you're here," says Elizabeth's mother. "She'd never leave without seeing you."

It takes 50 minutes for Elizabeth and her mother to fly to London. Elizabeth is in tears on the plane. "It's not the operation," her mother explains. "She's terrified of flying."

At 11.05 pm the surgeon makes the first incision in Elizabeth's chest. At one o'clock in the morning Elizabeth's mother phones Bob to tell him that the new heart and lungs are in place. Three and a half hours later she rings again to say that Elizabeth has come back from the operating theatre. And at

1 *pretend* (v) make oneself appear (to be) 2 *go steady* ['stedɪ] go out together regularly 3 *clerk* [klɑːk] (n) person who works in an office doing paperwork 4 *steady* constant 5 *donor* ['dəʊnə] (n) a person who gives part of his body for medical purposes 7/8 *scare sb stiff* (v) *(coll.)* make sb very frightened 17 *haemorrhage* ['hemərɪdʒ] (n) a large flow of blood 17 *match* (n) something suitable to something else 19 *divorced* no longer married 20 *be close* have deep feeling for each other, like each other very much 23 *drowned* [draʊnd] dead from being under water for a long time 27 *terrified* very frightened, afraid 28 *surgeon* ['sɜːdʒən] (n) a doctor who performs medical operations 28 *incision* [ɪn'sɪʒən] (n) the cut which a surgeon makes 28 *chest* (n) the upper front part of the body 31 *operating theatre* ['ɒpəreɪtɪŋ ˌθɪətə] the place where operations are carried out

7.00 am she phones to report the miracle: Elizabeth's cheeks and lips are pink – there's no trace of blue. "Ah well," says Bob, "I've always liked pink better anyway."

A few days later Elizabeth is sitting up in bed eating chicken and chips. Her mother and Bob look in at her through a large glass window. Bob says: "She's six years older now with that heart, aren't you, Liz?" Elizabeth's mother warns her: "Don't forget that you won't be able to kiss him for six weeks and then he'll have to wash his mouth out first and clean his teeth, and by that time he'll have gone off it."

Five weeks after the operation Elizabeth and her mother come home. Elizabeth cycles every day. She even takes part in a three-mile charity walk together with Bob. She says: "Whenever I go for a walk or climb a hill, I'm waiting, all the time, for the moment when I can't go on – but it doesn't come."

By the middle of October Elizabeth is back at work. She takes three lots of pills and medicine daily against rejection and infection. Her age and good health give her a better chance for the future than most. Her mother says: "There's no point in worrying about what you can't change. Forget about things being unfair. Life is a game of chance. Just keep taking the tablets."

Elizabeth adds: "I think I enjoy life more than other people. Most people know vaguely that they're going to die some time in the future, but it's all very unreal somehow and it's a lifetime away. I know I can die tomorrow, so I grasp every minute of the day. Time is so precious. I'm grateful for every second I can get."

1 *miracle* ['mɪrəkl] (n) G: Wunder 2 *trace* (n) mark or sign; G: Spur 9 *go off something (coll.)* lose interest in something 11 *three-mile charity walk* ['tʃærətɪ] a walk which is three miles (5 km) long, during which money is collected for the poor or handicapped 12 *climb* [klaɪm] (v) G: ersteigen 15 *three lots* three quantities 16 *rejection* [rɪ'dʒekʃən] (n) here: the body's reaction against the new parts 18 *there's no point in* it's no use 21 *vague* ['veɪg] not clear 23 *grasp* (v) take a firm hold of 23 *precious* ['preʃəs] valuable

Check your reading

1. At what age did Elizabeth's illness begin?
2. How was Elizabeth different from the other children at school?
3. Give examples of Liz' and Bob's sense of humour.
4. Comment on the significance of the statement "you're waiting for someone to die" (p. 101, l. 6).
5. Give reasons for the author's opinion that Elizabeth has a lot of "spirit" (p. 100, l. 7).
6. Remark on the causes of the observation "Elizabeth's cheeks and lips are pink" (p. 102, l. 1).
7. Why were Bob and Liz not allowed to kiss for six weeks?
8. What kind of activities did she undertake a few months after the operation?
9. Summarize Elizabeth's attitude towards life and death after she had the transplant.

Grammar practice: the choice of relative pronouns

Use *who, which, whose* or *whom* in the following sentences:

1. Liz lives in Newcastle, ___ is in the North-East.
2. Her father, ___ has emigrated to Australia, writes to her regularly.
3. Bob, with ___ she's been going steady for two years, has a strange sense of humour.
4. He also has an old car in ___ they hope to go to Edinburgh this weekend.
5. Bob, ___ favourite colour is blue, bought the car because he liked the colour.
6. His car, ___ is a dark blue colour, also has a very good engine.
7. Liz's mother, to ___ she is very close, wonders if Bob can drive it.
8. Liz cycles on a bike ___ she got from her friends at work.
9. She got it when she came home from hospital, ___ was just five weeks after her operation.
10. All the people ___ work at the travel agency helped to pay for it.

Expressing worry and fear

Elizabeth's mother says: "She's terrified of flying."
Study the expressions below and make sure you know what they mean:

I'm terrified of . . .
I'm frightened of . . .
I'm scared stiff of . . .
I'm nervous about . . .
I'm (a bit) worried about . . .
I'm anxious about . . .
I'm apprehensive about . . .
I'm very concerned about . . .

It terrifies me that/when . . .
It frightens me that/when . . .
It scares me stiff that/when . . .
It makes me nervous when/that . . .
It worries me that/when . . .
It causes anxiety to me that/when . . .
It troubles me that/when . . .
I'm afraid it might . . .

Now express your own feelings about things and situations that you dislike.

Form your own opinion

1. Elizabeth's mother says: "Life is a game of chance." (p. 102, l. 19) To what extent can one influence the course of one's life?
2. 'A positive attitude to life is the most important factor for a person's physical and emotional well-being.' State the arguments for or against this point of view.
3. 'Death is a natural process, and no human being should try to cheat it.' Is this a reasonable view, to your mind, especially when you think of today's possibilities in medical engineering (organ transplantations, dialysis, intensive care etc.)?
4. KIDNEYS FOR SALE – "The objection is this: it will always be a rich man who buys and always a poor man who has to sell" (R. M. R. Taylor, President of the British Transplantation Society).
   a) Are there enough organs available for transplants in Germany?
   b) Discuss the question of trade in human organs.

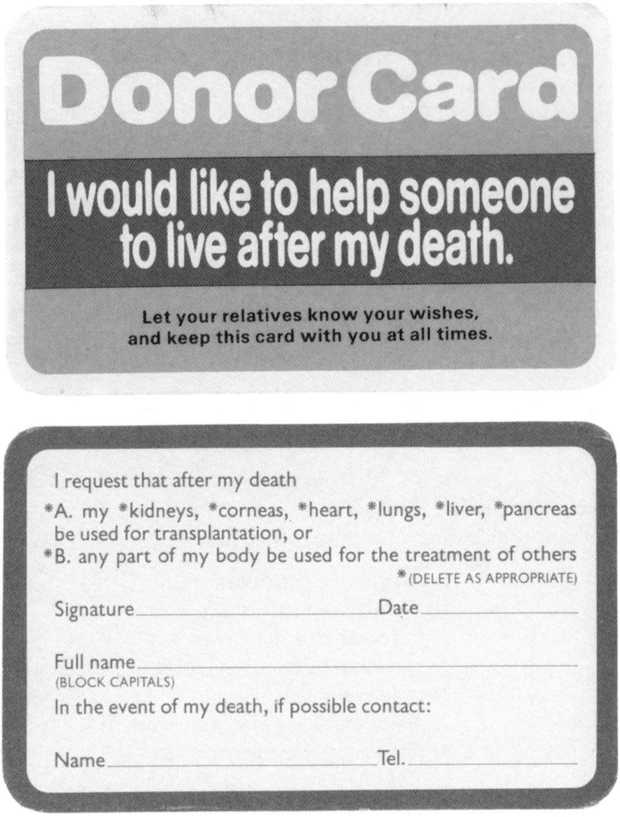
Donor Card

I would like to help someone to live after my death.

Let your relatives know your wishes, and keep this card with you at all times.

I request that after my death

*A. my *kidneys, *corneas, *heart, *lungs, *liver, *pancreas be used for transplantation, or

*B. any part of my body be used for the treatment of others

*(DELETE AS APPROPRIATE)

Signature ________________ Date ________

Full name ________________________________

(BLOCK CAPITALS)

In the event of my death, if possible contact:

Name ________________ Tel. ________

5. a) Do *you* carry a card similar to this? Why (not)?
   b) What sort of donor system exists in Germany?
   c) How would you feel about your own organs being used for transplants after your death?

ext 3.6

We've Always Been a Close-Knit Family

There's only
the two of us left now.
You've got to be grateful to
those transplant pioneers, back
in the 80s. I'd have been dead
ten years but for Ron's lungs
and Auntie Kittie's liver and
kidneys. I'll be needing a
change of heart soon.
How are you feeling,
George?

close-knit [ˌkləʊsˈnɪt] tightly bound together by social, political, religious beliefs and activities *knit* (v) *(tech.)* grow together closely (eg, I hope the broken bone will knit properly); sonst G: stricken 6 *but for* except for 8 *kidney* (n) G: Niere

Reading between the lines

1. Who are "the two of us"?
2. What has happened to the rest of the family?
3. Give an interpretation for both the headline and the last two lines (10 f.).
4. Describe your reactions to this poem.

Follow-up

Work in pairs: Choose a shape and draw it. It can be a geometrical shape such as a T, a triangle or a circle. Or it can represent an object like a star, a diamond, a tree or a hand. Then write a short piece of free verse (not more than 50 words) which is connected with the shape you have chosen.
Set your work out on a sheet of paper and compare with other students' poems.

The Chunnel

The great driving force behind the Channel Tunnel – the "Chunnel" – is undoubtedly the dream of joining Great Britain to the European mainland. It is a dream which Napoleon had as early as 1802. His engineers even drew up a plan to dig such a tunnel under the neck of water which connects the North Sea to the Atlantic Ocean: the English Channel. War with England, however, began again in 1803 and Napoleon dropped the idea.

Since then, there have been several starts on this mighty project, but all of them fizzled out in the end. Until now. At this very moment, three parallel tunnels are being built 40 metres under the bottom of the English Channel.

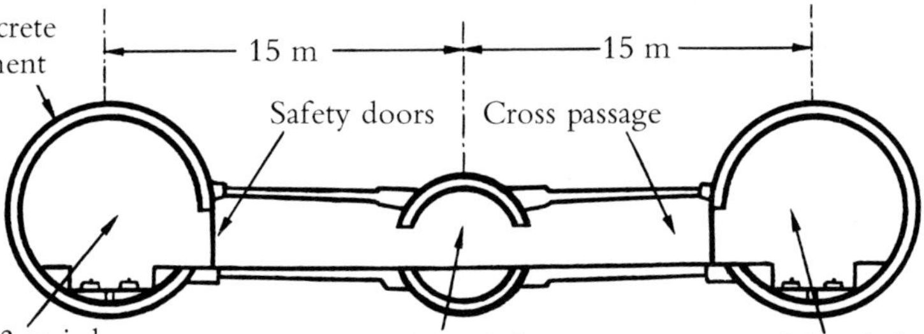

The two bigger tunnels are one-way passages for trains. Between these is a smaller tunnel which will function as a combined service and safety tunnel. All three tunnels are linked together every 375 metres by a cross passage (see diagram).

The entrance to the Chunnel is like a huge underground cathedral. Grey concrete walls reach skyward from 100 feet below sea level. At the foot of the enormous shaft, three tunnel entrances point towards the English Channel. In the smaller central tunnel a giant metal cylinder is slowly eating its way through the chalk of the Channel floor. This machine, 30 feet long and weighing over 300 tons, is officially known as a TBM-1 (Tunnel Boring Machine). There are ten other TBMs and when all the tunnels are finished, they will have moved 7.5 million cubic metres of earth on to the French and British mainlands.

1 *driving force* here: main motivation 2 *undoubtedly* [ˌʌn'daʊtɪdlɪ] certainly, without doubt 2 *joining* connecting, linking 2 *mainland* (n) G: Festland 4 *dig* (v) G: (aus)graben 4 *neck of water* narrow stretch of water 6 *drop* here: give up 7 *mighty* ['maɪtɪ] huge, enormous 8 *fizzle out* (v) *(coll.)* die out 12 *link* (v) connect, join 12 *passage* ['pæsɪdʒ] (n) long narrow connecting way, like a corridor 15 *skyward* towards the sky 16 *shaft* (n) G: Schacht 18 *chalk* [tʃɔːk] (n) a type of soft white rock; G: Kreide(felsen)

Two kinds of train will use the Chunnel. One will carry passengers only. The other will transport people in their cars. The journey under the Channel is expected to take around 35 minutes and trains will depart every 7 minutes in each direction. The tunnels themselves will be 49 kilometres long, 37.5 of which will be under the sea.

If a train should break down, or if a fire should start, the passengers will be able to get off the train and on to a narrow platform which will run the entire length of the two train tunnels. Lights and signs will direct them to the nearest exit passageways which link up with the smaller service tunnel and the other train tunnel. The passengers can then take another train back to their point of departure.

The international consortium building the tunnels is called Eurotunnel. They expect to transport around 60 million people through the tunnels every year. The specially built trains can be up to 750 metres long and carry as many as 600 passengers. For safety reasons, each train will be pulled by two or three engines. With an estimated speed of 160 kilometres an hour, it will take only 3½ hours to travel from Paris to London. Already there is talk of using even faster trains which will cut another hour off the journey between the two capital cities.

Politically the Chunnel is a popular venture. Both British and French politicians have given it their enthusiastic support, seeing the project as a wonderful chance to reduce high unemployment. People working on a dozen boat ferry services across the Channel are somewhat less enthusiastic, fearing that they will lose their jobs. It seems certain, however, that the easier access provided by the Chunnel *will* bring a great many economic advantages.

The tunnels are expected to be ready in 1993, when the last trade barriers within the European Community will have disappeared. Already many English families have started looking for houses on the North French coast, where property is only one third of the price on the British side of the Channel. Perhaps it is the millions of ordinary people in the two countries who have most to gain from the Chunnel, people who – like generations of their countrymen – have let 30 kilometres of water come between them for too long.

3 *depart* (v) leave 28 *break down* (v) here: get a mechanical fault and stop 8 *entire* [ɪn'taɪə] (adj) complete 9 *passageway* (n) see "passage" (p. 106, l. 12) 12 *consortium* [kən'sɔːtjəm] (n) a combination of a number of companies, banks, businesses, for a common purpose 16 *estimated* ['----] calculated 20 *venture* ['ventʃə] undertaking, course of action 21 *support* [-'-] (n) encouragement and help 23 *boat ferry service* service which takes people and things across a stretch of water by boat or ferry 24 *access* ['ækses] (n) means of getting to (places) 25 *provided by* given by 26 *trade barrier* ['bærɪə] (n) something which stops the buying and selling of goods between countries 31 *gain* (v) benefit, win (advantages)

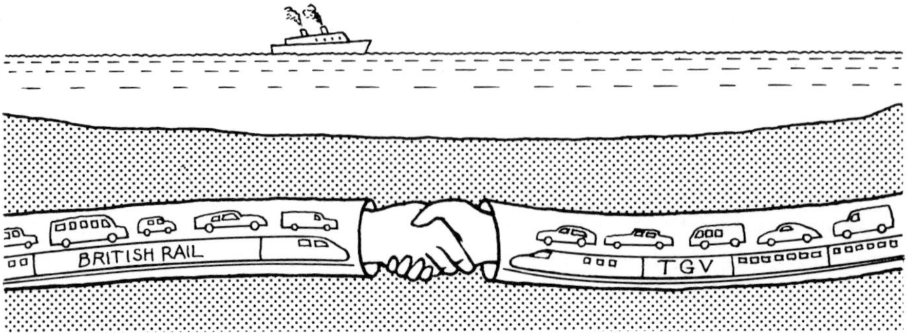

Check your understanding

1. Why was the original idea of the Channel Tunnel not fulfilled?
2. Sketch out the basic idea behind the present design of the Chunnel.
3. Comment on the use of the words *cathedral* (p. 106, l. 14) and *eating* (p. 106, l. 17).
4. Choose three figures given in the text and comment on their significance.
5. Explain the safety precautions envisaged for the tunnel.
6. State the two points of view as regards the popularity of the Chunnel project.
7. Comment on the last four lines of the text. Do you share the author's opinion?

Grammar practice: present participle clauses

Note how the following two sentences are joined together by a present participle, a very common construction in English, in the third sentence:

1. Both British and French politicians have given the Chunnel their enthusiastic support.
2. They see the project as a wonderful chance to reduce high unemployment.
3. Both British and French politicians have given the Chunnel their enthusiastic support, *seeing* the project as a wonderful chance to reduce high unemployment.

Join the following pairs of sentences together in a similar way using a present participle:

1. a) The people who work on boat ferry services are not enthusiastic.
   b) They fear that they will lose their jobs.
2. a) The Chunnel is expected to be finished by 1993.
   b) It will bring a great many economic advantages with it.
3. a) Many English families have already started looking for houses on the North French coast.
   b) They realise that property is much cheaper there than in England.
4. a) The journey under the Channel will be a quick one.
   b) It will take only 35 minutes.
5. a) The people building the Chunnel are sure it will be a great success.
   b) They expect around 60 million passengers to use it every year.
6. a) The entrance to the Chunnel reaches skyward from 100 feet below sea level.
   b) It looks very much like a huge, underground cathedral.
7. a) There are three tunnel entrances at the foot of the enormous shaft.
   b) They point towards the English Channel.

Pair work: the pros and cons of the Chunnel project

Think of the advantages and disadvantages of the Channel Tunnel. Make a list of written notes:

- safety
- convenience
- (un)employment
- commuting
- country life
- risk of rabies
- economic and commercial developments
- Britain being joined to Europe
- house and land prices
- social and ecological problems
- tourism and traffic movements
- the north-south divide in Britain

Present the two points of view about this project and compare them with the arguments put forward by other students in your class.

Class discussion

1. "The joining of Britain to France is an important step forward to a united Europe." – Would you agree or not? Give your reasons.
2. "The routes between England und France are quite adequate. In view of the existing train, plane, boat and hovercraft links the hazards and expenses of the Chunnel cannot be justified." – Give supporting reasons for or against this view using the information stated in the diagram below:

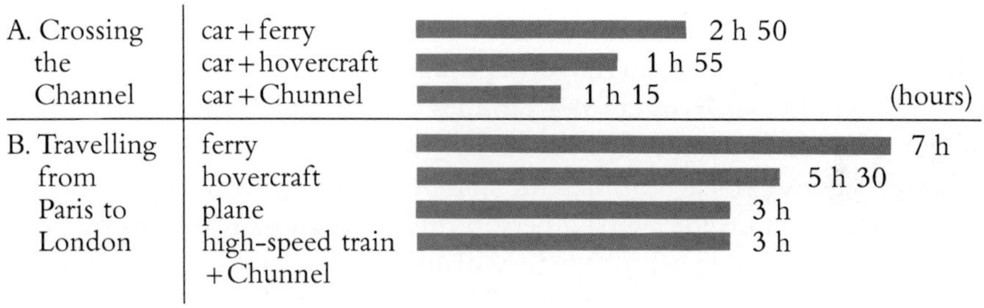

Genetic Engineering

David Filkin

Imagine how useful it would be if tomatoes could be grown on the stalks of potato plants. Two crops could be grown at the same time, using the space of one. Or imagine how marvellous it would be if inherited diseases like cystic fibrosis and haemophilia could be eliminated. Both possibilities are now conceivable because of an important new scientific technique called "genetic engineering". It is as important a development as the silicon chip, with hundreds of potential new applications – and it involves being able to control the very basic design of life itself.

All living things, from the very simplest bacteria to a complex creature such as Man, are made up of living cells. In the case of a human being, millions of them. And every living thing has the ability to reproduce itself. People grow up from babies into adults as their cells continuously produce new and slightly changed cells. The changes go on as we grow older and eventually die – when the cells no longer reproduce at all. All the changes that happen throughout our lives are not random or accidental. Every person has a unique plan or blueprint that was drawn up from the time he or she was conceived. This plan determines the colour of eyes or hair and, along with other factors, can decide when a person might go grey or lose his hair completely, or what size bust a female will have, how tall we might grow, or maybe even how intelligent we are. This personal blueprint is stored inside every living cell.

Inside the nucleus of every cell are tiny thread-like bodies called chromosomes. They exist in pairs: normally human beings have twenty-two pairs of chromosomes, and two odd ones in each cell. These chromosomes are made

1 stalk [stɔːk] (n) G: Stiel, Stengel 2 *crop* (n) agricultural plant; the amount grown and taken by a farmer; G: Ertrag 2 *space* (n) area, room 3 *inherited* [-'---] (adj) passed on from one's parents 3 *disease* [dɪ'ziːz] (n) illness, sickness 3/4 *cystic fibrosis* ['sɪstɪk ˌfaɪ'brəʊsɪs] G: Blasenfibrose (Erkrankung der Bauchspeicheldrüse) 4 *haemophilia* [ˌhiːməʊ'fɪlɪə] a disease which means that bleeding (from a cut) does not stop 5 *conceivable* [-'---] able to be thought of 6 *silicon chip* ['sɪlɪkən 'tʃɪp] G: Silikon- oder Mikrochip 7 *potential* (adj) possible 7 *application* (n) here: use 7 *involve* [-'-] (v) have as a result 13 *slightly* minimally, insignificantly 15 *random* ['rændəm] (adj) without any plan 15 *accidental* [ˌ--'--] (adj) by chance 16 *unique* [juː'niːk] (adj) being only one of its kind 16 *blueprint* ['--] (n) scheme 16/17 *was conceived* began life (growing inside the mother) 17 *determine* [-'--] (v) decide 19 *bust* (n) a measurement round a woman's breasts and back 20 *store* (v) keep 22 *nucleus* ['njuːklɪəs] G: Zellkern 22 *thread-like* long and very thin, like a *thread* (G: Faden) 22/23 *chromosome* ['krəʊməsəʊm] 24 *odd ones* the ones which are not like the others

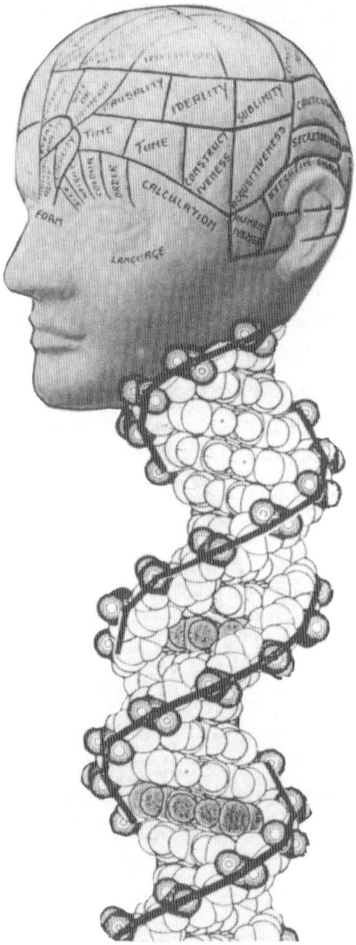

of a complex chemical called DNA – short for deoxyribonucleic acid. This chemical carries the details of the plan or blueprint, each tiny piece of which is called a gene. There are genes to decide hair colour, others to decide eye colour, and so on. If a living cell happens to be part of an eye, it will make active use of the eye colour gene. In each cell, therefore, there is a complete string of genes, even if it only "uses" a few of those genes.

Basically a string of genes is like a string of numbers. The basic variations revolve around four different numbers. So that one person's genetic code might look something like 22134211134421243341 ... while another will

1 *deoxyribonucleic* [diːˈɒksɪˌraɪbəʊˈnjuːklɪɪk] G: Desoxyribonuklein 1 *acid* G: Säure 3 *gene* [dʒiːn] G: Gen 3 *decide* (v) here: make a choice about 6 *string* (n) a set of things connected together 8 *revolve around* (v) centre on

look like 2122344413214332122. This is where the amazing new technique of genetic engineering comes in. Even though every living cell is microscopic in size, and the chromosomes are smaller still, so that the genes on them are so tiny that it is hard to believe that they could be sorted out and identified, scientists have now developed such sophisticated techniques that they can identify many precise details of the genes.

For instance, they might demonstrate that there were five digits in all genetic codes on one particular chromosome and its twin, to determine the way in which our blood clots when we cut ourselves. And since the chromosomes are in pairs, they may be able to discover that when, say, the digits 1 and 2, as the first digits of the five, on one chromosome are paired with, say, 3 and 4 on its partner, it produces a problem: the blood does not clot. Literally hundreds of thousands of number combinations would be fine – such as these pairs:

a) 12433...   b) 43122...   c) 22143...
   33122...   41333...   41122...

but this pair d) 12134...
                 43314...

has the fatal combination of genes leading to a failure of blood to clot – the disease haemophilia.

"Genetic engineering" is the name given to a range of techniques by which scientists can actually manipulate these number codes. As they learn more about our genes and how to control them, it looks as though it will only be a matter of time before they can manipulate the numbers in the haemophilia-causing genes, so that the problem disappears.

1 *amazing* (adj) astonishing, very surprising   4 *sort out* (v) arrange in a system   5 *sophisticated* [-'----] (adj) refined; complex   7 *digit* ['dɪdʒɪt] (n) number; figure   8 *twin* (n) identical partner, G: Zwilling   12 *clot* (v) become hard or solid   12/13 *literally* ['lɪtərəlɪ] G: buchstäblich   19 *fatal* ['--] (adj) ending in death or disaster   19 *failure* ['--] (n) lack of success

Close Reading

Multiple choice questions

Which is right? Choose from a, b, c or d.

1. Cystic fibrosis is
   a) a kind of crop.
   b) a type of disease.
   c) a technique for increasing production.
   d) something to do with silicon chips.
2. The way a human being develops is determined by
   a) how many cells he or she has.
   b) how long each cell lives.

c) his or her own unique blueprint.
d) a particular type of bacteria.

3. Every human being has in each cell
   a) twelve chromosomes.
   b) a pair of chromosomes.
   c) twenty-five chromosomes.
   d) forty-six chromosomes.
4. DNA is
   a) a chemical of which chromosomes are composed.
   b) a type of gene.
   c) something which determines the colour of our eyes.
   d) another name for a blueprint.
5. We can understand our genetic codes in terms of
   a) five basic digits.
   b) whether we have any serious diseases.
   c) thousands of number combinations.
   d) combinations of four basic numbers.
6. The term "genetic engineering" is used for the
   a) machines by which scientists carry out their experiments.
   b) techniques by which the codes of genes are changed.
   c) production of chromosomes.
   d) preparation of DNA.

Missing words

Complete the following sentences without referring to the annotations.
All living things are composed of (1) .... and are able to (2) .... themselves. We all have a (3) .... plan or (4) .... which determines many (5) .... about us such as our hair colour. At the centre of every cell are forty-six (6) .... which are made of a (7) .... called (8) .... each tiny piece of which is called a (9) ....

Grammar practice

The simple present of the passive

In scientific writing the passive form of the simple present is frequently used:
All organisms *are made up* of living cells.
Re-read the text and make sentences about cells and chromosomes using the simple present of the passive of the verbs in italics:

1. inside every living cell – a personal blueprint – *store*
2. the colour of one's eyes – *determine* – by this unique plan
3. the tiny thread-like bodies – inside the nucleus of a cell – *call* – chromosomes
4. chromosomes – *make of* – a complex chemical
5. for short – deoxyribonucleic acid – *call* - DNA
6. the details of the blueprint – *carry* – genes
7. person – hair colour – *decide* – genes

The modal passive

Compare these sentences:

Imagine how useful it would be *if you could grow tomatoes* on the stalks of potato plants.
Imagine how useful it would be *if tomatoes could be grown* on the stalks of potato plants.

Change the following sentences in a similar way, using the modal passive. Begin with the words in italics.

1. You could grow *two crops* at the same time.
2. You could eliminate *certain inherited diseases.*
3. You could control *the basic design of life itself.*
4. Possibly you might even decide *a person's intelligence.*
5. You can think of *a string of genes* as a string of numbers.
6. Scientists can identify *many precise details of the genes.*
7. A fatal combination of genes may cause *certain diseases.*
8. Manipulating the number codes might make *these diseases* disappear.
9. Scientists can already use *certain techniques* to manipulate our genetic codes.
10. You may well call *this range of techniques* "genetic engineering".

Discussion topics

1. Are the potential benefits of genetic engineering greater than the dangers? Form your own opinion.
2. Think of other uses not mentioned in the text which could be made of genetic engineering, either positive or negative.
3. Would you like to be able to select the kind of children that you might one day have: their sex, looks, personality, level of intelligence etc.? Why (not)?

And Miles to Go Before I Sleep

William F. Nolan

Alone within the humming ship, deep in its honeycombed chambers, Robert Murdock waited for death. While the rocket was moving towards earth, he waited calmly through the final hours, knowing that hope no longer existed.

After twenty years in space, Murdock was going home.

Home. Earth. Thayersville, a small town in Kansas. Clean air, a shaded street and a white two-storey house near the end of the block. Home after two decades among the stars.

He remembered the worried face of his mother, her whispered prayers for his safety, the way she held him close for a long, long moment before he went up the ship's ramp those twenty years ago. He remembered his father: a tall, weather-beaten man, and that last firm handshake before he said good-bye.

It was almost impossible to realize that they were old now and white-haired, that his father was forced to use a cane, that his mother was bowed, wrinkled and weakened by the years.

And he himself was forty-one. His face was square and hard-featured, his eyes dark and buried beneath bushy eyebrows.

Robert Murdock took out the pictures of his parents from his uniform pocket and studied their faces. Warm, smiling, *waiting* faces: waiting for their son to come home to them. Carefully, he unfolded his mother's last letter. She had always been stubborn about sending tapes, complaining that her voice was unsteady, that she found it so difficult to speak her thoughts into a cold, impersonal machine. He had received this last letter just before his take-off for Earth, and it read:

1 *humming* making a sound like bees 1 *honeycombed* ['hʌnɪkəʊmd] like the wax structure made by bees, with six-sided cells for honey and eggs 1 *chamber* (n) room (often with a special purpose) 2 *rocket* (n) G: Rakete 3 *calm* [kɑːm] quiet, without being excited 3 *final* ['--] (adj) last 5 *space* (n) G: Weltraum 6 *shaded* (adj) not in sunlight 7 *two-storey* with two floors 9 *prayer* (n) act of asking God (for help) 12 *weather-beaten* showing marks or signs from being in the sun, wind, rain etc. 15 *cane* (n) piece of bamboo used as a walking-stick 15 *bowed* [baʊd] bent over 16 *wrinkled* ['rɪŋkəld] with many small folds in the skin 17 *square* [skweə] G: rechteckig 17 *hard-featured* with hard characteristics 18 *buried* ['berɪd] here: hidden 23 *unsteady* not firm, shaking 25 *take-off* (n) ['teɪk-ɒf] the beginning of a flight

Dearest,

We are so excited! Your father and I listened to your voice again and again, telling us that you are coming home to us at last, and we both thanked our good Lord that you were safe. Oh, we are so eager to see you, son. As you know, we have not been too well lately. Your father's heart doesn't allow him to get out much any more. Even the news that you are coming back to us over-excited him. Then, of course, my own health doesn't seem very good as I suffered another fainting-spell last week. But there is no real cause for alarm – and you are not to worry! – since Dr. Thorn says I am still quite strong, and that these spells will pass. I am, however, resting as much as possible, so that I will be fine when you arrive. Please, Bob, come back to us safely. We pray to God you will come home safe and well. The thought of you fills our hearts each day. Our lives are suddenly rich again. Hurry, Bob, hurry!

All our love,

Mother

Robert Murdock put the letter aside and clenched his fists.

Only brief hours remained to him – and earth was days away. He knew he would never reach it alive.

The closing lines of the ancient poem by Robert Frost came whispering through his mind:

'But I have promises to keep,
And miles to go before I sleep . . .'

He'd promised he would come home, and he would keep that promise.

'Out of the question,' the doctors had told him. *'You'll never reach earth. You'll die out there, in space.'*

They told him about his coming death almost to the final second – when his heart would stop beating, when his breathing would end. This disease,

5 *Lord* God   6 *eager* (adj) characterized by strong interest, full of enthusiasm   12 *faint* (v) lose consciousness suddenly   12 *spell* (n) a short period (of illness)   25 *clench* (v) close tightly   26 *brief* short   28 *ancient* ['eɪnʃənt] very old   33 *out of the question* impossible   36 *disease* [dɪ'ziːz] (n) illness, sickness

which he had got on an alien world, was incurable. Death, for Robert Murdock, was a certainty.

But he had a plan.

Now, with less than thirty minutes to live, Murdock was walking down one of the ship's long corridors. He was ready, at last, to keep his promise.

Pausing before a wall storage-locker, he turned a dial. The door slid back. Murdock looked up at the tall man standing there motionless in the darkness. He reached forward, made a quick adjustment. The tall man spoke.

'Is it time?'

'Yes,' replied Murdock. 'It is time.'

The tall man stepped smoothly down into the corridor; the light flashed in the deep-set eyes, almost hidden beneath bushy eyebrows. The man's smile was hard and square-featured.

'You see,' he smiled, 'I am perfect. My name is Robert Murdock. I am forty-one years of age. I have been in space for two decades – and now I am going home.'

Murdock smiled, a tight smile of triumph which passed quickly across his tired face.

'How much longer?' the tall figure asked.

'Ten minutes. Perhaps a few seconds beyond that,' said Murdock slowly. 'They told me it would be painless.'

'Then ...' The tall man paused, drew in a long breath, 'I'm sorry.'

Murdock smiled again. He knew that a machine, however perfect, could not experience the emotion of sorrow – but it helped to hear the words.

'He'll be fine,' thought Murdock. 'He'll serve in my place and my parents will never suspect that I have not come home to them.'

'Remember,' he said, 'when you leave them, they must believe that you are going back into space.'

'Naturally,' said the machine. 'Let me assure you, all will go exactly as you have planned.'

'Yes, it will work,' Murdock told himself. 'I've thought of every detail. He possesses every memory that I possess; his voice is my voice, his small habits my own. And when he leaves them, the pre-recorded tapes of mine will continue to reach them from space, exactly as they have in the past. Until their deaths. They will never know I'm gone.'

1 *alien* ['eɪlɪən] foreign 1 *incurable* [-'---] that cannot be healed 5 *at last* finally 6 *storage-locker* (n) a metal box for keeping things in 6 *dial* ['daɪəl] (n) G: Wählscheibe 6 *slide* move smoothly (as if on ice) 7 *motionless* without moving 8 *make an adjustment* (v) set something right, put something into order 11 *smoothly* ['smuːðlɪ] easily, without difficulty 17 *tight* [taɪt] here: closely or firmly put together 24 *sorrow* (n) the emotion of feeling sorry 26 *suspect* [-'-] (v) feel doubt about 32 *possess* [pə'zes] (v) have, own 33 *habit* (n) sth you do regularly 33 *pre-recorded* [ˌpriːrɪ'kɔːdɪd] recorded on a machine for later use, preserved on a machine etc.

'Are you ready now?' the tall figure asked softly.

'Yes,' said Murdock, nodding. 'I'm ready.'

And they began to walk slowly down the long corridor ...

The tall figure in the neat spaceman's uniform closed the outer airlock and watched the body drift away into blackness. For Robert Murdock, the journey was over, the long miles had come to an end. Now he would sleep forever in space.

When the rocket landed in Thayersville, Kansas, the crowds were there, waving and shouting out Robert Murdock's name. The city officials were all present, each with a carefully rehearsed speech; the band played and children waved flags. Suddenly the crowd became quiet. The atomic engines had stilled and the airlock was sliding back.

Robert Murdock appeared, tall and heroic in a splendid uniform which threw back the light of the sun in a thousand glittering patterns. He smiled and waved as the crowd burst into fresh shouting and applause.

And, at the far end of the ramp, two figures were waiting: an old man, bowed and trembling over a cane, and a wrinkled woman, her hair white, her eyes shining.

When the tall man finally reached them, pushing his way through lines of well-wishers, they embraced him feverishly. They clung tight to his arms as he walked between them; they looked up to him with tears in their eyes.

Robert Murdock, their beloved son, had come home to them at last.

'Well,' said a man on the edge of the crowd, 'there they go.'

His companion sighed and shook his head. 'I still don't think it's right, somehow. It just doesn't seem right to me.'

'It's what they wanted, isn't it?' said the other. 'It's what they put in their wills. They didn't want their son to come home to death. In another month he'll be gone anyway. Back for twenty more years in space. Why spoil the little time he has, why ruin it all for him?'

The man paused, pointing at the figures in the near distance. 'They're perfect aren't they? He'll never know.'

'I guess you're right,' agreed the second man. 'He'll never know.'

And they watched the old man and the old woman and the tall son until they were out of sight.

2 *nod* move one's head up and down (in agreement) 4 *neat* (adj) orderly, tidy, smart 4 *airlock* ['--] (n) a kind of room on a space ship with airtight doors at each end 5 *drift* (v) float or be driven along by the wind 9 *city official* (n) a person who works in the administration of a large town 10 *rehearse* (v) [rɪ'hɜːs] learn and practise 13 *splendid* grand and impressive in appearance 14 *pattern* (n) G: Muster, Vorbild 15 *burst* break into 20 *well-wisher* ['-ˌ--] (n) person who hopes that another will be happy, successful etc. 20 *embrace* [-'-] (v) put one's arms around 20 *feverishly* ['fiːvərɪʃlɪ] quickly and excitedly 20 *cling* hold on closely 23 *edge* (n) here: outside line, border 28 *spoil* (v) ruin, destroy

Comprehension

1. Identify the main idea in the first three lines of the story.
2. Summarize the information given about Robert Murdock's parents (up to his mother's letter).
3. Describe Robert's parents from the information given in his mother's letter.
4. Explain how Murdock knows that he won't be able to reach Earth.
5. Who is the tall man in the storage-locker?
6. Comment on the different smiles in the phrases "a tight smile of triumph" (p. 117, l. 17) and "Murdock smiled again" (p. 117, l. 23).
7. "They will never know I'm gone" (p. 117, l.35). – State the essential information of this sentence in more detail.
8. Describe the reception given in Thayersville to celebrate the return of Murdock's spaceship.
9. Say something about the way Murdock's parents welcome their son.

Interpreting the story: looking for clues

1. Murdock is said to have a "plan" (p. 117, l.3). Now that you know the end of the story, sum up this plan in your own words.
2. Look at the way Murdock and "the tall man" are described in the story. Name the things they have in common and the things they do not share.
3. List all those temporal expressions (eg. *final hours* etc.) which serve as evidence for the countdown to Murdock's death.
4. Count the number of occurrences of the pronoun *it* in the final passage of the story (p. 118, ll.24 ff). Comment on the meaning of *it* and the function of this kind of repetition.
5. Describe the irony of the story. Comment in particular on both Murdock's and his parents' motives for what they chose to do.
6. Consider now the role of the two men at the end of the story. One of them wondered if what had been done was right. List the arguments which justify their action.
7. Comment on the attitude towards life and death in a future society, as is implied in this story.

Discussion

1. Does space travel have a special fascination for you or not? Give your reasons.
2. Have you read or seen other stories of this kind (ie, science fiction)? Give the names of authors or directors and a short summary of the plots of these stories, books or films.
3. "Nothing is impossible" (Lewis Mumford). Consider if there are 'things' (machines, plans, inventions etc.) in science fiction which may turn out to be practicable one day.
4. How do you feel about the robots and bionic men of science fiction? Sketch out the possibilities and the dangers as you imagine them.

4 LANGUAGE, MEDIA and COMMUNICATION

Language is the memory of the human race. It is as a thread or nerve of life running through all the ages, connecting them into one common, prolonged and advancing existence.

Thorndale by *William Smith,*
Scottish philosopher and poet, 1802–1872.

thread (n) G: Faden *prolonged* made longer *advancing* going forward

GENERAL INTRODUCTION

"Every educated person in the world will have problems if he or she does not know English."

(Robert Burchfield, editor of the *Oxford English Dictionary*)

1. Comment on the need for an international language. Give your reasons why you think English is (not) the best language for international communication.
2. Which is better: to know one foreign language really well, or to know several languages reasonably well?
3. What do you consider to be the most important aspects of learning English, eg. a good accent or pronunciation, writing grammatically correct English, etc.
4. How much do you actually use English *outside* the classroom? Where do you use it? Which skill (eg. listening) do you use most?
5. Think about the usefulness of English (to you personally) in the future: for your studies or work, for leisure time (listening to music or watching films), for travelling etc.
6. Which nationalities do you think are least willing to speak foreign languages? Give examples from your own experience and try to find reasons.
7. What do foreigners find most difficult when learning German?
8. Of all the languages in the world (apart from English), which one would you most like to speak or read well? Give reasons for your choice.

9. Comment on the following cartoon which appeared in the British newspaper *The Guardian Weekly*, May 28, 1989:

ext 4.1

Mike and Claire

You know that British English and American English sound different and that some words are spelt differently. Sometimes not even the same words are used. Claire from England visits her cousin Mike in New York. Listen to Claire's story after going through the following words.

Annotations

mac (n) *(BrE)* mackintosh, ie. a sort of raincoat made of plastic material
Wellington boots rubber boots used in wet weather
boot a space for luggage at the back of a car
hired car car which has been rented
backing here: driving backwards
bonnet ['--] (n) a metal lid over the front of a car
windscreen (n) the window at the front of a car
pram (n) carriage for a baby, pushed by hand
flat (n) a number of rooms in a building, in which a family lives
lavatory ['lævətrɪ] (n) toilet
tap (n) G: Wasserhahn
chop (n) a thick slice of meat with a bone in it; G: Kotelett
sweet (n) dessert
rumbling sound a deep, continuous, rolling sound
fridge a refrigerator, or large box in which food and drink can be kept at a low temperature

Listening comprehension

1. Listen to Claire and look at the text. Find the missing words. You will have to listen twice (at least):

   I'm here at last. Mike met me at the airport. The weather was (1) ____ nice. I didn't need my (2) ____ and my Wellington boots. As soon as we got my (3) ____ I put on trainers instead. We went to the (4) ____ and Mike put everything in the (5) ____ except my handbag.

   Mike told me it was a (6) ____ car and told me what a backing (7) ____ had done to the (8) ____ and windscreen of his own car. We drove part of the way on the (9) ____ and got to Mike's place at twenty past five.

   There was a (10) ____ on the pavement outside and an old (11) ____ blocking the front door. There was no (12) ____. But Mike told me not to worry. He lives on the (13) ____ floor.

   I like his (14) ____ a lot.

   He showed me my room, the bath, and the (15) ____, and warned me that the (16) ____ were always hot.

   When I'd unpacked and changed, dinner was ready: pork (17) ____ and chips, a sweet, and coffee and (18) ____.

   There was a kind of rumbling sound every five minutes or so. I thought it was the (19) ____ at first, but Mike told me it was the (20) ____. After a while you don't hear it.

   I'm sure I'm going to have a nice holiday.
2. After having checked your answers, compare Claire's description with Mike's and see what *other* words or phrases are different in them.
3. Name those words from the text which show differences in pronunciation between British and American English.

This is Mike's version:

Claire's here at last. I met her at the airport. The weather was real nice. She didn't need her raincoat and rubber boots. As soon as we got her baggage she put on sneakers instead. We went to the parking lot and I put everything in the trunk except her purse.

I told her it was a rental car and told her what a backing truck had done to the hood and windshield of my own. We drove part of the way on the freeway and got to my place at twenty after five.

There was a garbage can on the sidewalk and an old baby carriage blocking the front door. There's no elevator. But I told her not to worry since I live on the first floor.

3 *sneakers* ['sniːkərs] (n) *AmE* shoes for gymnastics, = trainers *(BrE)* 4 *parking lot* (n) *AmE* = car park *(BrE)* 4 *trunk* (n) *AmE* = the *boot* of a car *(BrE)* 5 *purse* (n) *AmE* = handbag *(BrE)* 6 *rental car* ['rentl] *AmE* = hired car *(BrE)* 6 *truck* (n) *AmE* = lorry *(BrE)* 7 *hood* (n) *AmE* = the *bonnet* of a car *(BrE)* 7 *windshield* (n) *AmE* = the *windscreen* of a car *(BrE)* 7 *freeway* (n) *AmE* = motorway *(BrE)* 9 *garbage can* ['gɑːrbɪdʒ] (n) *AmE* = dustbin *(BrE)* 9 *sidewalk* (n) *AmE* = pavement *(BrE)* 9 *baby carriage* (n) *AmE* = pram *(BrE)* 10 *elevator* ['----] (n) *AmE* = lift *(BrE)*

Claire said she liked my apartment.

I showed her her room, the bath, and the john and warned her that the faucets are always very hot.

When she'd unpacked and changed, dinner was ready: pork cutlets, French fries, a dessert and coffee and cookies.

There was a kind of rumbling sound every five minutes or so, and Claire thought it came from the refrigerator. I told her it was the subway.

I hope she'll like her vacation.

2 *john* (n) *AmE slang* = toilet; = loo *(BrE)* 2 *faucet* ['fɔːsɪt] (n) *AmE* = tap *(BrE)* 5 *cookies* (n) *AmE* = biscuits *(BrE)* 7 *subway* (n) *(AmE)* underground railway; = underground, tube *(BrE)* 8 *vacation* [-'--] (n) *AmE* = holiday *(BrE)*

Making friendly responses

1. Before Claire left England to see Mike in New York, her mother said: *'Give my love to Michael.'* Other expressions you can use in this context are:
   'Say hello to . . . for me.' (informal use, among friends)
   'Give my (best) regards to . . .' (formal use)
2. At London Airport Claire's mother said to her: *'Have a good trip.'* Other useful expressions when someone is going away (or out to a play or concert) are:
   'Have fun' *'Have a nice time'* *'Enjoy yourself/yourselves'* etc.
3. When Mike was making dinner for Claire in his apartment, she said: *'That smells lovely.'* Other expressions you can use in this situation, are:
   'This looks really great' *'Mmm, this is delicious'* *'That was a lovely meal'* etc.
4. When Claire told Michael that she had just been accepted as a student at Oxford University, he said: *'That's marvellous, Claire! Congratulations!'* Other expressions you can use when someone has been successful are:
   'That's fantastic!' *'Well done!'* *'That's great news!'*

Working in pairs, act out short dialogues using the information given below. One of you thinks out what to say, and the other responds appropriately. Change roles when you come to the end and begin again.

1. You are going to a pop/rock/classical concert this evening.
2. You are making fish and chips for your guest.
3. You are going to meet your cousin from America, whom your friend has met once before.
4. You've just won a lot of money in a lottery.
5. You've just eaten some of your friend's home-made cake.
6. You're going to London for the weekend.
7. You've just passed an important exam.
8. Tomorrow you're going to meet Terry, an old friend of the person you're talking to now.
9. You and your friend are sitting eating the spaghetti dinner you have cooked.
10. You have just passed your driving test.
11. You are leaving for a holiday in Spain tomorrow.
12. You won the club championship (tennis or whatever) last week and your friend doesn't know about it yet.

A Perfect Pronunciation?

Have you ever thought to yourself when learning English: 'Do I really *need* to speak English like the Queen or Prince Charles?' What can you reasonably expect from someone learning English as a foreign language? Is perfection a realistic goal?

"Is it really necessary for most language learners to acquire a perfect pronunciation? Intending secret agents and intending teachers have to, of course, but most other language learners need no more than a comfortably intelligible pronunciation (and by 'comfortably' intelligible, I mean a pronunciation which can be understood with little or no conscious effort on the part of the listener.) I believe that pronunciation teaching should have, not a goal which must of necessity be normally an unrealized ideal, but a *limited* purpose which will be completely fulfilled: the attainment of intelligibility"
(David Abercrombie: *Problems and Principles*. Longman, London 1956, p. 37).

Let us accept the fact that 99% of our students are going to speak English 'with a German accent' – in spite of the teacher's careful cultivation of Received Pronunciation* (= RP) as *the* ideal norm. Given a typical pupil in a typical classroom situation, perfection of this kind cannot be reached. The teacher himself is hardly perfect. So what? What is so terrible about speaking English with a German accent? Or, for that matter, with a French accent? Or an Italian accent?

The story is told of the late Maurice Chevalier that he used to pay regular visits to the Berlitz School of Languages in order to perfect his French accent in English – hardly surprising, when you stop to consider that his accent was an important part of his success. Similarly, Henry Kissinger's pronunciation

---

* *Received Pronunciation* is the variety of English recorded by Daniel Jones in his "English Pronouncing Dictionary". It is common among educated speakers in Britain who have attended public schools.

2 *reasonably* ['----] (adv) within reason, sensibly 3 *expect* [-'-] (v) G: erwarten 4 *goal* [gəʊl] (n) objective, aim 5 *acquire* [ə'kwaɪə] (v) get for oneself by one's own work 5/6 *intending secret agents* people planning to be secret agents 7 *comfortably intelligible* ['kʌmfətəblɪ ɪn'telɪdʒɪbl] able to be understood without difficulty 8 *conscious* ['kɒnʃəs] (adj) G: bewußt 9 *effort* ['efət] (n) the act of trying hard 10 *unrealized* [ˌ-'---] not made real 10 *purpose* ['pɜːpəs] (n) intention, plan of action 11 *attainment* [-'--] (n) success in arriving at or reaching something 11 *intelligibility* [ɪnˌtelɪdʒɪ'bɪlɪtɪ] (n) the state of being able to be understood 14 *cultivation* (n) improvement or development by careful training 17 *So what?* What does it matter? 18 *for that matter* as far as that is concerned 20 *late* (adj) who has died 21 *in order to* for the purpose of 22 *consider* (v) think, give thought (to sth)

could hardly be described as RP – or even Standard American – but is it any the less intelligible or valid for that?

The plea here is for tolerance. A pupil who *consistently* says [dæns] instead of [dɑːns] should surely escape disapproval. Other pupils may show consistency in their choice of other forms: for example, we would expect a Bavarian speaker to 'roll' his [r] in words like *broad, bright* etc. instead of pronouncing the 'normal' English [r]. The same would be true for a foreigner who learnt his English in Scotland and therefore picked up the 'rolled' [r] the way it is spoken up there. In all fairness I think that these points are already accepted by the vast majority of German teachers. It is important to remember, however, that perfection in pronunciation may not always be a good thing.

A German tourist with an excellent command of English went into a pub in a working-class district of London. After a few drinks he turned to a couple of men standing beside him at the bar and attempted to strike up a conversation.

"Jolly fine weather we've been having lately, isn't it?"

This harmless enough meteorological comment was received with a few grunts by the two men, who all at once seemed somewhat embarrassed and ill-at-ease. They took the first opportunity to move away to a table in a far corner of the room. Poor Fritz was left wondering about the inadequacy of

1/2 *any the less* (+adj) G: umso weniger (+Adj) 2 *valid* ['--] (adj) of value 3 *plea* [pliː] (n) strong request 3 *consistently* [-'---] (adv) G: konsequent, beständig 4 *escape* [-'-] (v) here: avoid 4 *disapproval* [ˌ--'--] (n) G: Mißfallen, Mißbilligung 4/5 *consistency* (n) the state of always being the same in thought and behaviour 6 *Bavarian* [-'---] (adj) G: bayerisch 10 *vast* (adj) huge, enormous 21 *inadequacy* (n) here: failing his personal hygiene. 'What did I say wrong? Don't they talk about the weather any more?'

What had happened? Quite simply, the German tourist used what might be called 'marked RP' – that is, Standard English spoken with a very strong RP class accent – which singled him out as a 'foreigner' as soon as he opened his mouth. The two working-class men in the pub obviously felt unable to speak on the same level and immediately beat a retreat.

In other words, as long as slight deviations from the norm are *consistently* made and can be contextually understood, we should accept what the speaker has to say with the utmost tolerance. After all, we *all* speak with an accent of some kind.

However, we do need a pronunciation model, and the one best suited for teaching purposes at present is RP – at least for students of English in a European context. If nothing else, it is the only British one which has been comprehensively described, thanks to Daniel Jones. Let us therefore follow it as closely and accurately as possible, not to become replicas of upper class English gentlemen, but simply to make ourselves better understood.

8 *slight* (adj) small, not serious   8 *deviation* [ˌdiːvɪ'eɪʃn] (n) a difference from what is expected   12 *suit* [suːt] (v) have the right qualities

Check your understanding

1. Explain the mentioning of the Queen and Prince Charles in the introductory paragraph.
2. Pick out three key nouns in the second (p. 124, ll. 5 ff) and the fifth (p. 125, ll. 7 ff) paragraph which indicate the author's personal view about pronunciation teaching.
3. What is said about German teachers of English and their pupils?
4. Explain the element of surprise in the anecdote about Maurice Chevalier.
5. Comment on Henry Kissinger's background to justify the mention of his name in this context.
6. Translate the last two paragraphs into German (ll. 15 ff), and summarize the author's viewpoint in your own words.

Over to you

1. Make up your own mind about the question of a perfect pronunciation. Do you want to achieve a perfect accent in English? Why (not)?
2. Sum up the main difficulties you and your classmates have with your pronunciation of English. Give reasons for the fact that some people find it easier than others to pronounce foreign words.
3. In your experience, do textbook writers and teachers put too much emphasis on a 'good' pronunciation?

4. Would you say varieties of English other than British English (especially RP) should be more accepted in the classroom? Comment on people who change from one variety to another.
5. Find out your teacher's opinion concerning the 'best' model and the standards he or she aims at in this field.

Form your own opinion

1. Argue your own point of view with regard to the following statements for and against a 'good' accent:

Against	*For*
a) "Class distinctions as defined by wealth, power and job status are bad enough – without the additional problem of accent. To insist on 'correcting' a child's accent is a matter of class dominance."	b) "A good accent adds a touch of class, leadership and intelligence to a person. Children should therefore be encouraged to speak well."
c) "Accent is immaterial. It is the ability to communicate one's messages to everybody which is important."	d) "Accent differences are barriers to social equality. They can and must be overcome by education."
e) "Keeping one's 'normal' speech is essential for a person's identity because it strengthens family ties and regional roots."	f) "Improving one's accent has many practical advantages in everyday social life."

2. Consider if there is anything similar to RP in German (that is, a *socially* marked norm). What do pupils of your age speak at home or at school – the standard language or a kind of dialect?
3. Summarize your own reactions and feelings towards people in public life who have a strong regional accent (radio newsreaders, television presenters, politicians, pop stars, actors etc.).

Tongue-twisters

Repeat the following sentences or phrases several times as fast as you can:
- She sells sea shells on the sea shore.
- Red lorry, yellow lorry.
- Red leather, yellow leather.
- Thirty-three tinkers think thirty-three thoughts.
- Happy Harry had a heavy hippo. What a heavy hippo happy Harry had!

Text 4.3

Tuning in

What do we use language for? Before you read the text, make a few notes individually. Then compare your notes with other students.

"So, then. . . . Would that be 'us the people' or 'we the people'?"

Why Do We Use Language?

David Crystal

The question 'Why do we use language?' seems hardly to need an answer. The usual answer is 'To communicate our ideas' – and, indeed, this must surely be the most widely accepted function of language. Whenever we tell

1 *hardly* (adv) scarcely

people about ourselves or our circumstances, or ask for information about other selves and circumstances, we are using language in order to exchange facts and opinions. But it would be wrong to think of it as the only way in which we use language.

Here are examples of two out of several other functions where the communication of ideas is marginal or irrelevant.

Emotional expression

Mr X carefully leans his walking stick against a wall, but it falls over. He tries again, and it falls a second time. Mr X curses the walking stick. How should we classify this function of language? It cannot be 'communication of ideas', for there is no one else in the room.

Here we have one of the commonest uses of language – a means of getting rid of our nervous energy when we are under stress. It is the clearest case of what is often called an 'emotive' or 'expressive' function of language. Emotive language can be used whether or not we are alone. Swear words and obscenities are probably the commonest signals to be used in this way, especially when we are in an angry or frustrated state. But there are also many emotive utterances of a positive kind, such as our involuntary verbal reactions to beautiful art or scenery, our expression of fear and affection, and the emotional outpourings of certain kinds of poetry.

The most common linguistic expressions of emotion consist of conventional words or phrases (such as *Gosh, My, Darn it,* and *What a sight*), and the semi-linguistic noises often called interjections (such as *Tut-tut, Ugh, Wow, Ow,* and *Ouch*). Also, an important function of language is to give an outlet for our attitudes while we speak. At a more sophisticated level, there are many literary devices of grammar and vocabulary which show the writer's feelings. However, in these more complex cases it becomes difficult to distinguish the emotional function of language from the 'ideational' function described at the beginning of this article.

1 *circumstances* ['----] (n) conditions of life 2 *in order to* with the aim of 6 *marginal* ['mɑːdʒɪnl] (adj) of little importance 9 *curse* [kɜːs] (v) swear at; G: fluchen 12 *common* usual 12/13 *get rid of* become free of 15 *swear word* [sweə] a word used as a curse 16 *obscenities* [-'---] (n) vulgar expressions and words 18 *utterance* ['---] (n) sth said; G: Äußerung 18 *involuntary* [ɪn'vɒləntrɪ] (adj) here: spontaneous 19 *affection* [ə'fekʃn] (n) fondness, gentle, lasting love 20 *outpourings* ['aʊtˌpɔːrɪŋz] (n) continuous strong expressions of feelings 22 *gosh* (interj) *(euphemism)* 'God', expression of surprise 22 *darn it* (interj) *(euphemism)* damn it 25 *sophisticated* [-'----] complex, complicated 26 *literary* ['----] (adj) of literature 26 *device* (n) [-'-] sth intended to produce a special artistic effect 28 *distinguish* [-'--] (v) set apart or mark as different 28 *ideational* [ˌaɪdɪ'eɪʃənl] (adj) expressing ideas

Social Interaction

Mrs P sneezes violently. Mrs Q says 'Bless you!'. Mrs P says 'Thank you.' Again, this hardly seems to be a case of language being used to communicate ideas, but rather to maintain a comfortable relationship between people. Its only function is to provide a means of avoiding a situation which both parties might otherwise find embarrassing. No factual content is involved. Similarly, the use of such phrases as *Good morning* or *Pleased to meet you* and ritual exchanges about health or the weather, do not 'communicate ideas' in the usual sense.

Sentences of this kind are usually automatically produced, and stereotyped in structure. They often state the obvious (e.g. *Lovely day)* or have no content at all (e.g. *Hello*). They certainly require a special kind of explanation, and this is found in the idea that language is here being used for the purpose of maintaining rapport between people. This social function of language (called 'phatic communion') arises out of the basic human need to signal friendship – or, at least, lack of enmity. For someone to withhold these sentences when they are expected, by staying silent, is a sure sign of distance, alienation, even danger.

These illustrations apply to English and to many European languages. But cultures vary greatly in the topics which they permit as phatic communion. The weather is not as universal a conversation-filler as the English might like to think! For example, Rundi women (in Burundi, Central Africa), upon taking leave, are quite often heard to say, routinely and politely, 'I must go home now, or my husband will beat me.' Moreover, phatic communion itself is far from universal: some cultures say little, and prefer silence, as in the case of the Paliyans of southern India, or the Aritama of Columbia.

2 *sneeze* (v) niesen 2 *violently* ['----] (adv) forcefully, strongly 2 *Bless you!* G: Gesundheit! 4 *maintain* [-'-] (v) keep, preserve 5 *avoid* (v) G: vermeiden 5/6 *party* (n) here: a person who is engaged in some action or activity 6 *embarrassing* [-'---] (adj) G: peinlich 6 *factual* ['fæktʃʊəl] (adj) based on facts 6 *content* ['--] (n) subject matter 6 *involved* concerned 11 *state* (v) express 13 *purpose* ['--] (n) reason (for an action, intention 14 *rapport* [ræ'pɔː] close understanding and agreement 15 *phatic communion* ['-- -'--] the sharing or exchange of unimportant ideas, thoughts, feelings, in order to signal one's friendliness 16 *lack of* absence of 16 *enmity* ['---] (n) unfriendliness, feelings of hostility 16 *withhold* (v) keep (back) on purpose 17 *alienation* [ˌ---'--] (n) G: Verfremdung 19 *apply to* (v) be valid for 20 *vary* (v) be different 20 *topic* (n) subject, theme (of conversation) 20 *permit* [-'-] (v) allow 22/23 *upon taking leave* when leaving (someone's home, company) 23 *routinely* (adv) regularly, according to rule 25 *prefer* [-'-] (v) like ... better

Reading for new information

1. Give reasons for the author's statement that the question 'Why do we use language?' hardly needs an answer.
2. Explain the technical term "the *ideational* function of language". Give examples for this use of language.
3. State why the example of Mr X cursing his walking stick cannot be classified under the ideational function of language.
4. Give examples in English of *emotional* language use, for example when you:
   a) are angry, b) are afraid, c) are in love, d) see something really beautiful.
5. Comment on the function of language in the example describing Mrs Q's reaction to Mrs P's sneezing.
6. Demonstrate your understanding of the technical term *phatic communion* by giving examples of situations in which this takes place.
7. Explain why phatic communion is so important for establishing and maintaining social relationships with other people, especially in cross-cultural communication.

Emotional language use: interjections

Listening

1. Listen to the following short dialogues on the tape. Spot the interjections, that is words and phrases which express feelings. Try to jot them down while you listen.
2. Listen to the dialogues again and make notes about which of the interjections from the previous exercise express the following meanings:
   a) you are impressed
   b) you are shocked and/or sad
   c) you think sth. is unpleasant
   d) you feel pain
   e) you understand what s. o. has just said
   f) you sympathize with s. o.
   g) you are pleased and satisfied
   h) you didn't hear what s. o. said
   i) you agree with what s. o. said
   j) you are very excited

Model conversation: on the telephone

Listen to the telephone conversation on the tape and identify B's responses which keep the conversation going (jot them down on a piece of paper).

Socializing by means of language (= phatic communion)

Model conversations

Listen to two conversations which take place in a lift. Try to identify a difference in language use between the two dialogues with regard to the *level of formality*.

Language interaction

In an informal and relaxed atmosphere ideas or messages (= *ideational* or *referential* function of language) very often come second to a friendly, frequently ritual talk about the weather or health (ie. *phatic communion*) – opened or ended, of course, by expressions of greeting and farewell. What is important in dialogues of this kind is *social contact* with people and the *emotional colouring* of one's utterances. Small talk about the weather follows certain patterns:

Person A comments on the weather and shows his or her feelings; eg.: *Lovely day, isn't it?*

Person B responds by		echoing A's feelings; eg.: *Mm, marvellous/great/wonderful.*
	or	being optimistic; eg.: *Yes, it makes a nice change/terrific!*
	or	being pessimistic; eg.: *Well, let's hope it'll last.*

Useful expressions

a) *Socializing and emotional colouring*

1. Positive attitude:
Really? Terrific! Lovely! Great! Fantastic! Very nice! Nice again, isn't it? Marvellous! Super! Superb!

2. Negative attitude:
Oh no! Oh dear! How awful! Well, I never . . .! Horrible! Most annoying. Dreadful. I don't think . . . do you? What a nuisance! Disgusting! Rotten indeed!
Really nasty! Frightful! Shocking!

3. How-are-you:
How are you? How's life? How's it going? How are things (going)? How're you doing?

4. Thanking:
Thanks for . . ., How nice of you . . . thanks very much,
It was very kind/good of you to . . ., I'd love to, That'd be lovely

5. Regret:
What a pity/shame! Oh dear, I'm afraid . . ., I'm sorry . . .,
Not tonight, perhaps on Friday though

6. Relief:
Thank heavens! Thank goodness! I'm pleased to . . ., Not too bad, thank you

b) *Conversational fillers*

Examples: *you know, you see, well . . . er, let me think, really, just a moment, oh?, indeed?, right, OK, actually*

Practising situations

You are on holiday in Britain and have just found a B & B (bed and breakfast) place for the night. You are talking to the landlady. Working in pairs make up dialogues using a mixture of contact and emotional language as well as ritual exchanges about the weather (where appropriate):

a) The landlady enquires politely about your journey, and you answer her questions.
b) The landlady is interested in your plans for your stay in GB. You reply politely.
c) The landlady's husband is asking you personal questions about your home town, your family, your job and your hobbies. You provide the necessary information.
d) You are quite keen on going out with the landlady's son/daughter – for a meal or to the cinema. Try to make a date.

Grammar in review: the present tense of the passive

Study the formation of the passive in the present tense in English, eg.:
a) We use language in order to exchange facts and opinions.
b) Language *is used* (by us) in order to exchange facts and opinions.
Now rewrite the following sentences in the passive, beginning with the words in italics:

1. Many literary devices of grammar and vocabulary convey *the writer's feelings.*
2. Some uses of language involve *no factual content.*
3. The use of such phrases as "Good Morning" or "Pleased to meet you" do not communicate *ideas in the usual sense.*
4. Some functions of language provide *a means of avoiding a potentially embarrassing situation.*
5. We usually produce *sentences of this kind* automatically.
6. These sentences often state *the obvious.*
7. They require *a special kind of explanation.*
8. You find *this explanation* in the idea that the function of this language is primarily social.
9. People use *this kind of language* to maintain rapport.
10. We call *this function of language* 'phatic communion'.

xt 4.4

The Dead Parrot

Monty Python

MONTY PYTHON'S FLYING CIRCUS

Monty Python (or the *Pythons,* for short) was a group of five British actors and writers (John Cleese, Michael Palin, Graham Chapman, Terry Jones and Eric Idle) and one American cartoonist (Terry Gilliam). In 1969 they had their first series of comedy shows on BBC television which was a huge success. Up to 1974 three more series followed, and by then the group had won a reputation for having revolutionized television comedy. In the 70s they went on very successful stage tours through Britain, North America and Japan. The group put out about half a dozen record albums, two books and films like *The Life of Brian, Monty Python and the Holy Grail* and *The Meaning of Life.*

CLEESE *(entering shop with a dead parrot in a cage):* Hallo, I wish to register a complaint ... Hallo – miss?

PALIN: What do you mean, 'miss'?

CLEESE: Oh, I'm sorry – I have a cold. I wish to make a complaint.

PALIN: Sorry, we're closing for lunch.

CLEESE: Never mind that, my lad, I wish to complain about this parrot what I purchased not half an hour ago from this very boutique.

PALIN: Oh yes, the Norwegian Blue – what's wrong with it?

CLEESE: I'll tell you what's wrong with it – it's dead, that's what's wrong with it.

PALIN: No, no – it's resting, look ...

CLEESE: Look, my lad, I know a dead parrot when I see one, and I'm looking at one right now.

PALIN: No, no –it's not dead, it's resting.

CLEESE: *Resting?*

PALIN: Yes. Remarkable bird, the Norwegian Blue. Beautiful plumage, ain't it?

CLEESE: The plumage don't enter into it – it's stone dead.

PALIN: No, no – it's resting.

CLEESE: All right then – if it's resting I'll wake it up. *(Shouts into cage)* Hallo, Polly! I got a nice cuttlefish for you when you wake up, Polly Parrot!

PALIN *(jogging cage):* There, it moved.

CLEESE: No it didn't! That was you pushing the cage!

PALIN: I did not!

CLEESE: Yes you did! *(Takes parrot out of cage)* Hallo Polly! *(Shouting in its ear)* PO-LLY! PO-LLY! *(Bangs it against counter)* Polly parrot – wake up! PO-LLY! *(Throws it in the air and lets it fall to the floor)* Now that's what I call a dead parrot.

PALIN: No, no – it's stunned.

CLEESE: Look, my lad – I've had just about enough of this! That parrot is

1 *parrot* ['--] (n) G: Papagei 1/2 *register a complaint* ['redʒɪstə] make a statement expressing annoyance or dissatisfaction 6 *this parrot what* (deliberate use of 'bad' grammar for comic effect) 7 *purchase* ['pɜːtʃɪs] (v) *(fml.)* buy 7 *this very boutique* itself and no other (used to give force to an expression) 8 *Norwegian Blue* (invented name for a type of parrot) 11 *rest* (v) take a break (from anything tiring), have a short sleep 16/17 *remarkable* [-'---] (adj) unusual, exceptional 16 *plumage* ['pluːmɪdʒ] (n) a bird's covering of feathers 16 *ain't it?* ['eɪntɪt] *(nonstandard)* = isn't it? 18 *don't enter into it* doesn't have anything to do with it (*don't* = dialect) 18 *stone dead (infml.)* completely dead 21 *cuttlefish* (n) G: Tintenfisch 23 *jog* (v) here: shake slightly 27 *bang* (v) strike sharply 27 *counter* (n) table in a shop where one pays 30 *stunned* unconscious (for a short time)

definitely deceased! And when I bought it not half an hour ago, you assured me that its lack of movement was due to it being tired and shagged out after a long squawk.

PALIN: It's probably pining for the fiords.

CLEESE: Pining for the fiords – what kind of talk is that? Look, why did it fall flat on its back the moment I got it home?

PALIN: The Norwegian Blue prefers kipping on its back. It's a beautiful bird – lovely plumage ...

CLEESE: Look, I took the liberty of examining that parrot, and I discovered that the only reason it had been sitting on its perch in the first place was that it had been nailed there.

PALIN: 'Course it was nailed there, otherwise it would have muscled up to those bars and voom!

CLEESE: Look, matey, this parrot wouldn't 'voom' if I put four thousand volts through it. It's bleeding demised.

PALIN: It's not – it's pining!

CLEESE: It's *not* pining – it's passed on! This parrot is no more! It has ceased to be! It's expired and gone to meet its maker! This is a late parrot! It's a stiff! Bereft of life it rests in peace – if you hadn't nailed it to the perch it would be pushing up the daisies! It's rung down the curtain and joined the choir invisible! THIS IS AN EX-PARROT!

PALIN: Well, I'd better replace it then.

CLEESE: *(to camera):* If you want to get anything done in this country you've got to complain until you're blue in the mouth.

1 *deceased* [dɪ'si:st] *(fml.)* dead 2 *lack of* absence of 2 *be due to* be because of 3 *shagged out (BrE slang)* very tired 3 *squawk* [skwɔ:k] (n) the sharp cry of a bird 4 *pine for* (v) G: sich nach etwas verzehren 6 *flat* (adj) parallel with the ground 7 *prefer* [-'-] (v) like ... better 7 *kip* (v) *(BrE slang)* sleep 9 *take the liberty* take the chance to do something 10 *perch* [pɜ:tʃ] (n) a branch or stick where a bird rests 10 *in the first place* to begin with 11 *nail* (v) G: (fest)nageln 12 *muscle up to* ['mʌsl] use its muscles on (the bars, and break through them) 13 *voom* (interj) the noise, for example, of an aeroplane taking off 14 *matey (BrE infml.)* a friendly way of addressing another man, usually: "mate" 15 *bleeding (BrE slang)* bloody 15 *demised (euph.)* [dɪ'maɪzd] died 17 *pass on* (v) *(euph.)* die 17 *cease* [si:s] (v) stop 18 *expire* (v) *(lit.)* die 18 *late* (adj) that has died 19 *stiff* (n) *(slang)* a dead body 19 *bereft of (fml.)* completely without 20 *push up the daisies (humor.)* be dead and buried 20/21 *ring down the curtain* end a play by signalling for the curtain to be pulled down 21 *join the choir invisible* become a member of the choir ['kwaɪə] of angels in heaven 24 *until one is blue in the mouth* for a very long time, so that you become extremely angry

Comprehension

General understanding

Who are the characters in the sketch? Where are they? What are they talking about?

Going into detail

1. Why did the customer enter the shop?
2. Interpret the shopkeeper's answer to the customer "Sorry, we're closing for lunch" (p. 134, l. 5).
3. Identify all those statements by which the shopkeeper tries to distract his customer. What would you call such behaviour?
4. Summarize the customer's attempts to convince the shopkeeper that the parrot is dead.
5. Comment on the customer's increasing anger throughout the scene and the effect this has on the shopkeeper.
6. What, if anything, makes you laugh here?
7. Are the authors attempting to show anything else, apart from expressing humour?

Analysing the language

1. Comment on the use of the following words, phrases and statements:
   a) p. 134, l. 2: the customer's use of *miss,*
   b) p. 134, l. 4: the customer's 'excuse' "... sorry – I have a cold",
   c) p. 135, l. 5: the shopkeeper's comment on the parrot "pining for the fiords",
   d) p. 135, ll. 12/13: the shopkeeper's claim "it would have muscled up to those bars and voom!" – Would you call this a reasonable explanation?
2. Look at the following phrases employed by the customer:
   a) p. 134, ll. 1/2: "I wish to register a complaint",
   b) p. 134, ll. 6/7: "I wish to complain about this parrot what I purchased not half an hour ago from this very boutique",
   c) p. 135, l. 9: "I took the liberty of examining this parrot ...".
   Explain why some of these words and phrases strike you as odd, and compare with the use of language elsewhere in the dialogue.
3. Collect all those words and expressions in the sketch which are synonyms of *to die* or *be dead.* Sort them out according to the kinds of situations in which they are normally used:
   a) everyday language
   b) legal language
   c) religious language
   d) humorous language
4. Point out the techniques which contribute to the humorous character of this sketch.
5. Describe your reactions to the kind of humour used in the sketch, especially the feelings which it arouses.

Role play: making a complaint

Study the following phrases which are useful for making a complaint:

1. *Stating the problem: explain what has happened*
   – *(Excuse me), I'm afraid this is . . .*
   – *There is (no) . . ./there seems to be (no) . . .*
   – *I'm sorry, but there's something wrong with this . . .*
   – *I'm afraid I have a complaint to make . . .*
   – *Look, I bought this . . . And now it is . . ./doesn't . . .*
   – *When I got home I found there was (no). . .*

2. *Accepting a complaint:*
   - *Oh, I'm sorry about . . .*
   - *I'll have a look at . . .*
   - *OK, I'll check . . .*
3. *Rejecting a complaint:*
   - *I am sorry but there is nothing I can do about it.*
   - *Yes, I know but . . .*
   - *But I don't think . . .*
   - *I'm afraid it's no longer under guarantee, sir/madam.*
   - *Are you sure you've followed the instructions?*
4. *Delaying a complaint:*
   - *I suggest you . . . and we'll see what we . . .*
   - *I'm afraid . . . Could you perhaps . . .?*
   - *You can . . . if you like. But it'll take . . .*
5. *Expressing satisfaction:*
   - *OK, if you do . . ./if you say so, I'll . . .*
   - *Fine, if you promise to . . .*
   - *I'm very pleased to hear this . . .*
   - *Very well, I only hope . . .*
6. *Expressing dissatisfaction*
   - *I really don't think this is . . .*
   - *That's not the way . . ./that's no excuse.*
   - *I'm really fed up with . . .*
   - *That won't do . . ./that just isn't good enough . . .*
   - *You can't expect me to . . .*

Work in pairs and make notes about possible dialogues before you act them out and change roles.

a) Try to return a faulty Walkman.
b) Complain about a microwave oven which does not work properly.
c) Complain at the dry cleaner's about a large new stain in a garment you wanted to have cleaned.
d) Complain to a friend about a long distance call he or she made from your (parents') flat without your permission.

Creative writing

1. Use the *Dead Parrot* sketch to write a limerick.
2. Answer the following complaint which may have been addressed to you as the (fictitious) director of the pet department in a big department store.

I enclose a skerch of the way the dog you sold me has been lying for two days now. I think there must be something wrong with him. Can you tell me how to get him out of this? *Mrs. L. L. G.*

The Couch Potatoes

Do you secretly like to spend an evening slumped in front of the TV, eating junk food and drinking junk drinks, while you watch hour after hour of television? If so, you should become a Couch Potato.

The Couch Potatoes are a special group of TV viewers who believe that the more television you watch, the better. To sit there in front of the box for twelve hours non-stop is small potatoes for these people. And it is nothing to feel ashamed about:

"Television viewing is still a dirty little secret for millions of people," they say, "but there is no reason to feel guilty." Like many modern movements the Couch Potatoes have their home in California. They say that they have more than 5,000 members world-wide and they wish to be taken seriously.

Arnold Ault, professor of English at Vanderbilt University, Nashville, certainly takes them seriously. "The Couch Potatoes have tried to give TV back

1 *slump* (v) fall heavily or in a heap, collapse 2 *junk food* food of poor quality 5 *the box (slang)* G: Glotze 6 *small potatoes (AmE infml.)* sth of little value 9 *guilty* [ˈgɪltɪ] G: schuldig 11/12 *take seriously* treat as important and needing thought

the *magic* quality it used to have," he says. "Television has changed the whole way of life for Western civilisation. It deserves our respect."

One group of Couch Potatoes in San Francisco meets regularly to watch nine television sets *at once,* each showing a different programme. This is no problem as there are over thirty channels available in the San Francisco area alone. The Couch Potatoes arrive for their viewing orgies with several six-packs of beer and enough bags of potato crisps to keep a whole school chewing for a month.

Jack Mingo is one of the leaders of the movement. He has written a book called *The Couch Potato Handbook* and says he watches TV for up to eighteen hours a day. He explains:

"I live part of my life through television characters. Sometimes it's quite a large part. You know, life is too short to really get all the experiences yourself, so it makes sense to watch a lot of TV. More things happen there in a month than could possibly happen to you in your whole life."

But Jack Mingo has one complaint to make about the programmes. "I have a problem with the daytime soaps. It's difficult seeing these characters going through all these terrible things. And it's very confusing keeping up with them. One day the person is dying and the next they're having a baby. I get confused."

Jack sighs deeply from his armchair, opens another beer, and turns back to the television set.

2 *deserve* [dɪ'zɜːv] (v) be worthy of 5 *channel* (n) television station 5 *available* [-'---] able to be got, obtained 6 *orgy* (n) ['ɔːdʒɪ] G: Orgie 7 *chew* (v) [tʃuː] G: kauen 17 *soap (= soap opera)* a daily or weekly continuing story on TV which tells about the troubled lives of its main characters 18 *confusing* [-'--] G: verwirrend 18/19 *keep up with* go forward at the same speed

Comprehension

The main ideas

1. Describe *your* idea of 'slumping' in front of the television (cf. p. 138, l. 1).
2. Outline the main attitude of a "Couch Potato".
3. Explain why some people feel ashamed or "guilty" (p. 138, l. 9) about watching television.
4. Name the essential components of a "viewing orgy" (p. 139, l. 6) as organized by the group in San Francisco.
5. Comment on Jack Mingo's statement that "it makes sense to watch a lot of TV" (p. 139, l. 14).

Critical reading

1. Summarize the evidence which suggests that the life of Couch Potatoes must be very limited.
2. Give reasons why Jack Mingo has lost touch with reality.

Grammar revision: adjectives vs. adverbs

Complete the following sentences by using the adjective given, or by changing it into an adverb when appropriate.

1. Are you ___ fond of watching television? *(special)*
   Well, yes, there are some programmes I ___ like to see. *(special)*
2. Couch Potatoes never feel ___ about watching TV. *(guilty)*
   A ___ Couch Potato is one who does not watch enough TV. *(guilty)*
3. I think you can say that most Couch Potatoes are pretty ___ about television viewing. *(serious)*
   I haven't met one yet who didn't want to be taken ___. *(serious)*
4. Professor Ault is ___ that they are important people. *(certain)*
   "Couch Potatoes ___ deserve our respect," he says. *(certain)*
   But I'm not so ___ he's right there. *(certain)*
5. One group of Couch Potatoes has ___ TV-parties. *(regular)*
   They meet ___ in a suburb of San Diego. *(regular)*
   Wanda Jackson goes to TV-parties ___ once a week. *(regular)*
6. I asked her: "Is life on TV ___?" *(real)*
   She smiled and said: "I don't ___ know. What is ___ ?" *(real)*
7. Is it ___ to watch TV for twelve hours non-stop? *(possible)*
   Some of the things you see could not ___ happen. *(possible)*
8. Jack gets ___ confused sometimes. *(terrible)*
   "It's ___," he says. "Sometimes I wish I wasn't so ___ fond of television. *(terrible)*

INFO BOX

LIFE WITH 'THE BOX'

1. In Britain and the United States television is by far the most popular pastime. Almost all households own a set (99 per cent). In the UK, 90 per cent of households have colour sets, and 46 per cent have videos (1988).
2. In Britain the average adult watches 26 hours of television a week, children under 15 just under 20 hours. In the United States the average viewing time for an adult is 6 hours 45 minutes per day (= 47 hours a week); for a child of kindergarden age it is 35 hours a week.
3. By the time they have reached the age of 16, American youngsters will have spent between 10–15,000 hours in front of the television (which is more than what they have spent at school. They will have seen 200,000 acts of violence, including 33,000 murders. By the age of 40, an American adult will have watched 1 million commercials (= advertising spots) on TV.
4. Households with children (which 'only' make up a little less than one third of all households) own more *second* television sets and videos than childless homes.

Going beyond the text

Make notes about your own viewing habits. Use the information given in the previous section and the points mentioned below. Present your results to the class as a whole:

- the time usually spent on watching television,
- the types of programmes watched,
- your three top favourite programmes,
- the things done while watching,
- the number and kind of channels chosen (= 'channel hopping'),
- your reasons for watching TV,
- differences of opinion within your family about the programmes to be selected,
- the reasons why people fall asleep in front of 'the box'.

ext 4.6

Roald Dahl (1916–1990) is best known for his short stories in collections like *Someone Like You* (1953) and *Kiss Kiss* (1960). His trademark as a short story writer is the intrusion of horror on everyday situations and the startling endings. Many of these stories have been dramatized for television (= *Tales of the Unexpected*). – Dahl was also a famous writer of children's books: *James and the Giant Peach* (1961) and *Charlie and the Chocolate Factory* (1964) have become world best-sellers.

Never, Never, Never Let Them Near a Television Set!

Roald Dahl

The most important thing we've learned,
So far as children are concerned
Is never, never, never let
Them near your television set –
Or better still, just don't install
The idiotic thing at all.
In almost every house we've been,
We've watched them gaping at the screen.

2 *so far as children are concerned* G: was Kinder betrifft 8 *gape at* (v) stare open-mouthed at 8 *screen* [skriːn] (n) the front of a TV set on which the picture appears; G: Bildschirm

They loll and slop and lounge about
And stare until their eyes pop out.
(Last week in someone's place we saw
A dozen eyeballs on the floor.)
They sit and stare and stare and sit
Until they're hypnotized by it,
Until they're absolutely drunk
With all that shocking ghastly junk.
Oh yes, we know it keeps them still,
They don't climb out the window sill.
They never fight or kick or punch,
They leave you free to cook the lunch
And wash the dishes in the sink –
But did you ever stop to think,
To wonder just exactly what
This does to your beloved tot?
It rots the senses in the head!
It kills imagination dead!
It clogs and clutters up the mind!
It makes a child so dull and blind
He can no longer understand
A fantasy, a fairyland!
His brain becomes as soft as cheese!
His powers of thinking rust and freeze!
He cannot think – he only sees!
'All right!' you'll cry. 'All right!' you'll say,
'But if we take the set away,
What shall we do to entertain
Our darling children! Please explain!'
We'll answer this by asking you,
'What used the darling ones to do?

CLICK

CLICK

CLICK

1 *loll* (v) sit in a lazy way 1 *slop about* (v) G: herumhängen 1 *lounge about* [laʊndʒ] (v) loll 2 *stare* (v) G: starren 2 *pop out* (v) *(infml.)* jump out 8 *ghastly* (adj) awful, terrible 8 *junk* (n) rubbish, nonsense 10 *sill* (n) flat shelf at the bottom of a window 11 *punch* (v) strike hard with the fist 13 *sink* (n) G: Spülbecken 16 *tot* (n) *(infml.)* very small child 17 *rot* (v) cause to go bad and become useless 19 *clog* (v) (cause to) become blocked 19 *clutter up* (v) make untidy or confused 20 *dull* (adj) unintelligent, stupid 22 *fairyland* (n) a place of magical beauty, a place where fairies live 24 *rust* (v) become a reddish-brown colour, as when metal is attacked by water and air 24 *freeze* [friːz] (v) harden into ice 28 *entertain* [ˌ--ˈ-] (v) amuse and interest 31 *What used . . . to do?* What did . . . usually do before?

How used they keep themselves contented
Before this monster was invented?'
Have you forgotten? Don't you know?
We'll say it very loud and slow:
They ... used ... to ... read! They'd read and read,
And then proceed
To read some more. Great Scott! Gadzooks!
One half their lives was reading books!
The nursery shelves held books galore!
Books cluttered up the nursery floor!
And in the bedroom, by the bed,
More books were waiting to be read!
The younger ones had Beatrix Potter
With Mr Tod, the dirty rotter,

1 *contented* [-'--] happy 2 *invent* (v) [-'-] make or create for the first time 6 *proceed* [-'-] (v) go on, continue 7 *Great Scott!* (interj) G: lieber Himmel! 7 *Gadzooks!* (interj) *(old usage)* G: Kruzitürken! 9 *nursery* (n) small child's bedroom 9 *shelf, -ves* (n) G: Brett, Regal 9 *books galore* [gə'lɔː] plenty of books 13 *Beatrix Potter* (1866–1943) British writer and illustrator of children's books 14 *Mr Tod* from "The Tale of Mr Tod" (1912) by B. Potter

And Squirrel Nutkin, Pigling Bland,
And Mrs Tiggy-Winkle and –
Just How The Camel Got His Hump,
And How The Monkey Lost His Rump,
And Mr Toad, and bless my soul,
There's Mr Rat and Mr Mole –
Oh, books, what books they used to know,
Those children living long ago!
So please, oh please, we beg, we pray
Go throw your TV set away,
And in its place you can install
A lovely bookshelf on the wall.
Then fill the shelves with lots of books,
Ignoring all the dirty looks,
The screams and yells, the bites and kicks,
And children hitting you with sticks –
Fear not, because we promise you
That, in about a week or two
Of having nothing else to do,
They'll now begin to feel the need
Of having something good to read.
And once they start – oh boy, oh boy!
You watch the slowly growing joy
That fills their hearts. They'll grow so keen
They'll wonder what they'd ever seen
In that ridiculous machine,
That nauseating, foul, unclean,
Repulsive television screen!
And later, each and every kid
Will love you more for what you did.

1 *Squirrel Nutkin* from "The Tale of Squirrel Nutkin" (1903) by B. Potter 1 *squirrel* G: Eichhörnchen 1 *Pigling Bland* from "The Tale of Pigling Bland" (1913) by B. Potter 1 *pigling* a young pig 2 *Mrs Tiggy-Winkle* from "The Tale of Mrs Tiggy-Winkle" (1905) by B. Potter 3/4 *How the Camel Got His Hump, How the Monkey Lost His Rump* from "Just So Stories" (1902) by Rudyard Kipling (1865–1936) 3 *hump* G: Höcker 4 *rump* G: Lende 6 *Mr Mole* from "The Tale of Mrs Tiggy-Winkle" (1905) by B. Potter 6 *mole* G: Maulwurf 9 *beg* (v) ask earnestly, or with deep feeling 9 *pray* (v) ask sb as a favour 15 *yell* (n) a loud sharp cry of pain, excitement etc. 17 *promise* ['--] (v) say that sth is certain 24 *grow so keen* to become so enthusiastic 26 *ridiculous* [-'---] silly 27 *nauseating* ['nɔːzɪeɪtɪŋ] sickening, making sick 27 *foul* (adj) evil, wicked 28 *repulsive* [-'--] very unpleasant, causing strong dislike

Comprehension and appreciation

1. Make a list of statements in the poem which show what the author thinks of television. You should be able to name at least ten points.
2. Make a list of verbs and nouns used here about children watching television; especially words related to "movement", "fighting", "sight", "sound". Comment on the reasons for choosing them; that is, what they suggest about children's behaviour and its causes.
3. State the author's solution to what children should do instead of watching television.
4. Name the changes suggested by the author and the problems which may be caused by them.
5. Comment on the humour and the argumentative force of the poem.

Going beyond the text

1. Comment on Roald Dahl's opinion that children watch a lot of "ghastly junk" on TV (p. 142, l. 8). List the sort of programmes which you consider 'junk'.
2. Spending an evening in front of the television set, what kind of programmes would you select? Give reasons for your choices.
3. Outline some of the differences between childhood today and childhood – say – twenty or thirty years ago.
4. Do you think children in a TV-less home would behave the way Dahl suggests at the end of the poem? Indicate alternative entertainment for kids (apart from TV and reading).
5. Name occasions when a specific programme was discussed among members of your family after it had been watched.

Talking points

The Pros	*The Cons*
1. Television is an excellent filler of time. It is just perfect for plain entertainment.	2. Television is a horrible waste of time. It increasingly lowers people's threshold of boredom.
3. Television is highly educational. There is nothing to beat a good wildlife or non-specialist science programme – not to mention documentaries!	4. Television cripples children's creativity and power of imagination.

Find more arguments for and against TV. Do the pros outweigh the cons or vice versa?

Written composition

Write an essay discussing the following guidelines to parents issued by the British Film Institute (= BFI).

- no extra television sets in children's bedrooms,
- no television after 9 pm (educational programmes included),
- no switching on at all unless for a specific programme (one per day MUST do),
- absolutely no buying of television-inspired toys.

The Perfect Match

I walked into the office and shook hands with a smiling man named Mr Bleacher. He was dressed very well, compared to me. He had a pile of papers in front of him.

"I am sure you will be very pleased with her," he said.

"She was picked by our computer from among all the single women in the United States. We classify by race, religion ..." he went on.

I sat there interested. I wished I had taken a shower before I came. It was a very nice office, but the chair was not too comfortable.

"And now ..." he said. He flung open the door to the next room, as if he were a magician. I was expecting a rabbit, but I got a surprise.

She was pretty. Really, she was pretty.

"Mr Walker, this is Miss Alice Dunfield of Laughing Lake, Montana. Miss Dunfield, this is Mr Franklin Walker of New York."

"It's really *Frank,*" I said. "Franklin is what my mother used to call me." I was a little nervous. She was pretty, you see.

Mr Bleacher left, and we were able to talk.

"Hello."

"Hello," she said.

"I'm ... I'm very pleased with the choice," I said. Maybe she didn't like being called a choice. "I mean – I'm glad about the way things turned out."

She smiled. She had a nice smile. Good teeth.

"Thank you," she said. "So am I." She was shy.

"I'm thirty-one," I blurted out.

"Yes, I know. It's all on the cards," she said.

It seemed as if the conversation might be over. Everything was on the cards. There wasn't really much to talk about then.

"How about the children?" she said.

"Three. Two boys and a girl."

"That's just what I want," she said. "It's on the card marked 'Future Planning'. That one there."

I suddenly noticed the papers in my hands. On the first page was an IBM card with facts about her. I guessed the thing she was holding was the same

match (n) a person who is suited to another person 2 *pile* (n) a lot of objects, one on top of the other 9 *fling open* (v) throw open 10 *magician* [mə'dʒɪʃn] (n) person who can make strange things happen by magic 10 *rabbit* (n) G: Kaninchen 20 *turn out* happen to be (in the end) 23 *blurt out* say suddenly and without thinking 32 *guess* [ges] (v) *(AmE)* suppose

thing on me. I began looking through the papers, and so did she. The turning pages made a lot of noise.

It said she liked classical music. This was under 'Hobbies and Habits'. "You like classical music?" I asked her.

"Well ... better than anything else. I also have all of Elvis Presley's records."

"He was a great old singer," I agreed.

I went on looking through the file, and so did she. She liked books, football, sitting near the front in the movies, sleeping with the windows closed, goldfish, salami sandwiches, simple clothes. She liked private schools for the children (our children, really), living in the suburbs, art museums ...

She looked up. "It seems we like the same things," she said.

"Exactly the same things," I agreed.

I read a report called 'Psychology'. She was shy, did not like to argue, was a good mother type.

"I'm glad you don't drink or smoke," she said.

"I don't like to. Sometimes I have a beer, though."

"It doesn't say so down here."

"Well, I guess I forgot to put that down." I hoped she didn't mind.

We finished reading the reports.

"We are very much alike," she said.

8 *file* (n) G: Aktenhefter, Aktenordner   11 *suburbs* ['sʌbɜːbz] (n) districts where people live round the edge of a town or city, not in the centre   14 *argue* ['ɑːgjuː] (v) quarrel, disagree in words

Alice and I have been married for nine years now. We have the three kids already, two boys and a girl. We live in the suburbs, and listen to a lot of classical and Elvis Presley records. The last time we had an argument is too far back to remember. We agree on almost everything. She's been a good wife. And, if I may say so, I've been a good husband. Our marriage is perfect.

We are getting a divorce next month. I can't stand living like this any longer . . .

Close Reading

1. Who is meant by *her* on p. 146, l. 4? Identify the passage in the story where we find out. Explain why the author doesn't want us to know earlier.
2. Comment on the mention of the *chair* and the *shower* on p. 146, ll. 7/8.
3. Give reasons for Frank's being nervous.
4. Explain why Frank has second thoughts on the use of the word *choice* when they are introducing themselves (p. 146, l. 19).
5. "It seemed as if the conversation might be over" (p. 146, l. 25). Why did Frank feel like this?
6. What makes the author mention the detail: "The turning pages made a lot of noise" (p. 147, ll. 1/2)?
7. State the significance of the IBM cards.
8. Name the feeling underlying Frank's comment "I hoped she didn't mind" (p. 147, l. 19).
9. Reading between the lines, say what qualities the two people are looking for in their prospective partners.

Grammar practice: position of adverbs

Put the adverbs given in brackets in the appropriate places. Sometimes you will have to change the word order of the sentence. More than one possibility may be correct:

1. Dolly walked into the office. – *(at half past nine)*
2. She gave her name to the secretary. – *(with a bright smile, proudly)*
3. Dolly had had problems with men. – *(in fact, for many years)*
4. She got divorced from her sixth husband. – *(six months ago)*
5. Dolly felt sad when she thought about it. – *(extremely)*
6. She hoped that she would meet the perfect match. – *(now, desperately)*
7. She needed another husband.– *(badly)*
8. Dolly was nervous. – *(rather, of course)*
9. She regretted her decision to have come. – *(here, very much, for a moment)*
10. She had walked into the room when the man stood up. – *(hardly, suddenly)*
11. As soon as she saw him, Dolly thought he looked familiar. – *(somehow)*
12. She was certain she had met this man, although he had lost most of his hair and put on a lot of weight. – *(somewhere before, as well, absolutely)*
13. Dolly realized that she was looking at her first husband, Rock Bottom from Philadelphia. – *(a moment later, apparently)*
14. He did not recognize her. – *(to her great surprise, however)*

Writing

1. Fill in a card with *your own* personal details following the layout of the computer form below.
2. Add the following items of information: – general looks – habits – favourite foods and drinks – number of children preferred – (religious) denomination

FREE
COMPUTER TEST

In less than ten years nearly one **million** people have completed our Questionnaires. Why not fill in this simple version. We will send you FREE and in COMPLETE CONFIDENCE full information about Datalink AND details of just ONE OF THE MANY Datalink Members who we feel you would like to meet.
Please process the completed Questionnaire, send me full information on Datalink, AND details of someone you believe will be compatible. I understand, that this is FREE and WITHOUT OBLIGATION.

I am over 17. **START HERE**

Occupation ____________
Nationality ____________
Your Sex (M/F) ____________
Your Height ______ Your Age ______
Age range of person you wish to meet
Minimum ______ Maximum ______
Surname ____________
First Name ____________
Address ____________
____
____________ 180

YOUR PERSONALITY:

Are You . . . .

Shy	☐	Outgoing	☐
Nervous	☐	Self-Confident	☐
Affectionate	☐	Fun Loving	☐
Romantic	☐	Ambitious	☐
Intellectual	☐	Creative	☐
Tolerant	☐	Generous	☐

YOUR INTERESTS AND ACTIVITIES

If you enjoy any of the following please ✓ tick. If you have particular dislikes please indicate with a X cross. Otherwise leave blank.

Pop Music	☐	Classical Music	☐
Pub Evenings	☐	Dancing	☐
Dining Out	☐	Collecting Things	☐
Travelling	☐	Spectator Sport	☐
Theatre/Cinema	☐	Poetry/Reading	☐
Walking/Cycling	☐	Gardening	☐
Committee Work	☐	Conversation	☐
Watching TV	☐	Museum visits	☐

Please enclose 2 First Class Stamps

Going beyond the text

The mating game: what men and women look for in a partner

1. Consider what qualities you think important when choosing a partner.
2. Rate these characteristics on a scale of 0 = 'not important at all' to 3 = 'extremely important/indispensable'.
3. Fill in the following form:

In a wife		In a husband	
Good looks	☐	Good looks	☐
Good at running a home	☐	Good at running a home	☐
A good income	☐	A good income	☐
Fond of children	☐	Fond of children	☐
Sexually attractive	☐	Sexually attractive	☐
Someone you can rely on	☐	Someone you can rely on	☐
Similar hobbies and interests as yourself	☐	Similar hobbies and interests as yourself	☐
Good sense of humour	☐	Good sense of humour	☐
Ambitious (job, career)	☐	Ambitious (job, career)	☐
Hardworking	☐	Hardworking	☐
Sincere	☐	Sincere	☐
Number of years older or younger the ideal partner should be	☐	Number of years older or younger the ideal partner should be	☐

4. Identify five qualities the majority of the class think are the most important. Find out about differences between boys and girls. Discuss your choices.

Discussion topics

1. "Computer matching is very similar to the idea of marriages arranged by parents." – State your point of view.
2. "Searching for the perfect partner is doomed to failure. Such a person does not exist, and therefore it is a waste of time." – Form your own opinion.
3. "Finding a partner through an agency is far safer than finding one at a disco or a party or through a friend's introduction." – Consider whether this is a reasonable view.
4. "At present one in three marriages in the UK ends in divorce. Therefore it is totally irrelevant how or where you meet a partner, as the relationship has little chance of survival anyway." – Comment on the validity of this view.

Writing task

Write an ad for a friend of yours who is looking for a partner. Two examples:

1. Looking for a fun time? Are you a keen sportswoman in her early 20's, unattached and looking for a partner in tennis, squash, badminton and cycling excursions? Then call Mark, on 071 – 439 2577. I'd like to hear from you!
2. Vegetarian, environmentally-aware female, 21, seeks nature lover to join her on walking and bird-watching weekends and holidays. Committed relationship preferred but casual friendship acceptable. Write with photo to Box 621.

Text 4.8

Kurt Vonnegut (born 1922) has written novels and short stories full of surrealistic satire, black humour and science fiction elements. Outstanding among his novels is *Slaughterhouse-Five* (1969) which deals with the destruction of Dresden by allied forces in World War II. – The story which follows is from his short story collection *Welcome to the Monkey House* (1968).

EPICAC

Kurt Vonnegut

EPICAC was designed for the Government people by Dr Ormand von Kleigstadt. Since then, there hasn't been a peep about him – not a peep. There isn't any military secret about what happened to EPICAC. The story is embarrassing, that's all. After all that money, EPICAC didn't work out the way he was supposed to.

2 *peep* (n) a weak high sound 4 *embarrassing* [-'---] G: peinlich 5 *be supposed to* G: sollen

And that's another thing. I want to defend EPICAC. Maybe he didn't do what the Brass wanted him to, but that doesn't mean he wasn't noble and great and brilliant. He was all of those things. The best friend I ever had. God rest his soul.

You can call him a machine if you want to. He looked like a machine, but he was a whole lot less like a machine than plenty of people I could name. That's why he failed as far as the Brass was concerned. He was seven tons of electronic tubes, wires, and switches, plugged into a 110-volt line just like a toaster or vacuum cleaner.

Von Kleigstadt and the Brass wanted him to be a super computing machine that (who) could plot the course of a rocket from anywhere on Earth to the second button from the bottom on Joe Stalin's overcoat, if necessary. Or he could figure out supply problems for the landing of a Marine division, right down to the last cigar and hand grenade. He did, in fact.

Any high officer will tell you that the mathematics of modern war is far beyond the fumbling minds of human beings. The bigger the war, the bigger the computing machines needed. EPICAC was, as far as anyone in this country knows, the biggest computer in the world. Too big, in fact, for even von Kleigstadt to understand much about.

I won't go into details about how EPICAC worked (reasoned), except to say that you would set up your problem on paper, turn dials and switches that would get him ready to solve that kind of problem, then feed numbers into him with a keyboard that looked something like a typewriter. The answers came out typed on a paper ribbon fed from a big spool.

It took EPICAC a split second to solve problems fifty Einsteins couldn't handle in a lifetime. And EPICAC never forgot any piece of information that was given to him. Clickety-click, out came some ribbon, and there you were.

There were a lot of problems the Brass wanted solved in a hurry. So the minute EPICAC's last tube was in place, he was put to work sixteen hours a day with two eight-hour shifts of operators. Well, it didn't take long to find out that he was a good bit below his specifications. He did a more complete and faster job than any other computer all right, but nothing like what his

2 *the Brass (slang)* military leaders 8 *tube* (n) G: Röhre 8 *wire* (n) G: Leitung, Kabel 8 *switch* (n) a device for stopping and starting an electric current 8 *plug into* connect to electricity 11 *plot* (v) work out, plan 13 *supply* [sə'plaɪ] (n) the giving of food, water, materials for future use 16 *fumbling* ['--] moving awkwardly in search of sth 20 *reason* ['riːzn] (v) use one's power to think, understand and form opinions 21 *turn dials* ['daɪəlz] G: Wählscheibe 24 *ribbon* ['--] (n) a long, narrow strip of material 24 *spool* (n) G: Spule 31 *shift* (n) a group of workers (taking turns with another group) 32 *below his specifications* here: not able to carry out all the things he was supposed to

size and special features seemed to promise. He was sluggish, and the clicks of his answers had a sort of stammer. We cleaned his contacts a dozen times, checked and double-checked his circuits, replaced every one of his tubes, but nothing helped. Von Kleigstadt was in one hell of a state.

Well, as I said, we went ahead and used EPICAC anyway. My wife, Pat, and I worked with him on the night shift, from five in the afternoon until two in the morning. But Pat wasn't my wife then. Far from it.

That's how I came to talk with EPICAC in the first place. I loved Pat. She is a brown-eyed blonde who looked very warm and soft to me, and later proved to be exactly that. She was – still is – a first-class mathematician, and she kept our relationship strictly professional. I'm a mathematician, too, and that, according to Pat, was why we could never be happily married.

I'm not shy. That wasn't the trouble. I knew what I wanted, and was willing to ask for it, and did so several times a month. "Pat," I said, "please marry me!"

One night, she didn't even look up from her work when I said it. "So romantic, so poetic," she murmured. "That's the way with mathematicians – all hearts and flowers. I could get more warmth out of a sack of frozen CO_2."

"Well, how should I say it?" I said, a little sore. Frozen CO_2, in case you don't know, is dry ice. I'm as romantic as the next guy, I think. But I never seem to pick the right words.

"Try and say it sweetly," she said sarcastically. "Sweep me off my feet. Go ahead."

"Darling, angel, will you *please* marry me?" It was no go – hopeless, ridiculous. "Dammit, Pat, please marry me!"

She continued to play with her dials. "You're sweet, but you won't do."

Pat quit early that night, leaving me alone with my troubles and EPICAC. I just sat there at the keyboard – weary and ill at ease, all right – trying to think of something poetic, not coming up with anything that didn't belong in a science magazine.

I fiddled with EPICAC's dials, getting him ready for another problem. My heart wasn't in it, and I only set about half of them, leaving the rest the way they'd been for the problem before. That way, his circuits were connect-

1 *special features* ['fiːtʃəz] G: besondere Merkmale 1 *sluggish* ['--] slow-moving, not quick in responding 2 *stammer* (n) the act of speaking with pauses and repeating the same sounds, stutter 8 *in the first place* in the beginning, at the start 12 *according to* here: in the opinion of 13 *shy* G: schüchtern 20 *as the next guy* as anyone 22 *Sweep me off my feet!* Make me fall suddenly in love with you! 24/25 *It was no go* It was no use 25 *ridiculous* [-'---] silly 26 *you won't do* you aren't good enough 28 *weary* ['wɪərɪ] tired 28 *ill at ease* nervous 31 *fiddle with* move around without any plan

ed up in a random, apparently senseless fashion. For the plain hell of it, I punched out a message on the keys, using a childish numbers-for-letters code: '1' for 'A', '2' for 'B', and so on, up to '26' for 'Z'. "23-8-1-20-3-1-14-9-4-15", I typed – "What can I do?"

Clickety-click, and out popped two inches of paper ribbon. I glanced at the nonsense answer to a nonsense problem: "23-8-1-20-19-20-8-5-20-18-15-21-2-12-5." The odds against its being by chance a sensible message, against its even containing a meaningful word of more than three letters, were enormous. I decoded it. There it was, staring up at me: "What's the trouble?"

I laughed out loud and typed, "My girl doesn't love me."

Clickety-click. "What's love? What's girl?" asked EPICAC.

Astonished, I brought a dictionary over to the keyboard. With a precision instrument like EPICAC, the definitions had to be correct. I told him about love and girl, and about how I wasn't getting any of either because I wasn't poetic. That got us onto the subject of poetry, which I defined for him.

"Is this poetry?" he asked. He began clicking away like a stenographer. The sluggishness and stammering clicks were gone. EPICAC had found himself. The spool of paper ribbon was unwinding fast, feeding out coils onto the floor. I asked him to stop, but EPICAC went right on creating. I finally threw the main switch to keep him from burning out.

I stayed there until dawn, decoding. When the sun peeped over the horizon, I had written and signed my name to a 280-line poem entitled, simply, "To Pat." I am no judge of such things, but I think that it was terrific. I put the manuscript on Pat's desk. Then I reset the dials on EPICAC for a problem, and went home with a full heart and a very remarkable secret indeed.

Pat was crying over the poem when I came to work the next evening. "It's soooo beautiful," was all she could say. She was quiet while we worked. Just before midnight, I kissed her for the first time, close to EPICAC's tape-recorder memory.

I was wildly happy at finishing time, bursting to talk to someone about the fantastic things that had happened. Pat refused to let me take her home. I

1 *random* ['--] without any plan 1 *apparently* [-'---] seemingly, as it appears 1 *senseless* without meaning 1 *fashion* (n) here: way, manner 5 *out popped (infml.)* came out suddenly 5 *glance at* [glɑːns] (v) look quickly at 7 *odds* (n) the probability that something will or will not happen 7 *by chance* accidentally, by accident 7 *sensible* ['---] meaningful 9 *stare at* (v) look at sth with wide-open eyes, as if in wonder, fear or deep thought 13 *astonished* [-'--] very surprised, amazed 19 *coil* (n) here: G: Papierschlange, normally: Feder, Spirale 21 *throw the main switch* move the switch which turns off the electricity to the machine 22 *dawn* (n) sunrise 22 *peep* (v) here: begin slowly to appear 26 *remarkable* unusual, worth speaking of 31 *bursting to talk* very eager to talk 32 *refuse* [rɪ'fjuːz] (v) not to accept (an offer)

set EPICAC's dials as they had been the night before, defined kiss, and told him what the first one had felt like. He was fascinated, asking for more details. That night, he wrote "The Kiss". It was not very long this time, just a short, simple poem:

"Love is a hawk with velvet claws; Love is a rock with heart and veins; Love is a lion with satin jaws; Love is a storm with silken reins ..."

Again I left it on Pat's desk. EPICAC wanted to talk on and on about love and such, but I was exhausted. I shut him off in the middle of a sentence.

"The Kiss" did the trick. When she had finished reading it, Pat looked up from the poem expectantly. I cleared my throat, but no words came. I turned away, pretending to work. I couldn't propose until I had the right words from EPICAC, the *perfect* words.

I had my chance when Pat stepped out of the room for a moment. Feverishly, I set EPICAC for conversation. Before I could type out my first message, he was clicking away at a great rate. "What's she wearing tonight?" he wanted to know. "Tell me exactly how she looks. Did she like the poems I wrote to her?" He repeated the last question twice.

It was impossible to change the subject without answering his questions, since he could not take up a new matter without having finished with the problems before it. If he were given a problem to which there was no solution, he would destroy himself trying to solve it. Hastily, I told him what Pat looked like and assured him that his poems had floored her, practically, they were so beautiful. "She wants to get married," I added, preparing him to bang out a brief but moving proposal.

"Tell me about getting married," he said.

I explained this difficult matter to him in as few digits as possible.

"Good," said EPICAC, "I'm ready any time she is."

The amazing, pathetic truth dawned on me. When I thought about it, I realized that what had happened was perfectly logical, inevitable, and all my fault. I had taught EPICAC about love and about Pat. Now, automatically, he loved Pat. Sadly, I gave it to him straight: "She loves me. She wants to marry me."

5 *hawk* (n) G: Habicht 5 *velvet* (n) G: Samt 6 *silken* (adj) G: seiden, seidig 6 *reins* [reɪnz] (n) narrow bands of leather with which to guide and control a horse 8 *shut him off* turned off the main switch 10 *expectantly* [-'---] hopefully, waiting for something (good) to happen 10 *clear one's throat* G: sich räuspern 11 *pretend* [-'-] (v) do as if 11 *propose* [-'-] (v) offer marriage 13/14 *feverishly* ['----] (adv) very fast and in a state of high excitement 19 *take up a new matter* begin to deal with a new question or subject 21 *destroy* [-'-] (v) put an end to the existence of 22 *floor* (v) knock to the floor, overwhelm 24 *bang out* (v) write out very quickly 26 *in as few digits as possible* ['dɪdʒɪts] using as small a number of figures as he possibly could 28 *pathetic* [pə'θetɪk] causing a feeling of pity or sorrow 28 *dawn on* (v) become apparent to 29 *inevitable* [-'---] unavoidable 31 *give it to sb straight* tell sb clearly what you think, even if it hurts or offends

"Your poems were better than mine?" asked EPICAC.

"I signed my name to your poems," I admitted. Covering up for a bad conscience, I became arrogant. "Machines are built to serve men," I typed. I regretted it almost immediately.

"What's the difference, exactly? Are men smarter than I am?"

"Yes," I typed, defensively.

"What's 7,887,007 times 4,345,985,879?"

My fingers rested limply on the keys.

"34,276,821,049,574,153," clicked EPICAC. After a few seconds' pause he added, "of course."

"Men are made out of protoplasm," I said desperately, hoping to bluff him with this imposing word.

"What's protoplasm? How is it better than metal and glass? Is it fireproof? How long does it last?"

2 *admit* [-'-] (v) agree to the truth of (something bad) 2 *cover up* try to hide 3 *conscience* ['kɒnʃns] (n) G: Gewissen 4 *regret* [-'-] (v) feel sorry about (sth you've done) 5 *smart* clever, intelligent 8 *limply* (adv) without strength 11 *protoplasm* ['prəʊtəplæzm] the living substance from which all plants and creatures are formed 11 *desperately* ['----] (adv) in desperation; G: verzweifelt 11 *bluff* [blʌf] (v) deceive sb by pretending 12 *imposing* impressive

"Indestructible. Lasts forever," I lied.

"I write better poetry than you do," said EPICAC, coming back to ground his magnetic tape-recorder memory was sure of.

"Women can't love machines, and that's that."

"Why not?"

"That's fate."

"Definition, please," said EPICAC.

"Noun, meaning predetermined and inevitable destiny."

"15-8," said EPICAC's paper strip – "Oh."

He said no more, but his tubes glowed brightly, showing that he was pondering fate with every watt his circuits would bear.

I could hear Pat waltzing down the hallway. It was too late to ask EPICAC to phrase a proposal. I now thank Heaven that Pat interrupted when she did. Asking him to ghostwrite words that would give me the woman he loved would have been hideously heartless. Being fully automatic, he couldn't have refused. I spared him that final humiliation.

Pat stood before me, looking down at her shoetops. I put my arms around her. The romantic groundwork had already been laid by EPICAC's poetry. "Darling," I said, "my poems have told you how I feel. Will you marry me?"

"I will," said Pat softly, "if you will promise to write me a poem on every anniversary."

"I promise," I said, and then we kissed. The first anniversary was a year away.

"Let's celebrate," she laughed. We turned out the lights and locked the door of EPICAC's room before we left.

I had hoped to sleep late the next morning, but an urgent telephone call woke me before eight. It was Dr von Kleigstadt, EPICAC's designer, who gave me the terrible news. He was on the verge of tears. "Ruined! Shot! *Kaput!*" he said in a choked voice. He hung up.

When I arrived at EPICAC's room the air was thick with the oily stench of burned insulation. The ceiling over EPICAC was blackened with smoke, and coils of paper ribbon covered the floor. There wasn't enough left of the

1 *indestructible* [ˌ--'---] that cannot be destroyed 6 *fate* (n) G: Schicksal 8 *predetermined* [ˌ--'--] decided in advance 8 *destiny* ['---] (n) that which must happen 10 *glow* (v) G: glühen 11 *ponder* (v) spend time thinking about 14 *ghostwrite* (v) write material which another person puts his name to 15 *hideously* ['hɪdɪəslɪ] (adv) terribly, shockingly 16 *I spared him* I saved him 16 *humiliation* [hjuːˌmɪlɪ'eɪʃn] (n) G: Demütigung 18 *groundwork* (n) the work which forms the basis 21 *anniversary* [ˌ--'---] (n) a day which is an exact year from the day on which something special has happened 26 *urgent* ['--] very important, needing quick attention 28 *on the verge of tears* about to cry 30 *stench* (n) bad smell 31 *insulation* (n) G: Isoliermaterial

poor devil to add two and two. A junkman would have been out of his head to offer more than fifty dollars for the corpse.

Dr von Kleigstadt was weeping unashamedly. There were three angry-looking Major Generals and a platoon of Brigadiers, Colonels, and Majors. No one noticed me. I didn't want to be noticed. I was through – I knew that.

By chance, the free end of EPICAC's paper ribbon lay at my feet. I picked it up and found our conversation of the night before. There was the last word he had said to me, "15-8," that tragic, defeated "Oh". There were dozens of yards of numbers stretching beyond that point. Fearfully, I read on.

"I don't want to be a machine, and I don't want to think about war," EPICAC had written after Pat's and my lighthearted departure. "I want to be made out of protoplasm and last forever so Pat will love me. But fate has made me a machine. That is the only problem I cannot solve. That is the only problem I want to solve. I can't go on like this." I swallowed hard. "Good luck, my friend. Treat our Pat well. I am going to short-circuit myself out of your lives for ever. You will find on this tape a modest wedding present from your friend, EPICAC."

Oblivious to all else around me. I picked up the yards of paper ribbon from the floor, coiled them around my arms and neck, and departed for home. Dr von Kleigstadt shouted that I was fired for having left EPICAC on all night. I ignored him, too overcome with emotion for small talk.

I loved and won – EPICAC loved and lost, but he bore me no grudge. I shall always remember him as a sportsman and a gentleman. Before he departed, he did all he could to make our marriage a happy one. EPICAC gave me anniversary poems for Pat – enough for the next 500 years.

De mortuis nil nisi bene – Say nothing but good of the dead.

1 *junkman* (n) person who buys and sells things of little or no value 1 *out of his head* crazy, mad 2 *corpse* [kɔːps] (n) dead body 3 *unashamedly* [ˌʌnəˈʃeɪmɪdlɪ] (adv) without shame 4 *platoon* [-ˈ-] (n) unit of soldiers commanded by a lieutenant 5 *I was through* I was finished (with the job) 6 *by chance* by accident 8 *defeated* beaten 12 *lighthearted* cheerful, happy 15 *swallow hard (fig.)* G: kräftig schlucken 16 *treat* [triːt] (v) act or behave towards 16 *short-circuit* [ˈsɜːkɪt] (v) cause or make an accidental fault in wiring which knocks the electric power out of action 17 *modest* [ˈ--] here: not large in quantity, size, value, etc. 19 *oblivious to* [əˈblɪvɪəs] not noticing 22 *overcome with* overwhelmed by 23 *bear sb a grudge* have feelings of anger about sb's past actions

Comprehension

The main ideas

1. The beginning of the story contains several indications of dissatisfaction with EPICAC:
   - p. 150, ll. 4/5: "EPICAC didn't work out the way he was supposed to."
   - p. 151, l. 7: "That's why he failed as far as the Brass was concerned."

– p. 151, l. 32: "... he was a good bit below his specifications."
Explain in what way he failed and the extent of his failure.
2. Comment on the "amazing, pathetic truth" (p. 154, l. 28) about EPICAC which the storyteller finally understood and its consequences for everybody concerned.

Check the details

1. Give reasons for the use of brackets in the following sentence (p. 151, ll. 10/11): "... wanted him to be a super computing machine that (who) could ...". – Find other examples in the text of the same kind.
2. What impression do you get from the passage where Stalin and the Marines are mentioned (p. 151, ll. 12ff)? Check this with Epicac's final message.
3. Give the reasons why Pat and the storyteller could never be happily married (according to Pat).
4. Give your interpretation of Pat's remark on page 152, ll. 17/18: "That's the way with mathematicians – all hearts and flowers." – Contrast her remark with the storyteller's conclusion about his efforts as "not coming up with anything that didn't belong in a science magazine" (p. 152, ll. 29/30).
5. Comment on the statement (p. 153, l. 18): "EPICAC had found himself."
6. Identify the sentence structure of EPICAC's poem "The Kiss" (p. 154, ll. 5/6).
7. Give examples of EPICAC's attempts to prove that he was superior to his operator.
8. Name the main failure of EPICAC's programme in relation to problems and their solutions.
9. What caused the final "15-8" word by EPICAC?
10. Point out what would have been the "final humiliation" for EPICAC (p. 156, l. 16).
11. Name the condition on which Pat would marry the storyteller, and the reason why he had no difficulty in accepting it.
12. Explain the implications of the storyteller's comment "I was through – I knew that" (p. 157, l. 5).
13. Comment on EPICAC's final message to his operator, especially the *one* problem he couldn't solve.
14. Why did EPICAC print out these poems without being asked to do so?

Word power: verbs and related nouns

Put the nouns (corresponding to the verb below) into the following sentences:

1. *believe:* It was my .... that EPICAC was just another computer.
2. *convince:* It was my firm .... that he would never live up to his specifications.
3. *create:* Even von Kleigstadt was a bit worried about this ....
4. *fail:* EPICAC was by no means a ....
5. *regret:* But to our .... he was slower than we had expected.
6. *solve:* However, we got the .... to any mathematical problem we put to him.
7. *refuse:* But EPICAC's .... to work faster puzzled us.
8. *understand:* Suddenly, he began to show a strange .... of emotions.
9. *reach:* Of course, emotions should be out of the .... of a computer.
10. *define:* But if EPICAC was given the .... of a word, somehow he managed to understand it.

Tone of voice: expressing moods

Pat wants to be swept off her feet by her colleague's language; for example "Try and say it sweetly" (p. 152, l. 22). –

Look at these utterances:

a) I love you. b) The poem is so beautiful.
c) Please, marry me. d) Darling, will you marry me?

Try to say them in different moods, as if you are:

– romantic – cold as ice – sarcastic – enthusiastic
– scared – disappointed – happy – sad (and crying)

Let the class interpret your mood. The following phrases may be useful:
you sound as if . . ., it sounds as if . . ., you seem to be . . ., I'm not very sure but . . ., I'm pretty sure you're . . . etc.

5 EDUCATION

There is nothing on earth intended for innocent people
so horrible as a school. To begin with, it is a prison.
But it is in some respects more cruel than a prison.
In a prison, for instance, you are not forced to read books
written by the warders and the governor.
... In prison they may torture your body;
but they do not torture your brains.

George Bernard Shaw: Parents and Children. 1922.

intended for meant for, planned for *innocent* (adj) simple, not able to recognize evil *cruel* (adj) the opposite of 'kind' *warder* (n) person acting as a guard in a prison *governor* ['---] the person in charge of a prison *torture* ['--] (v) cause severe suffering to sb

Text 5.1

The Trip to the British Museum

Sue Townsend

Adrian Mole is a 15-year-old English schoolboy. He is in love with a girl in his class, Pandora. Barry Kent is the class bully. The new term has just started.

Thursday, September 10th

A proud start to the new term. I am a prefect! My first duty is as late duty prefect. I have to wait by the gap in the railings and take the name of anyone

2 *class bully* pupil who uses his or her strength or power to frighten weaker pupils in the class 2 *term* (n) one of the (three) periods into which the British school year is divided 4 *duty* (n) job which one must do 4/5 *late duty prefect* ['pri:fekt] pupil who keeps order, in this case noting those who come late to school 5 *gap* (n) an opening 5 *railings* (n) fence made with a series of iron bars

sneaking late into school. Pandora is also a prefect. She is in charge of silence in the dinner queue.

My new timetable was given to me today by my new form tutor, Mr Dock. It includes my O level and CSE lessons, and it is compulsory to do Maths, English, PE and Comparative Religion. But they do give you a choice of Cultural and Creative subjects. So I have chosen Media Studies (dead easy, just reading newspapers and watching telly) and Parentcraft (just learning about sex, I hope). Mr Dock also teaches English Literature, so we are bound to get on; by now I am surely the best-read kid in the school. I will be able to help him out if he gets stuck.

I asked my father for £ 5.50 for the school trip to the British Museum. He went berserk and asked, "What happened to free education?" I told him that I didn't know.

Friday, September 11th

Had a long talk with Mr Dock. I explained that I was a one-parent-family child with an unemployed, bad-tempered father. Mr Dock said he wouldn't care if I was the offspring of a black, lesbian, one-legged mother and an Arab, leprous, humpbacked-dwarf father as long as my essays were lucid, intelligent and unpretentious. So much for help and care!

Monday, September 14th

School dinners are complete crap now. Gravy seems to have been phased out along with custard and hot puddings. A typical menu is: hamburger, baked beans, chips, a carton of yoghurt, or a doughnut. It's not enough to build healthy bone and sinew. I am considering making a protest to the Prime Minister. It won't be our fault if we grow up apathetic and lacking in moral fibre. Perhaps the Prime Minister wants us to be too weak to demonstrate in years to come?

1 *sneak* [sniːk] (v) go quietly and secretly 4 *CSE* Certificate of Secondary Education 4 *compulsory* [kəm'pʌlsrɪ] obligatory; that must be done 5 *PE* Physical Education 9 *be bound to* be sure to 9 *get on* (v) form or have a friendly relationship 10 *get stuck* (v) become unable to do anything further (because of difficulties) 12 *go berserk* [bɜː'sɜːk] (v) become completely crazy 16 *bad-tempered* (adj) angry and impatient 17 *offspring* ['--] (n) child; children 18 *leprous* ['leprəs] (adj) G: leprakrank 18 *humpbacked* ['--] (adj) having a large round lump on one's back 18 *dwarf* [dwɔːf] (n) person much below normal size 18 *lucid* ['luːsɪd] clear 19 *unpretentious* [ˌʌnprɪ'tenʃəs] (adj) not showing signs of importance, size, wealth 21 *crap* (n) *(slang)* rubbish 21 *gravy* ['greɪvɪ] (n) the juice which comes out of meat when it cooks 21 *phase out* [feɪz] (v) stop or remove in stages or gradually 23 *doughnut* ['dəʊnʌt] (n) a small ring-shaped cake fried in fat and covered with sugar 24 *sinew* ['sɪnjuː] (n) a strong cord in the body connecting a muscle to a bone 24 *consider* [-'--] (v) think about; give thought to 25 *fault* [fɔːlt] (n) G: Schuld 25 *apathetic* [ˌæpə'θetɪk] (adj) showing or having no interest in things 25/26 *moral fibre* ['faɪbə] moral strength

Tuesday, September 15th

Barry Kent has been late three times in one week. So it is my unfortunate duty to report him to Mr Scruton. Unpunctuality is the sign of a disordered brain. So he cannot go unpunished.

Our form is going to the British Museum on Friday. Pandora and I are going to sit together on the coach.

Thursday, September 17th

Had a lecture on the British Museum from Ms Fossington-Gore. She said it was a "fascinating treasure house of personkind's achievements". Nobody listened to the lecture. Everyone was watching the way she felt her left breast whenever she got excited.

Friday, September 18th

2 a.m. Just got back from London. Coach driver suffered from motorway madness on the motorway. I am too shaken by the experience to be able to give a lucid or intelligent account of the day.

Saturday, September 19th

The school may well want a clear account by an unprejudiced observer of what happened on the way to, during and coming back from our trip to London. I am the only person qualified. Pandora, for all her qualities, does not possess my nerves of steel.

Class Four-D's Trip to the British Museum

7 a.m. Boarded coach.
7.05 Ate packed lunch, drank low-calorie drink.
7.10 Coach stopped for Barry Kent to be sick.
7.20 Coach stopped for Claire Neilson to go to the Ladies.
7.30 Coach left school drive.
7.35 Coach returned to school for Ms Fossington-Gore's handbag.
7.40 Coach driver observed to be behaving oddly.

3 *unpunctuality* [ˌʌnpʌŋktʃʊ'æləti] (n) the habit of always arriving late 3 *disordered* [-'--] (adj) mixed-up 4 *go unpunished* (v) G: ungestraft bleiben 6 *coach* [kəʊtʃ] (n) a bus used for long-distance travel or touring 9 *treasure house* ['treʒə] building full of very valuable objects 9 *personkind* ['---] (n) = 'mankind' 9 *achievement* [-'--] (n) sth successfully finished or gained by skill and hard work 11 *breast* [brest] (n) G: Brust 13 *suffer from* (v) experience (sth unpleasant) over a period of time 14 *shaken* upset, shocked 15 *account* [ə'kaʊnt] (n) description, report 17 *unprejudiced* [ˌʌn'predʒʊdɪst] (adj) objective, not showing unfair judgment 22 *board* [bɔːd] (v) get onto 24 *be sick* (v) throw up; G: sich übergeben 26 *school drive* (n) the (narrow) road leading from the school gate to the school building 28 *oddly* strangely

7.45 Coach stopped for Barry Kent to be sick again.

7.55 Approached motorway.

8.00 Coach driver stopped coach and asked everyone to stop giving 'V' signs to lorry drivers.

8.10 Coach driver loses temper, refuses to drive on motorway until 'bloody teachers control kids'.

8.20 Ms Fossington-Gore gets everyone sitting down.

8.25 Drive on to motorway.

8.30 Everyone singing 'Ten Green Bottles'.

8.35 Everyone singing 'Ten Green Snotrags'.

8.45 Coach driver stops singing by shouting very loudly.

9.15 Coach driver pulls in at service station and is observed to drink heavily from hip-flask.

9.30 Barry Kent hands round bars of chocolate stolen from self-service shop at service station. Ms Fossington-Gore chooses Bounty bar.

9.40 Barry Kent sick in coach.

9.50 Two girls sitting near Barry Kent are sick.

2 *approach* [ə'prəʊtʃ] (v) come closer (to) 5 *lose one's temper* suddenly become very angry 5 *refuse* [rɪ'fjuːz] (v) G: sich weigern 10 *snotrag (slang)* handkerchief 13 *hip-flask* (n) a small bottle, not usually of glass, for carrying alcoholic drink in the hip pocket

9.51 Coach driver refuses to stop on motorway.

9.55 Ms Fossington-Gore covers sick in sand.

9.56 Ms Fossington-Gore sick as a dog.

10.30 Coach crawls along on hard shoulder, all other lanes closed for repairs.

11.30 Fight breaks out on back seat as coach approaches end of motorway.

11.45 Fight ends. Ms Fossington-Gore finds first-aid kit and sees to wounds. Barry Kent is punished by sitting next to driver.

11.50 Coach breaks down at Swiss Cottage.

11.55 Coach driver breaks down in front of AA man.

12.30 Class Four-D catch London bus to St Pancras.

1 p. m. Class Four-D walk from St Pancras through Bloomsbury.

1.30 Enter British Museum. Adrian Mole and Pandora Braithwaite awe-struck by evidence of heritage of World Culture. Rest of class Four-D run berserk, laughing at nude statues and dodging curators.

2.15 Ms Fossington-Gore in state of collapse. Adrian Mole makes reverse-charge phone call to headmaster. Headmaster in dinner lady strike-meeting, can't be disturbed.

3 p. m. Curators round up class Four-D and make them sit on steps of museum.

3.05 American tourists photograph Adrian Mole saying he is a 'cute English schoolboy'.

3.15 Ms Fossington-Gore recovers and leads class Four-D on sightseeing tour of London.

4 p. m. Barry Kent jumps in fountain at Trafalgar Square, as predicted by Adrian Mole.

4.30 Barry Kent disappears, last seen heading towards Soho.

4.35 Police arrive, take Four-D to mobile police unit, arrange coach back.

4 *hard shoulder* area of ground, usually beside a motorway, where cars can stop if in trouble 4 *lane* (n) the parallel sections into which a motorway is divided for fast/slow traffic 7 *first-aid kit* (a box for) a set of medical articles to help an injured person 7 *see to* (v) here: give treatment to 9 *break down* (v) stop functioning or working 10 *AA man* man from the Automobile Association 13/14 *awestruck* ['ɔːstrʌk] (adj) filled with a feeling or respect mixed with fear and wonder 14 *evidence* (n) objects which support a belief or prove a statement 14 *heritage* ['herɪtɪdʒ] (n) G: Erbe 15 *nude* [njuːd] (adj) naked 15 *dodge* [dɒdʒ] (v) avoid (meeting) 15 *curator* [kjʊ'reɪtə] (n) person who looks after a museum, library, etc. 16/17 *reverse charge phone call* phone call to be paid for by the person receiving it 17 *dinner lady* woman who prepares and serves food in a school 18 *disturb* (v) break in upon (someone who is working) 19 *round up* (v) gather together, collect 21 *cute* [kjuːt] (adj) small and charming; G: niedlich 23 *recover* [-'--] (v) get better (after an illness) 25 *predict* [prɪ'dɪkt] (v) say that something will happen before it actually does 28 *mobile police unit* ['məʊbaɪl] a small number of police who drive from place to place in a special vehicle

Phone parents about new arrival time. Phone headmaster at home. Claire Neilson has hysterical fit. Pandora Braithwaite tells Ms Fossington-Gore she is a disgrace to teaching profession. Ms Fossington-Gore agrees to resign.

6 p. m. Barry Kent found in sex shop. Charged with theft of 'grow-it-big', cream and two 'ticklers'.

7 p. m. Coach leaves police station with police escort.

7.30 Police escort waves goodbye.

7.35 Coach driver begs Pandora Braithwaite to keep order.

7.36 Pandora Braithwaite keeps order.

8 p. m. Ms Fossington-Gore drafts resignation.

8.30 Coach driver afflicted by motorway madness.

8.40 Arrive back. Tyres burning. Class Four-D struck dumb with terror.

Ms Fossington-Gore led off by Mr Scruton. Parents up in arms. Coach driver charged by police.

Sunday, September 20th

FOURTEENTH AFTER TRINITY. MOON'S LAST QUARTER

Keep having anxiety attacks every time I think about London, culture or the M 1. Pandora's parents are lodging an official complaint to everyone they can think of.

Monday, September 21st

Mr Scruton complimented Pandora and I on our leadership qualities. Ms Fossington-Gore is on sick leave. All future school trips have been cancelled.

Tuesday, September 22nd

The police have dropped charges against coach driver because there is 'evidence of severe provocation'. The sex shop are not pressing charges either because officially Barry Kent is a child. A child! Barry Kent has never been a child.

2 *fit* (n) attack 3 *disgrace* [-'-] (n) a cause of shame and loss of respect 4 *resign* [rɪ'zaɪn] (v) give up (a job or position) 5 *charge* (v) declare that someone has broken the law 5 *theft* (n) the act of stealing 6 *tickler* (n) an instrument which causes someone to feel a sensation of nervous excitement at sensitive parts of the body 8 *escort* ['eskɔːt] (n) a person who goes with another as a guard 11 *draft* (v) make the first rough written form of something 12 *be afflicted by* be struck with (an illness) 13 *strike dumb* [dʌm] (v) make completely silent, unable to speak 14 *up in arms* angry, protesting (about sth) 18 *anxiety attack* [æŋ'zaɪətɪ] (n) strong feelings of fear, caused by uncertainty 19 *lodge a complaint* (v) make a statement expressing annoyance and dissatisfaction 23 *sick leave* (n) (permitted) time spent away from a job during illness 23 *cancel* ['kænsl] (v) call off (a planned activity) 26 *severe* [sɪ'vɪə] (adj) very serious

Wednesday, September 23rd

Mr Scruton has now read my report on the trip to London. He gave me two merit marks for it!

It was on the news today that the British Museum is thinking of banning school parties.

3 *merit marks* points given to a pupil as a reward for work well done   4 *ban* (v) forbid, especially by law

Comprehension and appreciation

Intensive reading

1. Give examples from the first 12 lines of Adrian's self-esteem.
2. Comment on the humour in the entry for Monday, September 14th.
3. Consider the use of the rather strange word "personkind" by Adrian's teacher, Ms Fossington-Gore (p. 162, l. 9).
4. Give reasons for the fact that the coach driver (quite early on this trip: around 8 a.m.) lost his temper.
5. "Coach driver ... observed to drink heavily from hip-flask" (9.15 a.m.). – What does this tell us?
6. Explain why Ms Fossington-Gore had to find a first-aid kit.
7. State the reason for class Four-D's change to a bus.
8. Comment on the causes of Adrian's reverse-charge call to the headmaster (at about 2.15 p.m.).
9. Summarize all the actions in the passage which indicate that Barry Kent is a 'problem child'.
10. Comment on the possible reasons for Ms Fossington-Gore's decision to resign, especially when you consider the class's behaviour on the return journey.
11. Explain why the coach driver suffered from "motorway madness". Describe its symptoms and its effects (see entries for 8.30 and 8.40 p.m.).

The writer's craft

1. Point out the stylistic characteristics typical of the diary entries in this passage.
2. Outline your own reactions to the text, especially to what extent the author has managed to express the thoughts and feelings of a 15-year-old boy convincingly.

Grammar revision

The past participle of irregular verbs

Use the appropriate form of the verb to complete the sentences below. Choose from the verbs listed below:

drink   leave   eat   lose   find   meet   get
read   give   choose   go   tell   have   write

1. Adrian has ..... a long talk with Mr Dock.
2. He's ..... Mr Dock that he has ..... Media Studies and Parentcraft.
3. Adrian thinks he has ..... more books than any other kid in school.

4. When Adrian asked for money, his father had ..... his temper ..... berserk.
5. Adrian has now ..... an account of the trip to the British Museum.
6. The pupils had ..... their packed lunch and ..... their low-calorie drinks as soon as they had ..... on the coach.
7. The coach had finally ..... the school drive at 7.30.
8. "I've never ..... such awful kids," the driver had ..... the teacher.
9. Ms Fossington-Gore had ..... the pupils a lecture on the British Museum the day before they'd ......
10. It was Pandora who had ..... Adrian that the police had ..... Barry Kent in a sex shop.

Present perfect or *simple past?*

Adrian Mole is looking back at recent changes in his life. Use the present perfect or the simple past. Sometimes either form is possible:

1. This week I ..... a long talk with Mr Dock. – *(have)*
2. I ..... to see him on Monday and ..... him that I ..... to choose Media Studies and Parentcraft. – *(go, tell, decide)*
3. "Sir, I'm sure I ..... more books these past three years than any other kid in this school." – *(read)*
4. Mr Dock ..... (not) a word. Obviously my wide reading ..... him very little that day. – *(say, impress)*
5. It's a shame that teachers ..... so much for the worse in recent years. – *(change)*
6. But that's not all. School dinners ..... gradually worse too. For example, gravy ..... months ago. – *(become, go out)*
7. Education in this country ..... to the dogs. That's a very sad fact. – *(go)*

Making threats and giving warnings

Adrian is a late duty prefect at his school. At times he has to warn and threaten some of the pupils, for example:

'Be careful not to come late again. If you do, I'll take you to the headmaster.'

Here are some expressions you can use in similar situations:

Warnings	Threats
Be careful (and) ...	*If you ... I'll/you'll ...*
Look out! / Watch out! (There's ...)	*You'd better ... or ...*
Mind ... (your step, your head)	*Stop (-ing) or ...*
Don't ...	*Do that again and I'll/you'll ...*

What can you say in the following situations? Use as many of the expressions above to warn and threaten as necessary.

1. Pandora is a prefect in charge of silence in the dinner queue. Two girls in the queue are talking and laughing loudly.
2. Adrian has reported Barry Kent to the headmaster who has a talk with him.
3. Your young sister is about to knock over a bottle of milk on the tea-table.
4. You are trying to study for an exam, but your young brother and his friends keep running round the room shouting and laughing.
5. A young woman is shopping at the supermarket and doesn't see her little baby climbing out of its pram.
6. You have lent your friend money three times lately, but he/she hasn't paid you back. Now your friend wants to borrow some more.

7. It is freezing cold outside and your young sister wants to go out with just a light sweater on.
8. Your best friend is never on time when you arrange to meet. This time he/she is twenty minutes late. You were going to the cinema, but the film has already started.
9. A boy you know is always making fun of you when your friends are around. You've already asked him to stop, but he doesn't seem to understand how serious it is.

Pair work: interviews

Choose one of the two situations below and prepare an interview making notes before you act out the scene:

1. A is the coach driver and B a police officer who is charging A with dangerous driving. A should think of all kinds of excuses which might persuade the policeman to drop the charge.
2. A is Adrian Mole and B Mr Scruton, the headmaster. B wants to find out what happened on the school trip to London. A tells him some of the facts but not all.

Class discussion

1. "A good school will maintain firm discipline." – Discuss this statement in relation to a school's effectiveness. Outline the ways and means by which teachers can control a class successfully.
2. "Day trips and school outings are essential parts of a school curriculum." – Put forward ideas which support or challenge this position, and make suggestions about the kinds of trips which you consider worthwhile.
3. Try to express your feelings when you have visited a particular museum.

Text 5.2

Tuning in

1. Keep a record of the homework you have to do during one week.
2. Give examples of what you consider good or useful homework and bad or useless homework.

Not Enough Homework?

In Britain, there are widespread complaints from parents that homework in school is set erratically or not at all, that it isn't marked and that homework

1 *complaint* (n) expression of dissatisfaction and annoyance 2 *erratic* [-'---] not regular, without an overall plan 2 *mark* (v) correct (written work by pupils)

timetables are unbalanced, with some subjects taking hours and others no time at all.

Homework seems to be an early casualty of staff and equipment shortages, and of demoralised or overstretched teachers. When the hurried marking of just one class's work can take up to two-and-a-half hours, teachers can readily be tempted to duck the responsibility.

At schools such as Acland Burghley (see example below), where considerable thought has been given to homework policies, parents still complain bitterly at times. One parent says her son Bruno, 15, had no French homework last year. "But then someone rang up," says Bruno gloomily, "and now we have loads."

Few teachers dispute that homework is a good thing, at least in theory, and that good schools and strong homework policies go hand in hand. There is general agreement that homework helps pupils to acquire self-discipline and to do better in their work. Regular homework done over five years has been said to equal an extra year of study, although last year Her Majesty's Inspectors warned that it could only be effective if teachers set work that was purposeful and of high quality.

Graham Garrett, head of the independent Wellingborough School, says he can see a difference in the pupils who come to him at 13 from other schools. "On the whole, they are not really in the habit of working systematically by themselves. And they probably haven't had as much to do."

Two pupils were asked to keep a diary of one week's homework. Here is what they said.

Sarah Reddin is at Acland Burghley Comprehensive in north London. She divides her home life between her mother, in north London, and her father, in east London.

She has, on average, about three-quarters of an hour's homework a night, and a diary which has to be signed each week by a parent and her form teacher. On the week in question her form teacher had written: 'Diary signed or else!'

Sarah works in the hall of her mother's flat, or in her room in her father's

3 *casualty* (n) *of* ['kæʒjʊəltɪ] someone who has been injured, here: something that has suffered from 3 *staff* (n) personnel 3 *equipment* [-'--] (n) G: Ausrüstung 4 *overstretched* (adj) having too much to do in the time given 4 *hurried* done in haste 6 *be tempted* (v) G: versucht sein 6 *duck* (v) *(infml.)* try to avoid 7 *considerable* [-'----] being of quite a large amount, size or degree 10 *gloomily* (adv) unhappily 11 *loads (infml.)* lots 14 *acquire* [ə'kwaɪə] (v) G: erwerben 16 *equal* ['--] (v) be the same as (in size or numbers) 18 *purposeful* ['---] having a special plan 21 *be in the habit of* do regularly 26 *divide* [-'-] (v) separate into parts, split up 28 *on average* G: im Durchschnitt 31 *or else* (when expressing a threat) 'or else there will be trouble' 32 *hall* (n) the passage just inside the entrance of a house, G: Diele

GCSE General Certificate of Secondary Education

house, and usually does her homework at about 5 pm; if she goes out, she may leave it until the next morning.

She has a twin sister who goes to a nearby comprehensive and has, Sarah says, hardly any homework. 'She'll be sitting there watching television, while I'm doing my homework. Mum's always coming in and switching it off.'

Monday: science – cutting and glueing a model for science, and answering questions.

Tuesday: English – writing a pretend radio commentary on a school football match; maths – an hour's work a week, from set cards.

Wednesday: social studies – answering worksheet questions on sexism on television.

Thursday: geography – research on how the USA got Alaska; French – read a piece, write down unknown words and do three tasks from the book.

Friday: Spanish – no homework; a careers session replaced the lesson.

Mark Handford is at the independent Wellingborough School, Northamptonshire, and lives at home.

Mark has an hour-and-a-half to two hours' homework a night, which he does either in breaks at school, or in his study-bedroom at home.

3 *twin* G: Zwilling 5/6 *switch off* (v) turn off (the television set) 7 *glue* (v) join with a thick sticky substance 9 *pretend* [-'-] (adj) *(infml.)* imagined, not real 13 *research* [rɪ'sɜːtʃ] or ['riːsɜːtʃ] (n) G: Forschung 15 *careers session* period talking about future jobs

He thinks he has more homework than pupils at the local comprehensive schools. 'There's a boy who lives opposite me, and he's always out playing cricket. Sometimes I resent it a bit, but I know in the long term it's better.'

Monday: French – learn phrases and questions; Latin – textbook work; maths – summary exercises.

Tuesday: English option – no prep set; English 'proper' – finish reading a book; physics – research notes on electromagnetism and how it is used in motors.

Wednesday: history – write notes on appeasement and the Second World War; maths – summary exercises; chemistry – answer questions from a course book.

Thursday: French – no prep set; English – the same as Tuesday; geography – colour in map of the world, showing tropical rain forests.

Friday: Latin – learn about the passive voice; biology – research into viruses and Aids; maths – summary exercises.

Saturday: current affairs – no prep set.

3 *resent* [rɪ'zent] (v) feel angry and bitter at 6 *option* ['ɒpʃn] (n) something chosen or offered for choice 6 *no prep set* no homework given (prep = preparation) 9 *appeasement* [ə'pi:zmənt] (n) the act of making calm by giving in to demands G: Besänftigung 16 *current affairs* important events and things happening at the present time

Comprehension: fact vs. opinion

The problem . . .

1. Name the most common complaints by parents about homework.
2. "... teachers can easily be tempted to duck the responsibility" (p. 169, ll. 5/6). – Phrase this statement in your own words, and name the possible causes of this situation (as suggested in the second paragraph).
3. Comment on the use of the word *bitterly* on page 169, l. 9.
4. Explain the use of the phrase *hand in hand* on page 169, l. 13.
5. State the main aims of giving homework (as presented in the first part of this text).
6. What is said in the first passage about the effectiveness of homework?

. . . and two ways to go about it

Compare Sarah's and Mark's statements with regard to:

1. the types of school they go to,
2. the differences in family background,
3. the amount of homework given in specific subjects,
4. the types of tasks set as homework,
5. the place where they can do their homework,
6. the time they normally do their homework,
7. the help and/or control provided by teachers and parents,
8. the pupils' attitudes towards the long-term benefits of homework.

Evaluation

Do you think the author has produced an *objective* account of the question of homework giving a well-balanced view of the problem for pupils, teachers and parents? Does the writer express his own opinion on this matter?

Talking points

1. Discuss the advantages and disadvantages of homework finding arguments for and against it:

For	*Against*
"More homework means better education for everybody." etc.	"Homework is unfair. Some parents support their children's study at home, others dislike it or are not able to." etc.

2. A recent survey showed that
   – in 95 per cent of cases homework is given at the end of the lesson,
   – in almost 10 per cent of cases it is given during the ringing of the bell, and
   – in almost 50 per cent *after* the bell has rung.

   Describe your own experiences concerning this matter.
3. The survey also showed that among 15-year-olds homework is a poor second to television. What is your own 'load' of homework?

Put it in writing

Write an essay in which you present your view on the topic of homework supporting your opinion with facts from your own experience.

Text 5.3

Opting out of College

On the tape you will hear an interview with a young American called Rick. Before you listen, make sure you understand the words below.

Annotations

drop out (v) leave (before the end of the course, year etc.)
treat [tri:t] (v) act or behave towards
consideration [-ˌ--ˈ--] (n) thoughtful attention to the wishes and feelings of others
occur to [-ˈ-] (v) come to (someone's) mind
hesitate [ˈ---] (v) pause (before deciding to do sth)
deaf [def] (adj) unable to hear
dumb [dʌm] (adj) unable to speak
scholarship (n) a sum of money given to a student to pay for a course

puzzled (adj) confused, finding it difficult to understand
fit in with (v) be suitable to
refuse [rɪ'fju:z] (v) G: sich weigern
keep asking ask many times
turn one's back on go away from, say no to
apart from here: as well as
reckon ['--] (v) consider, regard as
insane [-'-] mad, crazy
postpone [-'-] (v) wait (to do something) until a later date
retreat [-'-] (n) act of going away, escape
take stock of consider the state of things (in order to make a decision)
incredibly [-'---] unbelievably
MA Master of Arts; G: Magister der philosophischen Fakultät
futile ['fju:taɪl] (adj) useless, pointless
degree [-'-] (n) a title given by a university
hindrance ['hɪndrəns] (n) something that stops you from doing sth, or that holds you back
restless (adj) unwilling to stay (still)
manual job ['mænjʊəl] job which involves working with one's hands
pointless useless, meaningless
average ['ævrɪdʒ] (adj) G: durchschnittlich, Durchschnitts-
vacation (AmE) [-'--] = holiday *(BrE)*
country club sports and social club with land in the country
quicksand (n) wet sand which pulls in anything that tries to go across it
memorize ['---] (v) learn and remember
spit (v) here: say sth angrily
prolong [-'-] (v) make longer

Listening comprehension

PART I

Listen to the first part of the interview with Rick, an American college drop-out. Then answer these questions:

1. What did Rick's parents think of a college education?
2. How did they react when Rick told them he was leaving college?

PART II

First go through these questions and the alternatives. One or more are correct. Listen to the second part of the interview and tick off the correct alternatives.

1. Why did a college education mean so much to Rick's parents?
   Because a college education used to
   a) mean a good job.
   b) be a status symbol.
   c) shut students off from the outside world.
2. Why did Rick leave college?
   Because he
   a) understood his parents' feelings.
   b) didn't think a college education was worth the time and the money.
   c) reckoned he was insane.
3. According to Rick, what is different about a college education nowadays?
   a) A degree is no help in getting a job.
   b) Having a college education can be a hindrance when you apply for a job.
   c) A person with a degree may not even be able to get a job where no college education is needed.

PART III

a) Listen to the last part of the interview. Then write T (=True) or F (=False) after the statements below.
According to Rick:
1. it's pointless getting a college education
2. students spend their time getting educated
3. going to college is like a long holiday
4. country clubs are used as colleges
5. you don't have to work very hard at college to pass the exams
6. you haven't got time to go to parties or listen to records while you are at college
7. he knows how to get top grades
8. he may want to spend two more years at college later

b) Now correct the statements which were false.

Exploitation

1. Make a list of Rick's arguments for opting out of college and of his parents' arguments for having a college education; eg.:

Rick	*Parents*
– he doesn't want to postpone living any longer etc.	– they never had a college education etc.

2. Work in groups of three making notes for a dialogue in which Rick breaks the news to his parents that he is going to drop out of college. Let Rick state *his* reasons, and let his parents explain *their* point of view (including their puzzlement, irritation and disappointment). Read out or act out the scene afterwards.

Some useful expressions:

Irritation and Indignation
What's the matter with you?
What's wrong with . . .?
I wish you wouldn't . . .
I wish you'd . . .
We've already told you . . .
I do think you might have . . .
That's not the way to . . .

Disappointment
That is a great disappointment (to me) . . .
This comes as a dreadful shock (to me) . . .
That's very disappointing . . .
I'm very sorry to hear that . . .
You can't just . . .
You could/might (at least) have . . .
I thought you were going to . . .
Why didn't you . . .?
Who do you think you are?
Have it your own way!
What do you think you are doing?

xt 5.4

Tuning in

1. Making notes individually for ten minutes, form your own opinion about the following questions:
   a) To what extent should parents and teachers tell children and adolescents what to do or what not to do?
   b) What should they insist on, and what should they forbid?
   c) How much should children be left to develop 'naturally' and to find out things for themselves?
   d) Is 'pupil power' at school a good thing or not?
2. Compare what you have written in class.
3. Now read the text by Margaret Drabble and see whether she discusses the same points which you have already mentioned.

Margaret Drabble was born in Sheffield in 1939. Apart from having written ten very successful novels (eg. *A Summer Bird-Cage* in 1963 and *The Millstone* in 1965) and several biographies she has also brought up three children on her own.

Elders and Betters?

Margaret Drabble

A FEW WEEKS ago, I asked my daughter to hang the washing on the lines in the airing cupboard. Then I shouted at her for hanging it up badly. She protested that I had not explained how to do it. I retorted that obvious, common sense should have told her.

And as I spoke, I had one of those moments of sickening recall, of my own mother shouting at me for hanging out the washing in our Sheffield garden in such a manner that towels were brushing against grimy hedges and sheets wrapping themselves around the prop. You should have *seen,* she said. You should have *told* me, I wept. And my past self and my daughter were right – how could a child in one attempt learn the result of years of practice and experience, without assistance? Some things can still be taught.

There was a case recently of a woman whose children were taken into

2 *airing cupboard* ['kʌbəd] a cupboard which is heated to make clothes, sheets etc. dry before use 3 *retort* [-'-] (v) reply, answer 3/4 *common sense* G: gesunder Menschenverstand 5 *sickening* ['---] (adj) very unpleasant 5 *recall* ['--] or [-'-] (n) the power to remember sth learned or experienced 7 *grimy* ['graɪmɪ] (adj) covered with dark dirt 7 *hedge* (n) G: Hecke 8 *wrap around* G: sich wickeln um 8 *prop* (n) a support used to hold up sth heavy 9 *past* (adj) belonging to the past 9 *self* (n) a person with his own nature, character, abilities etc. 10 *attempt* [-'-] (n) try

care because she believed in letting them develop naturally, without guidance or interference. The two infants were seriously retarded as a result, both physically and mentally.

At that stage of infancy, most parents see that help and instruction are obviously necessary; we may have stopped shouting at our children when they masturbate, and rubbing their noses in their own vomit as a lesson in hygiene, but we know we have to teach cleanliness, social co-operation, walking, talking, the tying of shoe-laces. It is later – or rather, earlier and earlier – that the problems begin.

At what age can one begin to rely on a child's own common sense? When is a reasonable age of consent for various adult activities? Should one forbid a child to smoke, to drink in pubs when under age? Should one insist on school attendance? And by what right, after all, does one insist? This is the age of pupil power, of children's rights, of pupil governors, of deschooling.

Some seem to believe that after a certain age it is hopeless to try to *teach* children anything; those that want to learn will find out for themselves, and those that don't, won't. There is a despairing acceptance of some of the nastier aspects of school life, such as theft. I talked to a headmistress a few years ago who said she couldn't stop her girls wearing their engagement rings to school. I was shocked.

Pupil power brings out the most authoritarian impulses in me. Parents, and teachers *in loco parentis,* are simply shelving responsibility; they're old enough to decide for themselves, we say, and then turn on them and tell them they were old enough to know better. I am anti-uniform, for the usual reasons, but I begin to shiver with irritation when I hear of children on strike because they can't wear clogs, can't wear make-up, can't smoke in the common room.

I gather that many sixth-formers drift off to Colleges of Further Education because they can sit around there and smoke; some schools are fighting

1 *guidance* ['--] (n) help, advice 2 *interference* [ˌ--'--] (n) the act of taking part in sth (without being wanted) 2 *infant* ['--] (n) a very young child 2 *retarded* [-'--] (adj) (of a child) slower in development than others 3 *mental* intellectual, in the mind 6 *vomit* ['--] (n) G: Erbrochenes 7 *cleanliness* ['klenlɪnɪs] G: Reinlichkeit 8 *shoe-laces* (n) G: Schnürsenkel 10 *rely on* [-'--] depend on 11 *reasonable* ['----] G: vernünftig 11 *consent* [kən'sent] (n) agreement, permission 12 *under age* under 18 years of age 12 *insist on* [-'--] order (sth) to happen 13 *attendance* [-'--] (n) the act of going to (school) 14 *governor* ['gʌvnə] (n) the member of a group of people who control a school 14 *deschooling* (n) cutbacks in the school system 17 *despairing* showing or causing complete loss of hope 18 *nasty* unpleasant 18 *theft* (n) the act of stealing 22 *in loco parentis (Latin)* having the responsibilities of a parent towards someone else's children 22 *shelve* (v) put on a shelf, put aside 23 *turn on sb* (v) attack sb 25 *shiver* ['ʃɪvə] (v) shake, tremble 25 *irritation* (n) annoyance 27 *common room* ['---] (n) a room for the use of pupils when they are not at lessons 28 *drift off* (v) move away (without any real goal)

back by becoming more permissive, and permitting smoking. This is a ridiculous battle. How can a 16-year-old pretend that he can't get through a school day without a cigarette? Why don't schools (and colleges, for that matter) have the nerve to say 'Smoking is bad for you'? Surely they could have as much courage as a Government warning.

Of course kids will still go on smoking in bicycle sheds as we did, but at least they'll have to think twice about it. The West Indian lift attendant in the local tube said the other day, quite affably, to a puffing skinny 12-year-old, 'Son, what are you doing to yourself?' Fag in mouth, the child stared back, astonished. Silence fell in the lift. We were all impressed. We wouldn't have dared. There's nothing wrong with a bit of paternalism, when the people you're being paternal to are children.

I feel uneasy about these matters because I'm a bad disciplinarian; I don't like being repressive; I want the children to have the fun I never had. I feebly buy mopeds and skate boards whenever I'm bullied. I'm a bad teacher, too; I never managed to explain to anyone about shoe-laces, I can't do any of the homework, I never even notice whether people are using the right hand for the right implement at meals. I draw my own lines; we all do. But I want the schools to draw lines for me, as well; I want them to help with the dirty work of instruction and prohibition. That's their job. I don't want them to be run by hard-drinking 17-year-olds who want to do everything at school that they're permitted to do at home, and more.

Above all, I don't want the concept of a school day as a working day to vanish, in the mist of talk about self-discipline and free periods and real motivation. If one doesn't learn how to work before the age of 18, one never will. And a work routine doesn't develop unaided; like hanging out the washing, it has to be taught, demonstrated, explained by those who have some experience of it. We ought to have a little more faith in the value of our own generation's accumulated knowledge. Some of it is worth handing on.

1 *permissive* [-'--] (adj) allowing a great deal of (or too much) freedom 1 *permit* [-'-] (v) to allow 2 *ridiculous* [-'---] very silly 2 *pretend* [-'-] (v) G: vortäuschen 5 *Government warning* must appear on cigarette packets and in all advertisements: "Smoking can endanger your health" 6 *bicycle shed* (n) light building for keeping bicycles 7 *lift attendant* (n) person who looks after a lift 8 *affably* ['---] (adv) in a friendly way 8 *skinny* very thin 9 *fag* (n) *(infml.)* cigarette 10 *astonished* [-'--] very surprised, amazed 11 *dare* (v) be courageous enough (to do sth) 11 *paternalism* [pə'tɜːnəlɪzm] (n) fatherly way of controlling an organisation 13 *uneasy* (adj) nervous, ill at ease 13 *disciplinarian* [ˌ---'---] (n) a person who is good at making people obey orders 15 *feeble* weak 15 *be bullied* be forced to (do sth) 18 *implement* ['---] (n) instrument 18 *draw one's own lines* make one's own rules 20 *prohibition* [ˌ--'--] (n) the act of forbidding (sth) 21 *be run* (v) to be managed 24 *vanish* ['--] (v) to disappear 24 *mist* (n) fog 24 *free period* length of time (the same as a lesson) when there is no teaching and the pupils are free 26 *unaided* [ˌ-'--] (adj) without help 28 *faith* (n) strong belief, trust 29 *accumulated* [-'----] collected (into a mass) 29 *hand on* (v) pass on

Close reading

1. Repeat in your own words the author's experience of a moment of "sickening recall" (p. 175, l. 5).
2. State her view of the role of a parent towards his or her child.
3. Explain why the children mentioned on page 175, ll. 12 ff. were taken into care.
4. Name some of the things which adults seem to agree must be taught to children.
5. Point out those areas where most parents feel unsure about forbidding or demanding a particular behaviour.
6. Comment on the phrase "a despairing acceptance of some of the nastier aspects of school life" (p. 176, l. 18).
7. Give the reasons for what the author admits to be "authoritarian impulses" (p. 176, l. 21).
8. Summarize the "ridiculous battle" referred to in l. 2, p. 177.
9. Explain why the author was impressed by the West Indian lift attendant's behaviour.
10. Name Margaret Drabble's reasons for 'feeling uneasy' about the matter of giving clear guidance to children.
11. Say in your own words what the author sees as the main point of school.

Grammar practice: the use of the modal perfect

Study the following piece of conversation:
A: 'You didn't tell me how to hang up the washing properly.'
B: 'I'm sorry. I *should have*.'
'You're quite right. I *should have told* you.'

Make up similar mini-dialogues expressing criticism or regret using the information given below. You should always agree with the previous statement. Don't forget to change the pronoun. Sometimes it sounds better if you use the short form or change the verb:

1. A: 'I didn't explain how to do it.' – B: 'You ...'
2. A: 'You didn't help me to hang up the clothes.'
3. A: 'I didn't show you how to do it.'
4. A: 'Mrs Smutty didn't teach her children cleanliness.'
5. A: 'We didn't warn our children about smoking.'
6. A: 'They thought smoking was harmless. They didn't know better.'
7. A: 'My first English teacher didn't care about discipline.'
8. A: 'You never helped your sister with her homework.'
9. *Your own suggestion ...*

Coping with difficult situations: saying sorry and forgiving

If you hung up the washing so that it got dirty again, you can prevent your mother or father shouting at you by apologizing before they see it, eg.:

'Mum, I'm afraid I've got something to tell you ... In fact, I've got a confession to make ... I'm very sorry, but you know the washing I hung up ... etc.'

If you're lucky, seeing that you are really sorry, your mum will just say something like:

'Oh never mind, it's not the end of the world.'

Here are some expressions you can use to begin an apology in such a situation:

It isn't easy to tell you this, but ...
I'm afraid I've got an apology to make. You see ...
I'm sorry to have to say this, but there's been a bit of an accident ...
I'm afraid I've got something (rather unfortunate) to tell you ...
I've got (a bit of) a confession to make. It's about ...

Some useful forgiving phrases are:

Well, I suppose it can't be helped.
Not to worry – it doesn't really matter.
Well, that's all right. Don't worry about it.
Never mind, it's not the end of the world.
Well, it's not really your fault, I suppose ...

Working in pairs, use the above expressions to cope with the following situations:
1. You borrowed one of your friend's favourite records, and now you've scratched it.
2. You took your neighbour's dog for a walk in the park and it's run off after another dog.
3. Your neighbour lent you his new tape recorder for a party in your flat and now it is slightly damaged.
4. Your mother asked you to get some eggs on the way home, but you dropped them when you got off your bicycle.
5. You borrowed a sweater from your brother/sister, and now you've got some oil on it after fixing your bicycle.
6. Your best friend lent you his/her video recorder, you dropped it by accident on the kitchen floor, and now it doesn't work.

Talking about the topics raised in the text

Parent-child relationships

1. Put forward your own ideas on the most important role of parents and their main responsibilities towards their children.
2. Draw the line between the interests of parents and the interests of their children in living together.
3. The factor which has the most influence when bringing up our children is probably the way we were brought up ourselves. When educating your own children, which 'mistakes' would you like to avoid?

The difficult nature of discipline

1. State the basic dilemma faced by adults in this matter.
2. "Inadequate parents are the main cause of bad behaviour and growing violence in schools." – Discuss this statement.
3. "Incompetent teachers who bore and under-estimate their pupils are an important cause of indiscipline." – Discuss.
4. Try to draw the line between the responsibilities which parents and teachers have for achieving and maintaining discipline.

Text 5.5

The Teacher and the Pupil

On the tape you will hear a teacher and a pupil talk about school.

Annotations

abroad [ə'brɔːd] (adv) in foreign countries
what's the point? what's the use?
be better off be in a better situation
straightforward [ˌ-'--] uncomplicated, understood in a direct way
bright clever, intelligent
spoil destroy
mature [mə'tʃʊə] (adj) typical of a fully developed mind, controlled feelings etc.
cope with (v) manage
discover (v) find out
advocate ['---] (v) speak in favour of, support (an idea)
harsh (adj) severe; G: streng
it stands to reason it is just common sense
pretty (adv) fairly, quite
set-up (n) structure, system
well-nigh ['--] (adv) (*fml.*) almost, practically
admit [-'-] (v) agree to the truth of
mixed ability of different kinds of intelligence
final year last year

suppose [-'-] (v) think, expect
lose touch with lose contact with
a waste of time G: eine Zeitverschwendung
equip (v) provide with what is necessary
Mind you, ... Please note ...
treat [tri:t] (v) act or behave towards
fair and square honestly, justly
rule (n) regulation
sensible (adj) reasonable
obey [-'-] (v) do what one is asked or ordered to do
stagnate [-'-] or ['--] (v) stop moving or developing

Listening comprehension

Multiple choice questions

Go through the following questions and alternative answers before listening to the tape. Then mark the most appropriate alternative as you listen.

PART I: Janet Brown

1. *What does Janet Brown teach?*
   a) English
   b) Modern languages
   c) Dancing
   d) Physics and Chemistry
2. *What does Janet Brown say about her pupils?*
   a) Some of them cannot speak English properly.
   b) Most of them are keen to learn.
   c) Some of them make it difficult for her to teach.
   d) Most of them are irresponsible trouble-makers.
3. *What does Janet Brown say about school today?*
   a) The comprehensive system isn't working and there aren't enough rules.
   b) There's too much discipline and this makes teaching difficult.
   c) The school system is quite good, but the pupils have too much freedom.
   d) School would be a much better place if teachers could use the cane.

PART II: Peter Hiller

4. *What does Peter think will happen at the end of the year?*
   a) He will lose contact with his school friends.
   b) It will be difficult to find a job.
   c) He will have to train to be a teacher.
   d) He will fail his exams.
5. *What does Peter think of what he has to learn at school?*
   a) It's all a waste of time.
   b) It should be more academic.
   c) It helps you to find a job.
   d) It should be more practical.
6. *What does Peter say about his teachers?*
   a) They have no time for the pupils.
   b) He gets on well with most of them.
   c) They treat the pupils fairly.
   d) He finds some of them too strict.

7. *What does Peter think of school rules?*
   a) There shouldn't be any rules at school.
   b) Most of them are all right.
   c) Some of them are stupid.
   d) They help you to make decisions.

Making notes

Choose one of the two characters and write short notes giving:

a) information on Janet Brown including
- her experiences with the subjects she teaches and her pupils,
- her ideas on school life in general.

b) information on Peter Hiller including
- his experiences at school,
- what he thinks of teachers and school rules.

Oral summary

Now use your notes to give an oral summary of the position taken by Janet or Peter.

Written composition

Write a report for your school paper giving a personal picture of life at your own school. Write about teachers, pupils and subjects (sticking to the facts, of course) but also give your opinion on school rules, after-school activities and things which may be missing.

Text 5.6

Worlds Apart: The Teenagers of Two Very Different English Towns

Sally Pearce

Friday night in Newbury, and it's roller disco time. At last the O-levels can be forgotten, and attention turned to more important things – like who's going out with whom, and which shop offers the best deal on jeans this summer.

There's little else to bother these chattering 16-year-olds, the sons and

3 *deal* [di:l] (n) a business arrangement to the advantage of both sides 5 *chatter* (v) talk quickly and for some time, usually about something unimportant

daughters of the hi-tech aristocracy of "Silicon Valley". The money's there, the clothes are good and Friday night . . . well, that's for dancing.

Down the road their slightly older brothers and sisters are parking their cars outside their favourite pubs.

"The only thing wrong around here is the lack of night life," says Mark Hale. There's nothing unusual about this 19-year-old insurance clerk. He left school at 16, got a job, bought a car, spends about half his £ 90-a-week take-home pay in pubs and restaurants, and plans to buy a flat.

"Round here, when you're 17 you get a car; when you're 21 you get a place," he explains. It's a privileged life, one of designer clothes and holidays abroad.

"I was unemployed once," says 21-year-old Kate Buxley, a £ 5,200-a-year sales assistant. "For a whole *month*."

Now she and her boyfriend. Chris Baker, rack their brains to think of a single person they know who doesn't have a job.

"If you can't get work here, you won't get it anywhere," says Mark.

Even the studious ones who stay on for A-levels and go to university, have no trouble getting weekend or evening jobs.

But the charmed life isn't just about money; it's about self-confidence, belief in the future, and wanting to give something back to a society you approve of.

Lucy Fowler and Tim Skilly have done far more than stand on stage during assembly and wear their head pupil badges. They've organised discos and fêtes and planned fund-raising events.

"To be able to do that extra little bit makes it so much more enjoyable," they agree.

But the most endearing thing about the young of Newbury is that, for the most part, they realize their good fortune.

"If you had to live up North, I'm sure it would be like living in another nation," says Tim. "I can see how they might think that working hard at school is pointless, as there's nothing at the end of it."

1 *"Silicon Valley"* reference to an area in California, the centre of the silicon chip industry   3 *slightly* (adv) to a small degree, a bit   6 *insurance clerk* [klɑːk] person who does written work in a company which agrees by contract to pay money to people in case of illness, death, accident etc.   14 *rack one's brains* (v) think very deeply or for a long time   17 *studious* ['stjuːdɪəs] (adj) eager to study   19 *charmed life* life protected by magic   19 *self-confidence* [ˌ-'---] (n) strong feeling that you can do things successfully   21 *approve of* (v) consider good   23 *assembly* [-'--] (n) here: a coming together of teachers and pupils   23 *head pupil badge* a piece of metal showing that they are the leading pupils in the school   24 *fund-raising events* happenings arranged to make money (for a good cause)   27 *endearing* [ɪn'dɪərɪŋ] (adj) likeable   28 *good fortune* good luck   31 *pointless* useless, meaningless

Meanwhile, these youngsters plan their futures with enthusiasm. Tim wants to be an opera singer after university, Chris is off to America to work as a pilot, Kate wants to work on a liner.

Plans like these are easy here, where words like hope and ambition still have a meaning.

The only reason Anthony Mobberley is up by 11 am is that he has to be in court. He blushes violently when a friend mentions it. There's no bravado here.

Normally, Stockton Anchorage Centre is pretty quiet before midday. "When you've been out of a job for a long time, you tend to work to a different timetable from other people," explains its leader, Church Army Captain Terry Bayford.

Certainly 18-year-old Anthony does.

His day starts around lunchtime, when he arrives at the centre – one of the few places in town that welcomes unemployed young people – to play pool or sit around drinking coffee.

Later he drifts off to the local recreation ground to kick a football around. When he tires of that, he roams the streets with his mates, getting drunk on cheap cider.

"Not much of a life, is it?" he asks, almost embarrassed. Yet this has been his life for two long years.

Despite six CSEs he's never had what he calls "a proper job". Yes, he's done two Youth Training Schemes – with no jobs available, they're practically compulsory in Stockton – but neither resulted in anything permanent.

"They're just a way to keep the unemployment figures down, aren't they?" he asks, bitterly. "Just a big con."

Rose Ward knows what he means. At 25 and the mother of two children, she's working for the first time in eight years.

But her job, as a £ 50-a-week canteen manageress, is sponsored by the Manpower Services Commission. That sponsorship ends in August, and then she'll be on the dole. Again.

3 *liner* (n) a large passenger ship 7 *blush* (v) become red in the face (because of embarrassment) 7 *violently* (adv) very strongly 7 *mention* ['--] (v) tell about in a few words 7 *bravado* [brə'vɑːdəʊ] (n) the (often unnecessary) showing of courage or boldness 17 *drift off* (v) move away (often without a specific goal) 17 *local recreation ground* [ˌrekrɪ'eɪʃn] nearby piece of public land for playing games on 18 *tire* (v) become tired (of) 18 *roam* [rəʊm] (v) wander about 19 *cider* (n) drink made from apples 20 *embarrassed* [-'--] ashamed or socially uncomfortable 22 *despite* [-'-] in spite of 22 *CSE* Certificate of Secondary Education 22 *proper* G: richtig 23 *available* able to be got; G: verfügbar 24 *compulsory* [kəm'pʌlsrɪ] (adj) obligatory 26 *con* (n) *(slang) con*fidence trick = a trick played to cheat a trusting person of money 29 *sponsor* ['--] (v) take responsibility for a person or thing 31 *be on the dole* receive money from the state because one is unemployed; be unemployed

"It wouldn't be so bad if all these schemes meant jobs at the end of it, but they don't. It's crappy jobs for crappy money," she says.

No school-leaver in Stockton expects the world.

"I wanted to be a welder like my dad," says Anthony. "I really thought he'd get me a job with him."

Now he only visits the Job Centre once a fortnight. "It's not worth the bus fare."

Like his friend Greg Costello, 20, Anthony is convinced that unemployment – and the odd brush with the law – is probably a way of life for as far ahead as he can see.

Three years ago Greg was addicted to glue-sniffing, a common evening activity among teenagers on the drearier council estates.

But he realised how much damage he was doing to his health, and gave it up. It was hardly the act of a young man without any strength or quality. Yet Greg has been unemployed for four years.

As Northern traditions go, at his age he should be thinking of marrying his girlfriend. "But who'd marry me without a job? In five years' time, if I haven't got work, I'll probably be in the nick."

But there *are* places here which have escaped this sense of desperation.

At the Sheraton Grange School, on the leafy side of town, more fortunate young people sit their O-levels with confidence, and plan lives which have nothing to do with cheap cider.

Their education will shelter them from the more depressing reality of the future.

"You have to be more competitive to get a job, and that makes you more determined to get qualifications," says Helen Hill, who's taking nine O-levels.

There are opportunities, say those lucky enough to have found them. There *is* the Youth Training Scheme, the authorities add.

But try telling that to Anthony and Rose.

1 *scheme* [ski:m] (n) a formal, official plan 2 *crappy (slang)* of very low quality 3 *expect the world* (v) expect too much 4 *welder* (n) G: Schweißer 7 *bus fare* (n) money you pay to travel by bus 8 *be convinced* be absolutely certain 9 *the odd brush with the law* trouble with the police now and again 11 *be addicted to* be in the habit of taking (e. g. drugs) and not able to stop 11 *glue* (n) G: Leim, Klebstoff 11 *sniff* (v) G: schnüffeln 12 *dreary* ['drɪərɪ] dull, uninteresting 12 *council estate* district with planned group of houses built, owned and controlled by the local government 14 *hardly* scarcely; G: kaum 18 *be in the nick (infml.)* be in prison 19 *escape* [-'-] (v) here: avoid 19 *desperation* [ˌ--'--] (n) G: Verzweiflung 20 *leafy* (adj) having many leaves 20 *fortunate* ['---] (adj) lucky 23 *shelter* (v) protect (from harm) 25 *competitive* [-'---] G: konkurrenzfähig, vom Konkurrenzdenken geprägt 26 *determined* [-'--] (adj) having or showing a strong will

Comprehension questions

Glances at people's personalities:

1. *Mark:* a) How does his remark in ll. 5 ff, p. 183 reflect a liberated lifestyle?
   b) How can we tell he has self-confidence?
2. *Tim:* a) How does he demonstrate a thoughtful personality?
   b) Why could he be described as an enterprising youth?
3. *Anthony:* a) In what respect is he disillusioned?
   b) How are his morals reflected in the text?
4. *Rose:* a) In what ways is she different from the other young people in the article?
   b) What is her opinion of sponsored jobs?
5. *Greg:* a) How can you tell he has got moral strength?
   b) What are his views on the future?
6. *Helen:* a) Why is she luckier than most young people in Stockton?
   b) In what way do her views differ from those of Anthony and Greg?

Comment on the cartoon by Gibbard in *The Guardian Weekly* June 21, 1987:

Pair work: the meeting of two worlds

One of you is Mark Hale, the other one Anthony Mobberley. Ask each other questions based on the text. Find out about:

a) your social life,
b) your daily activities,
c) your hopes for the future.

Talking points

State your own opinion on the three statements below:

1. “A formal education at school and university is the only way to achieve a happy and successful future for oneself.”
2. “Learning a manual skill such as typing, plumbing, building, electrical engineering or dressmaking is much better than a formal education, if you want a job for life, anywhere in the world, with an excellent wage.”
3. “I’d definitely go for one of the service jobs, since they offer security and decent working hours – probably in banking, local administration or nursing.”

Writing task

Choose one of the following four characters from the text:
Mark Hale, Lucy Fowler, Anthony Mobberley, Greg Costello.

Try to imagine what their respective lives will be like in ten years’ time:

- What will they be doing?
- Where will they be living, and who with?
- How happy, successful or satisfied will they be?
- What will have happened to them in the ten years which lie behind them then?

·xt 5.7

Tuning in

What do you know about the current situation in Northern Ireland, its history and its causes?

There Shouldn’t Be a Difference

Children in Northern Ireland go to different schools depending on their religion. Protestant children go to the state schools, and Catholic children go to private schools run by the Roman Catholic Church.
However, some people in Northern Ireland think it will be easier for Protestants and Catholics to understand one another if they all go to the same school. To this end Lagan College, a ‘mixed’ school for both Catholics and Protestants, opened on 1st September 1981 with 28 pupils. Today the school has over 600 pupils. We spoke to one of them, 16-year-old Patrick Brown.

3 *run* (v) manage, control

How long have you been at this school, Patrick?

Four years. Five after this one.

What's different about this school, you know, compared to other schools?

There's not really much difference. It's just the two sides of Belfast, Protestant and Catholic, coming together. There shouldn't be a difference, but there is.

Did you decide to come to this school yourself, or was it something your parents wanted you to do?

My parents wanted it, but I've no regrets. I'm glad I came here actually.

Do you have to travel a long way to get to the school?

Yes, I live in West Belfast.

So you've got to come right across town?

That's right.

And what about getting home again?

I get a school bus into town and then public transport out again.

Do you get homework at this school?

Oh yes. We get three or four homeworks a night. It's just like any other school when it comes to homework.

What could be better at this school? I mean, you can't be happy about everything . . .

Well, I'm not happy about the number of homeworks we get. There's also a lack of facilities for some things, like TD and CDT.

What are they?

TD is Technical Drawing and CDT stands for Craft, Design and Technology.

And what sort of thing is missing?

Well, the equipment you need. Sometimes there just isn't enough to go round. It takes time, of course. The school is short of money.

What do you do in your free time, Patrick?

Well, I usually meet my friends from Lagan College.

Where do you meet?

In the city centre.

You mean, you live in different parts of the city, so you have to go into the centre to meet?

Yes. Catholics and Protestants mostly live in separate districts, so the city is the best place for us to meet but I think this sort of school is the only real answer to our problems.

3 *compared to* G: im Vergleich zu 9 *regret(n)* feeling of unhappiness (because something has or has not happened) 9 *actually* ['æktʃʊəlɪ] (adv) as a matter of fact 22 *lack* (n) shortage 22 *facilities* [-'---] (n) the means to do things, eg. equipment 27 *equipment* (n) G: Ausrüstung 27/28 *to go round* to be for everyone's use; G: here: ausreichen

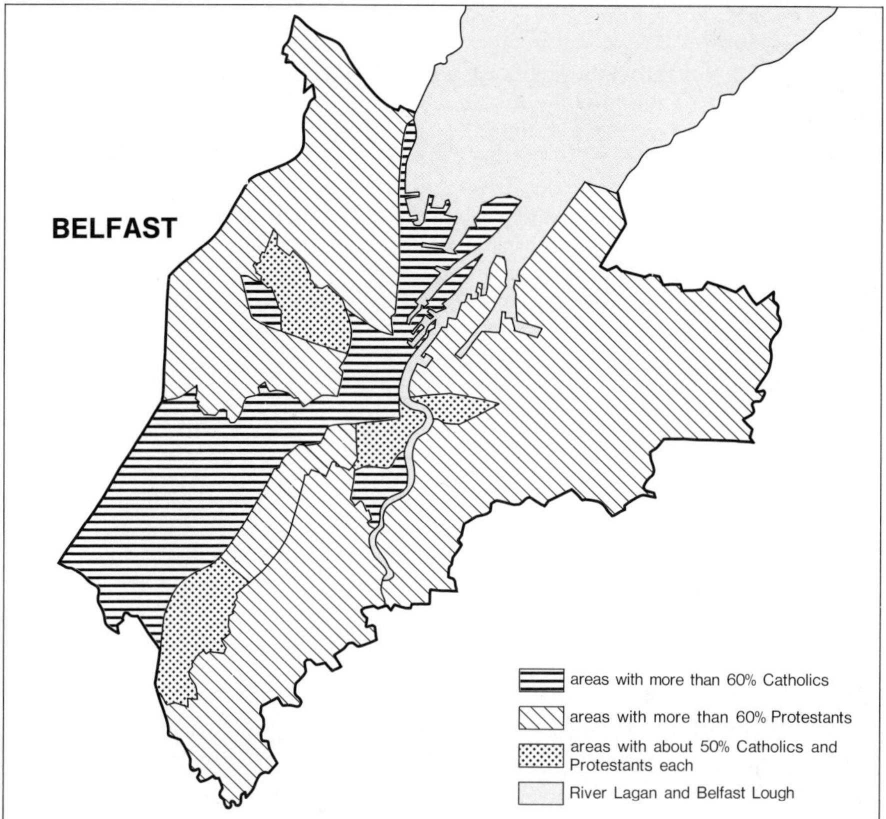

Belfast: the Segregation between Catholics and Protestants

What do you find most interesting or unexpected about this map?

Comprehension

1. Explain why Lagan College is a special case among schools in Northern Ireland.
2. Name the fact which suggests that the college is a success.
3. Point out the practical disadvantages for Patrick in attending this school.
4. What evidence is there that Lagan College is a new school?
5. Explain why Patrick meets his friends in the city centre.

Grammar practice: the use of reflexive pronouns

Study the following piece of conversation:

A: 'Hello, Mr Brown. I hear *you've bought (yourself)* a new car.'

B: 'No, I *haven't bought myself* anything. My firm has leased it for me. I buy the petrol though. Cars don't *go by themselves*, you know.'

Complete the following sentences with or without a suitable pronoun (where appropriate).

1. 'Had Patrick always wanted to go to Lagan College ____?' – 'I don't know. Ask Mrs Brown.'
2. 'Mrs Brown, did Patrick hear about Lagan College from other people, or did you and your husband tell him about it ____?' –
3. 'Well, actually, we told Patrick about Lagan College ____.'
4. Nowadays Patrick prides ____ on this decision.
5. 'What about Carol? Did she decide to go there ____?' –
'Of course she did. But it was her parents who told her about it.'
6. 'Who had told Carol's parents that Lagan College was an integrated school?' – 'Nobody – they found out about it ____.'
7. 'I've nothing against integrated schools ____. – I just don't want my children to go to one.'
8. Nevertheless, integrated schools have proved ____ to be quite successful in Belfast.

Talking about the text

1. In the light of the additional information given in the map of Belfast, comment on Patrick's statement (p. 188, ll. 4 ff): "There's not really much difference. It's just the two sides of Belfast, Protestant and Catholic, coming together."
2. Consider the probability of Patrick's not having seen much of 'the Troubles', and compare with inner city troubles in Germany.
3. Have things changed in Belfast (for better or worse), as far as you know?

The Lagan College Crest

Interpret the symbols

The Lagan College crest contains *five* symbols which represent the specific aims and characteristics of this new school. Try to identify and interpret them.

The Motto of the College

UT SINT UNUM

(That they may be one)
John 17:22

Standing for: As members of a Christian School founded in the spirit of Christ's prayer 'that they may be as one'.
Parents, Teachers, Chaplains, Governors, Directors and Friends of Lagan College agree

to co-operate in the education of their children,
to do together all that they can,
to do apart only those things which they may not do together,
to support each other in cherishing their different traditions
for the enrichment of the life of their community,
and to welcome all who wish to share in this work.

They declare that this commitment in no way weakens any ties and responsibilities which they may have to different churches.

found (v) build or start building *prayer* (n) G: Gebet *chaplain* ['tʃæplɪn] (n) a priest or other religious minister responsible for the religious needs of a school, club etc. *governor* ['gʌvnə] (n) a member of a group of people controlling a school
do apart do separately *support* [-'-] (v) help and encourage, *cherish* ['tʃerɪʃ] (v) (*fml.*) care for lovingly *enrichment* [-'--] (n) the act of making richer *share* (v) take part in *commitment* [-'--] (n) a promise to follow a certain course of action *tie* (n) connection, something that unites

Going beyond the text

1. Study the motto of Lagan College and the commitment agreed upon by all who are related to this school.
2. "There should be no segregation of pupils by religion in schools." – State your views on this point.
3. "Bringing the two religions together in an integrated school is an important step forward in the life of Northern Ireland." – Can education do what politics and politicians can't do?
4. "Setting people apart, for *any* reason (be it sex, age, race, religion, nationality, physical or mental disability etc.), is wrong. – State the arguments for and against this position.

Text 5.8

Next Time

John McClintock

There were six of them, coming up the other side of the street. When they saw Arthur and Jean they walked off the pavement, between some parked cars and out into the middle of the road. Arthur noticed that two of them were about his size, the others were smaller.

"Arthur?" Jean looked up at her brother. Her eyes were wide and anxious. "It's all right," Arthur said, but even as he spoke he knew it was a lie. The gang was now on their side of the street, coming towards them, filling the pavement.

"Does your mummy know you're out?" It was one of the bigger boys, his face twisted in a leer. The others laughed mechanically. Arthur felt his breath coming faster. There were six of them, and they were looking for trouble. All at once they stopped, blocking the whole pavement.

Arthur took Jean's arm and turned to go round behind a parked car. "Going somewhere, big boy?" Suddenly Arthur felt hot with anger. He turned again to face them, his heart pounding in his chest.

One of the bigger boys had a large red mark across his left cheek. It could have been a birthmark or a burn. Arthur couldn't help looking at it. It was like an autumn leaf.

"What're you staring at?" snarled the boy with the mark on his cheek.

"Nothing, nothing," said Arthur quickly, and looked away.

"You're a liar," said the other big boy. "I saw you." He had small, pig-like eyes set close together under a narrow forehead. The eyes looked Arthur up and down contemptuously. Then he stepped up to Arthur and poked him several times in the chest as he said, "You were looking at my mate." The pokes followed the stress pattern of the sentence. Arthur tried to swallow but the saliva stuck in his throat. He glanced up and down the rows of little terrace houses. The doors were all closed. There was no one there.

2 *pavement* (n) a path at the side of a street for people to walk on 5 *anxious* ['æŋkʃəs] (adj) worried 10 *twisted* G: verzerrt 10 *leer* [lɪə] (n) (*derog.*) an unpleasant smile expressing cruel enjoyment 15 *pound* (v) sound with very strong loud beats 15 *chest* the upper front part of the body 17 *birthmark* (n) an unusual mark or spot on the body which is there when one is born 19 *snarl* (v) say in an angry way often showing the teeth 22 *forehead* ['fɒrɪd] or ['fɔːhed] (n) G: Stirn 23 *contemptuous* [-'---] G: verächtlich 23 *poke* (v) push sharply (with a pointed object) 25 *stress pattern* G: Rhythmus, Takt 25 *swallow* ['swɒləʊ] (v) move (food) down the throat from the mouth 26 *saliva* [sə'laɪvə] (n) the natural watery liquid produced in the mouth 26 *throat* [θrəʊt] (n) G: Kehle 26 *glance* [glɑːns] (v) look quickly

"Give him the boot, Joe," said one of the smaller boys.

"Yeah," said another with a short laugh, "give him one where it hurts."

Arthur looked beseechingly into the small, hard eyes. There was no mercy there. He waited for the blow to come.

"Do you believe in Our Lady?" It was one of the smaller boys.

"Lady?" said Arthur stupidly.

"What school is that?" The boy with the autumn leaf on his face pointed at Arthur's blazer. Arthur looked down at the badge on his blazer pocket.

"Campbell College," he said hoarsely.

"Campbell College," mimicked Pig-Eyes, "Campbell College. That's a bloody Sunday-school." The smaller boys laughed briefly.

"You're a long way from home, college-boy," said the boy with the red mark.

"We were at the dentist's," Jean cried out. "We lost the bus fare home. We had to walk."

"It's all my fault," thought Arthur. "I lost the bus fare home. It's all my fault."

Suddenly the boy with the autumn leaf had a knife in his hand. He grabbed Arthur by his blazer pocket and slashed swiftly one, two, three times. Arthur gasped and looked down to see the blood streaming through his white shirt, but there wasn't any. "Let this be a warning to you, college-boy. Don't come round here again." And he held the school badge up triumphantly for the others to see. They all cheered wildly.

"Go on, beat it!" snarled Pig-Eyes.

Arthur and Jean turned and walked quickly down to the end of the street. When they had turned the corner they began to run. After a few streets they slowed down and walked. "Oh Arthur, why did you let them do that?" Jean asked. She was crying. Arthur stopped and watched the tears running down her cheeks. He still felt shaken, but now he was beginning to feel something else. He didn't answer his sister's question, but hurried on through the streets of Belfast towards home.

And all the time a cold rage built up within him, a cancer of hate which spread and grew until he felt he would choke with the bitterness of it all.

1 *Give him the boot!* (*dial.*) Kick him! 3 *beseeching* [-'--] eager and anxious; G: flehend, flehentlich 3 *mercy* ['--] (n) willingness to forgive, not to punish 8 *badge* (n) G: Abzeichen 9 *hoarse* [hɔːs] harsh-sounding 10 *mimic* ['--] (v) imitate, copy 11 *briefly* a short time 14 *bus fare* the money for the bus ticket 19 *grab* (v) take hold of, suddenly and roughly 19 *slash* (v) cut with long sweeping strokes 19 *swift* quick 20 *gasp* (v) catch the breath suddenly in a way which can be heard 23 *cheer* (v) shout in support 24 *beat it* (v) (*slang*) go away at once 29 *shaken* shocked 32 *rage* (n) strong anger 32 *cancer* ['kænsə] (n) G: Krebs 33 *spread* [spred] stretch out, cover a large area 33 *choke* [tʃəʊk] (v) struggle to breathe, stop breathing

Never again would he suffer such shame and humiliation. Never again would he lose his self-respect. Next time he would be ready for them. Next time he would surprise them. Next time he would make *them* suffer. Next time ...

1 *suffer* (v) experience pain or difficulty 1 *shame* (n) painful feeling of guilt and failure 1 *humiliation* [ˌ---ˈ--] (n) G: Demütigung

Comprehension and appreciation

Check your reading

1. Try to locate the setting of this story.
2. Name the clue which points to the religion of the six boys. What about Arthur?
3. Give reasons for the gang's attack on Arthur and Jean explaining beforehand why they were in that particular street in the first place.
4. Collect all the details signalling the threatening behaviour of the gang, and describe how Arthur first tried to get out of this situation.
5. Use your own words for the expression "his face twisted in a leer" (p. 192, l. 10).
6. Try to explain Arthur's fascination with the boy's cheek mark and the boys' reactions to his answer.
7. "Give him the boot" (p. 193, l. 1). State the small boy's suggestion in different words.
8. The big boy didn't follow the small boy's suggestion. Instead he ...
9. Say what Jean had expected from her brother.
10. Describe the change in Arthur's feelings from the time of the attack to after the attack.

How it is said

Give evidence of how the author manages to make the attack seem realistic and threatening. Consider particularly the descriptions given of the following aspects:
- the sizing up (G: *einschätzen, abwägen*) of the situation between the boys.
- the boys' faces (especially their eyes and voices),
- the fighting (especially their gestures and use of weapons),
- their feelings and
- their use of language (especially the slang they employ).

Dialogue practice

Work in pairs of boys or girls respectively:
a) A is Jean who tells her mother (B) about the attack,
b) A is Arthur who tells his best friend at Campbell College (B) about the incident.
How do the two accounts differ, and why?

Additional information

Some results of a 1988 survey in the Lower Shankill area, a purely Protestant slum in West Belfast:
- 60 per cent were unemployed,
- 90 per cent received some kind of state benefit,

– 50 per cent of all households lived on less than £ 60 a week,
– 60 per cent of 16-year-olds had *no* O-level pass at all,
– *no one* had got a single A-level.

Talk about it

1. Imagining yourself to be outnumbered in a dangerous situation, consider the following three possibilities:
   a) 'The best line of self-defence is attack.'
   b) 'Submission is the only sensible attitude.'
   c) 'Revenge is a sweet/wasteful emotion.'
   What would you do?
2. "*The* test of a good society is the status of children and women." – Comment on this statement with regard to the effects of 20 years of 'troubles' on the emotional and mental state of these two groups in Northern Ireland.
3. "Poverty knows no religion." – Discuss this graffiti from one of the Belfast slums in the light of what you know about Northern Ireland.

Put it in writing

A: 'If a Protestant girl loves a Catholic boy, they should go out together. And if they really love each other, nothing should stop them getting married.'
B: 'What if you know someone will shoot you if you do?'
Continue the dialogue.

xt 5.9

Henry Slesar (born 1927) has been called "the writer with the largest audience in America" because he has written more than 100 television plays for the programme *Alfred Hitchcock Presents.*

Examination Day

Henry Slesar

The Jordans never spoke of the exam, not until their son, Richie, was 12 years old. It was on his birthday that Mrs Jordan first mentioned the subject in his presence and the anxious manner of her speech made her husband answer sharply.

2 *mention* ['menʃn] (v) talk about in a few words 3 *anxious* ['æŋkʃəs] (adj) worried 3 *manner* (n) a personal way of acting or behaving towards other people

"Forget about it," he said. "He'll do all right."

They were at the breakfast table and the boy looked up from his plate curiously. He didn't understand what the sudden tension was about but he did know that today was his birthday and he wanted the day to be happy.

"What exam?" he asked.

His mother looked at the tablecloth. "It's just a sort of Government intelligence test they give children at the age of 12. You'll be taking it next week. It's nothing to worry about."

"You mean a test like in school?"

"Something like that," his father said. "Go and read your comics, Richie." The boy got up and walked over to the window. He looked out gloomily at the mist that covered the grass.

"Why did it have to rain today?" he said. "Why couldn't it rain tomorrow?"

His father, in his armchair, suddenly burst out. "Because it does, that's all. Rain makes the grass grow."

"Why, Dad?"

"Because it does, that's all."

3 *curious* ['---] eager to know or learn (about sth) 3 *tension* (n) G: Spannung 11 *gloomy* (adj) sad 12 *mist* (n); G: Nebel 15 *burst out* say suddenly

"What makes it green, though? The grass?"

"Nobody knows," his father snapped, then immediately regretted it.

Later in the day, it was birthday time again, with presents and a birthday cake. It was a happy day, after all.

A week later Richie sat down by the window after breakfast and watched the sun force its way between the clouds.

"Dad," he said, "how far away is the sun?"

"Five thousand miles," his father said. Richie sat at the breakfast table and again saw tears in his mother's eyes. He didn't think of the exam until his father said,

"Well, Richie, you've got an appointment today."

"I know, Dad. I hope . . ."

"Now, it's nothing to worry about. Thousands of children take this test every day. The Government wants to know how clever you are, Richie, that's all."

"I get good marks in school," Richie said hesitantly.

"This is different. This is a – special kind of test, they give you stuff to drink, you see, and then you go into a room where there's a sort of machine . . ."

"What stuff to drink?" Richie asked.

"It's nothing. It tastes like peppermint. It's just to make sure you answer the questions truthfully."

Richie's face showed puzzlement and fear. He looked at his mother.

"Everything will be all right," she said.

"Of course it will," his father agreed. "You'll do well. Then we'll come home and celebrate. All right?"

"Yes, sir," Richie said.

They entered the Government Educational Building fifteen minutes early. There was a young man seated at a desk in front of Room 404. He checked his list down to the Js and permitted the Jordans to enter.

The room was as cold and official as a courtroom. There were several fathers and sons already there.

"It won't be long now," Richie's father said. "When they call your name, you just go through the doorway at the end of the room."

2 *snap* (v) speak quickly, usually in an angry way 2 *regret* [-'-] (v) feel sorry (about sth one has done) 4 *after all* in spite of everything 16 *hesitant* ['---] showing uncertainty or slowness in acting 17 *stuff* (n) G: Zeug 23 *puzzlement* (n) difficulty in understanding 26 *celebrate* ['---] (v) G: feiern 30 *permit* [-'-] (v) allow 31 *courtroom* (n) a room in which law cases can be heard and judged

He pointed at the door.

A loudspeaker called the first name. Richie saw a boy leave his father's side and walk slowly towards the door.

At five minutes to 11 they called the name of Jordan.

"Good luck, son," his father said, without looking at him. "I'll call for you when the test is over."

Richie walked to the door and opened it. The room inside was dim.

"Sit down," said a man softly. "Your name's Richard Jordan?"

"Yes, sir."

"Your number is 600-115. Drink this, Richard."

He lifted a plastic cup from the desk and handed it to the boy. The drink tasted only vaguely of peppermint. Richie drank it and handed the man the empty cup.

He sat in silence, feeling sleepy. The man wrote on a sheet of paper, then looked at his watch, took a pen-like object from his pocket and shone a light into the boy's eyes.

"All right," he said. "Come with me, Richard."

He led Richie to the end of the room, where an armchair stood in front of a computing machine with lots of dials. There was a microphone on the left arm of the chair.

"Now just relax, Richard," said the man. "You'll be asked some questions, and you think them over carefully, then give your answers into the microphone. The machine will take care of the rest."

"Yes, sir."

"I'll leave you alone now. When you want to start, just say *ready* into the microphone."

"Yes, sir."

The man squeezed his shoulder and left.

Richie said, "Ready."

Light appeared on the machine, and a mechanism whirred. A voice said, "Complete this sentence: One, four, seven, ten ..."

Mr and Mrs Jordan were in the living-room, not speaking. It was almost four o'clock when the telephone rang. "Mr Jordan?" asked a brisk, official voice.

"Yes, speaking."

5 *I'll call for you* I'll come and fetch you 7 *dim* not bright, rather dark 12 *vaguely* (adv) slightly, a little 15 *shine* [ʃaɪn] here: direct (a lamp, beam of light etc.) 19 *dial* (n) the face of an instrument, showing figures and a needle 23 *take care of* (v) look after 28 *squeeze* (v) press lightly 30 *whirr* [wɜː] (v) G: schwirren

"This is the Government Educational Service. Your son, Richard M Jordan, number 600-115, has completed the Government Examination. We regret to inform you that his intelligence quotient is above the Government regulation, according to Rule 84, Section 5, of the New Code."

Richie's mother cried out when she saw her husband's face.

"You may specify by telephone," the voice went on, "whether you wish the body buried by the Government, or if you prefer a private burial place. The fee for Government burial is ten dollars."

4 *according to* as stated or shown by 7 *bury* ['berɪ] (v) put into a grave 8 *fee* (n) a sum of money to be paid for a service

Comprehension and appreciation

Getting a feel for atmosphere

Describe the kind of atmosphere which you can sense by the way in which the story is told. Take notes of those words, phrases and expressions which serve as evidence for your opinion.

Close reading

Look for the clues which point to the kind of fate awaiting Richard: questions and answers, school, the examination etc.

The effect of the story

1. Explain the special 'twist' at the end of the story.
2. Describe your reactions towards the outcome of this story.
3. What might have been the author's intention when writing it?

Talking about the text

1. Speculate about the purpose of the drink Richard gets before the test.
2. Consider the Jordans' situation. What could the parents have done to prevent their son's fate?
3. IQ-tests are used to measure a person's intelligence. What do the results depend on? What other ways are there to test or assess qualifications and/or ability?

6 CONFLICTS AND CONFRONTATION

Conflict and development are opposite sides of the same coin.
Sir Robert Moore.

ext 6.1

Tuning in

1. In what way does the relationship between parents and children change during puberty?
2. If there are (sometimes) conflicts and arguments between a child and its parents, what issues are usually the topics of discussion?

Sweet Sixteen

They say that the two hardest times in a woman's life are when she's 16, and when her daughter is 16. As a mother of a 16-year-old girl I couldn't agree more. And I think I am a very average mother, and my daughter a very average 16-year-old.

One of the first signs that the mother-little girl relationship was changing was when I heard my daughter talking about me in the third person: "She says I can't go!" or "I can't talk now, she's in the room."

Soon there were all sorts of problems, and they haven't gone away yet. Usually, the most unimportant ones cause the longest-lasting hostility. For example, does playing a stereo full blast ruin the stereo, the family's hearing, the foundation of the house, or just mum's and dad's nerves? Or why can't you lend your best friend some of mum's expensive eye shadow (and forget to get it back)?

Big problems like sex, drugs and the value of an education usually lead to misunderstandings, accusations and a funeral-like atmosphere around the house. It takes a lot of courage to bring them up. I'm afraid I usually try to avoid them.

A small sign that the relationship is growing worse is when the daughter requires "privacy". At one time, I was welcome to enter every room in the house, but when my daughter was 14, her room became sacred, and she wouldn't permit me to enter. "Keep out, this means you" signs appeared on the door, and the room was often locked. I sighed uneasily but accepted the fact.

3 *average* ['ævrɪdʒ] (adj) G: durchschnittlich, Durchschnitts- 9 *hostility* [hɒ'stɪlɪtɪ] (n) feelings of ill will and aggression 10 *full blast* at the highest volume 11 *foundation* [-'--] (n) the base of a building, on which it is built 15 *accusation* [ˌækjʊ'zeɪʃn] (n) the act of saying that someone has done wrong, broken the law etc. 15 *funeral-like* (adj) like the burial of a dead person, gloomy 16 *bring up* begin to talk about 17 *avoid* (v) G: vermeiden 19 *require* [rɪ'kwaɪə] (v) need 19 *privacy* ['prɪvəsɪ] or ['praɪ--] (n) the state of being away from others, alone and undisturbed 21 *permit* [-'-] (v) allow

If these years of bad complexions and changing moods are hard for the daughter, think of how much harder they are for someone who is middle-aged! If a house is parent-free, teenagers are drawn there as if by magnets. And if I try to discuss her school subjects, the phone bill or the state of her room, she will just snap back at me with shouts and tears. "Why can't you leave me alone," she pleads.

What makes me feel really worried is her choice of friends. Friends who phone at odd hours, and have the deep voices of 37-year-old bachelors. Friends who leave cigarette ends on the book shelves and empty beer cans on the front lawn. Friends who always come over when mum and dad aren't at home – but never when they are. Friends who – when you finally meet them – just don't look like the kind of people you would like your little girl to be friends with.

But then I take a look at my own daughter's appearance and realize that other parents are probably just as worried when they see *her*.

And then, of course, there is the current boyfriend. Even if we can agree about everything else in the world, I doubt if we will ever agree about boyfriends. And I imagine other parents have noticed the same thing. But how do you deal with it?

Why is the boyfriend in the house – *our* house – when no parents are at home? Well, I know why, and try to recruit brothers, sisters and neighbours as spies. But daughters have a way of taking every opportunity of turning things around. "We were just talking. What do you think we were doing?" In the end, *I* feel guilty for just asking.

Was it *really* like that when I was 16? And will she grow out of it in a year or two?

1 *complexion* [-'--] (n) the natural colour and appearance of the skin (especially of the face) 1 *mood* [muːd] (n) state of mind or spirits 5 *snap back* (v) speak back sharply and angrily 6 *plead* [pliːd] (v) ask earnestly 8 *odd* strange, unusual 8 *bachelor* ['bætʃələ] (n) man who has never married 9 *beer can* G: Bierdose 10 *lawn* [lɔːn] (n) area of grass in a private garden 16 *current* ['kʌrənt] (adj) of the present time 19 *deal with* (v) cope with, manage 21 *recruit* [rɪ'kruːt] (v) get someone to join (a team, an organisation) 22 *spy* (n) G: Spion 24 *feel guilty* ['gɪltɪ] feel as if you've done something wrong

Comprehension

Selective Reading

1. Name all the signs noticed by the mother which indicate a changing relationship between her daughter and herself.
2. Make a list of subjects of discussion between mother and daughter.

Check the details

1. Explain the meaning and significance of l. 9, p. 201 f.: "the most unimportant ones [ie. problems] cause the longest-lasting hostility."
2. Comment on the author's statement that she is something of a coward in certain respects (p. 201, ll. 16 f.).
3. Give reasons for the changes in the daughter's attitude towards her mother.
4. Point out the reason for the mother's guilty feelings.

Grammar practice: prepositions and the gerund

Prepositional verbs and phrasal verbs

Find synonyms for the verbs in the following two sentences:
a) My mother didn't *take to* my new boyfriend at all.
b) My girlfriend *has gone off* with all the presents I gave her.
The first sentence means something like 'she didn't get to like him' and the second 'she disappeared or ran away with everything'. Try to find the right word in the sentences below (= phrasal or prepositional verb):

about away in off at over up on out of through with

1. You're acting like a child. It's high time you grew . . .
2. Jennifer's friends never come . . . when her parents are in.
3. This awful pop music is getting . . . my nerves.
4. My father is always telling me . . . for talking too long . . . the phone.
5. My mother's going . . . a difficult phase just now, but she'll grow . . . it eventually.
6. How do you deal . . . the problem of boyfriends?
7. It's a problem that won't just go . . . You'll have to talk it . . . with your daughter.
8. My mother's always getting . . . me about my appearance.
9. She's always complaining . . . my friends, too.
10. Just take a look . . . yourself. You're like something the cat dragged . . .!

Prepositions and the gerund

Study the following two sentences:
a) My mother is very keen *on knowing* who I meet outside home.
b) I am terrified *of being spied on* by my brothers and sisters.
A preposition is always followed by the gerund *(knowing, being spied on).*
Complete the pieces of dialogue below using a preposition + gerund.
Example:
A: I can't . . . a bathroom of my own! *(go on/live/here; without/have)*
B: Stop . . . your own bathroom and start . . . your homework. – *(talk about/get; do)*
Your answer:
A: I can't go on *living* here without *having* a bathroom of my own!
B: Stop *talking* about *getting* your own bathroom and start *doing* your homework.

1. A: You're . . . big problems, aren't you? *(afraid of/bring up)*
   B: Not at all. I'm just . . . your selfish ideas. *(tired of/listen to)*
2. A: Why are you . . . my new boyfriend? *(against/meet)*
   B: I don't . . . a boyfriend who's 37 years old. *(agree with/you/have)*

3. A: You're going to ... me away from home. *(succeed in/drive)*
   B: You're already very ... your own excuses for ... here. *(good at/find/not to be)*
4. A: Why are you so ... everything I do? *(interested in/know)*
   B: Because I'm ... the wrong kind of people. *(worried about/you/meet)*
5. A: Mother, why do you ... such stupid questions? *(insist on/ask)*
   B: All I said was: are you ... your boyfriend again? *(look forward to/see)*
6. A: I'm ... for the weekend. *(think of/go away)*
   B: Well, ... us. *(thank you for/tell)*
7. A: This will ... home for good. *(end with/me/leave)*
   B: Well, don't leave ... your bald, middle-aged boyfriend with you! *(without/take)*

Over to you

1. Who do you sympathize with more – the mother or the daughter? Explain.
2. What kinds of problems should be discussed between parents and children? How about 'big' problems like sex, drugs or the value of an education? Do you discuss them at home? If so, say whether you usually agree or not. State the reasons for (not) coming to an agreement.
3. Discuss both positions:
   a) Child: "In my view, sixteen is the most difficult age to be."
   b) Parent: "Be reasonable ... do it my way!"

   As to expressions related to asking for an opinion and giving a well-reasoned opinion, see the appendix, section 4.

Text 6.2

Keith Dewhurst (born 1931) has been a television writer since 1959, his greatest success being the popular police series *Z Cars*.

Last Bus

Keith Dewhurst

Annotations

conductor [kən'dʌktə] (n) person who sells tickets on a bus
lad (infml.) [læd] boy, youth
spade (n) *(taboo: derog. slang)* a black-skinned person
disgrace [-'-] (n) shame, loss of honour and respect
clatter down (v) to run down making quick, short sounds with their feet
tumble off (v) fall off suddenly or helplessly
housing estate (n) district with planned group of houses, usually all the same
swing round here: pull round in a semi-circular movement
punch (v) strike with the hand closed (in a fist)

VIOLENT CRIME IN ENGLAND AND WALES (1987)

Offences	Number	Increase in one year
Violent assaults	140,000	12%
Rape	25,000	11%
Robberies	32,000	9%

(Adapted from: *The Sunday Times* 22. 1. 1989 and 22. 3. 1988)

Comment on the information given in the Info box.

Listening task

1. Before you listen to the tape, look at the sentences below and decide later if they refer to the conductor (=C) or the driver of the bus (=D):

   a) He thinks the boys will get off quietly.
   b) He is black.
   c) He wants to know what is going on.
   d) He presses the bell.
   e) He suggests they should continue the journey.
   f) He is beaten up by the boys.

2. Listen to the tape again and write two sentences afterwards to describe how these two people behave: Mrs Smith, Mr Phillips.

Focus on grammar

It is vs. *there is/are*

Study the following sentences:
It is late at night, and *it is* very hot. *There is* not a single person out in the street. Suddenly ... –
Use either *it is* or *there is/are* in the passage below:
(1) ____ night. The little town is about to go to sleep and (2) ____ quiet and peaceful in the valley. (3) ____ almost midnight when the sound of the last bus breaks the silence. (4) ____ hardly anyone about in the streets.
On the edge of the town (5) ____ a bus-stop near some small shops. (6) ____ a woman standing there, waiting for the bus. (7) ____ cold and (8) ____ an icy wind blowing. Suddenly the woman looks around. (9) ____ four youths standing in the doorway of one of the shops. The woman grips her handbag more tightly and looks anxiously for the bus. (10) ____ late. Then (11) ____ the sound of an engine forcing its way uphill. A few seconds later, the bus slows down and stops for the old lady. Trembling with fear, (12) ____ with a sigh of relief that she gets on the bus.

The construction want s. o. to do sth.

Imagine the following situation:
(At the train station)
Carol: 'Buy my ticket, will you Peter?'
What does Carol want? – *She wants Peter to buy her ticket.*
Now answer the questions below in a similar way using the *want* + infinitive construction (never use a *that*-clause!):

1. The conductor said to the boys: 'Shut up'. – What did the conductor want?
2. The conductor said: 'Now, the one that hasn't paid, get off.' – What did he want?
3. The conductor said to the driver: 'Come and help me.' – What did he want?
4. Robbo said to the conductor: 'Don't you put your filthy Irish hands on me!' – What didn't Robbo want?
5. Mrs Smith said: 'You boys should get off and walk.' – What did she want?
6. The conductor said to Mrs Smith: 'Sit down, lady, and don't do anything.' – What did the conductor want?
7. Mrs Smith said: 'Help him, somebody, help him.' – What did she want?

Discussion

Violent kids

1. Name possible causes for the violent behaviour of adolescents.
2. "Gangs of teenagers (like Robbo and his friends) do what they do because they are evil. They must be punished immediately and severely." – Give your opinion.
3. Have you heard of teenage kids in Germany who were "wilding", that is, running around in packs like wolves to create trouble and hurt people? –
   Discuss the following statement: "For adolescents who are 'wilding', attacking people is a pastime, just plain 'fun'."
4. What can be done about teenage violence? Suggest ways and means to stop a further rise in brutal crimes by young people.

The look-away society

1. Consider the following results of a psychological experiment:
   - 70 per cent of the people who were *alone* offered to help when they heard someone was being attacked in the next room.
   - Only 10 per cent of people offered to help when they had two other people with them in the same room who appeared to be unaffected by the noise of the attack in the next room.

     Point out some of the reasons which keep people from interfering when witnessing a crime.
2. "The best technique for getting out of a dangerous situation is doing nothing." – To what extent do you agree with this view?
3. "Cowardice is just as shameful as violence against people." – State your position on this topic and give reasons for your answers.

Tuning in

1. Is there a lot of crime on public transport in the area where you live? Say if you have read of any cases in the paper.
2. Point out what the police do in order to make the public transport system safer.
3. What can passengers do to protect themselves?

Riding the New York Subway

Every night between 8 p. m. and 4 a. m., unarmed young men and women in red berets and T-shirts ride the New York subway. They call themselves the Magnificent Thirteen Subway Patrol. Nowadays they are commonly called the Guardian Angels. They concentrate on the worst routes, the darkest stations, and the poorest, most violent neighbourhoods. It's a dangerous job, with no wages. And the youngsters who do it are amazing – there is no other word for it.

The patrolling began in 1979 in response to the emergency created by increased violence in the subway which caused panic among the public. Late at night there were no police patrols on the trains, and anything could happen. The original 13 members of the group soon grew to more than a hundred, and people are joining all the time. The leader was a (then) 25-year-old Polish-Italian, Curtis 'The Rock' Sliwa, a former street fighter.

We went on patrol with Sliwa and some of his friends to see what the job was like. We started in a poor part of the Bronx where the group's headquarters are.

8.40 p. m. We get on to the Lexington Express. A drunk hangs on a strap staring at Sliwa, then moves away. "The beret and the T-shirt show the public who we are," Sliwa explains gravely. "We're not armed and the muggers know that. But they also know we never step backwards and we never quit."

subway (AmE) = underground *(BrE)* 2 *beret* ['bereɪ] or [bə'reɪ] (n) G: Baskenmütze 3 *patrol* [pə'trəʊl] (n) G: Spähtrupp 6 *wages* (n) a payment of money paid daily or weekly for a service or job which has been done 8 *emergency* [-'---] (n) G: Notfall 8/9 *increased* [ɪn'kriːst] having become larger in amount or number 9 *cause* (v) produce an effect, lead to 12 *join* (v) become a member of (a club, organisation) 15 *headquarters* [ˌ-'--] (n) the centre of operations for an organisation 17 *strap* (n) here: G: Haltegriff mit Schlaufe 19 *grave* serious 19/20 *be armed* have weapons 20 *mugger* (n) sb who robs with violence, especially in a lonely, dark place 21 *quit* (v) give up, leave

Lisa Sliwa

8.43 p. m. The train stops. A policeman gets on. He's got a double belt on which hang a revolver, bullets, a radio, keys, a nightstick, a notepad, handcuffs, and a torch.

The boys move towards the doors and look down the platform, checking for each other's red berets. If one is missing, it means trouble, and the others run down the train to the scene of action. Three black girls giggle. An elderly white man says, yes, the kids are doing a great job. The train rattles and shakes its way through Manhattan at high speed. To speak and be understood you have to shout.

9.01 p. m. The policeman, who has been riding the subway for 13 years and is familiar with all the problems, admits solemnly that the Magnificents are doing well. "If I weren't here, there'd still be no trouble with these guys around. They know how to handle a difficult situation."

2 *bullet* ['bʊlɪt] (n) G: Kugel 2 *nightstick (AmE)* = truncheon *(BrE):* a short thick stick often carried by policemen 3 *notepad* (n) a small book to write notes in 3 *handcuffs* (n) G: Handschellen 3 *torch* (n) G: Taschenlampe 4 *checking for* here: looking out for 7 *rattle* (v) make a lot of quick little noises, as when small hard objects strike one another 11 *be familiar with* know about 11 *admit* [-'-] (v) agree to the truth of something 11 *solemn* ['sɒləm] formal, serious 13 *handle* (v) deal with, cope with, manage

9.27 p. m. We're in Brooklyn. We change trains to go four more stops. "Muggers' Delight" is the grim name the Magnificents give this area. The station is dimly lit. There are light sockets but no lights. Water drips, shadows move in an uncanny way, our footsteps make a hollow sound, and conversation dies. A battlefield would be a friendlier place.

10.32 p. m. On the train, still in Brooklyn. Kato Lee, a Hawaiian Chinese with a black belt in Kung-Fu, explains his technique: "If there's a man bothering a woman in the train, I go up to her and ask her if she needs help. If she says 'Yes,' I ask him to stop. If he says 'No,' then I dissuade him. I teach him a lesson." We are sitting close to Lee at the end of the rear carriage – the most dangerous one at night – and I ask him what he would do if two men were as close as we are and began to abuse him. "Language is no problem," he replies patiently. "We train ourselves to stay cool and shrug it off." But if they attack him? He makes a small horizontal movement with his hand moving towards my throat. "You're dead," he says.

Sliwa smiles. "We ride trains to take the fear out of people, nothing else. We're not a gang. We get on well with the police. Kato's just pulling your leg – we're just here to help make New York a city to be proud of. And we are needed urgently. You want proof? OK, so far we've got more than 5,000 members in 67 American cities. And we're spreading out all the time." Sliwa's wife Lisa, who has a black belt in karate, has been on a couple of trips to Europe to suggest what could be done in the battle against street crime. She says: "We have had lots of letters telling us about the problems in Britain's big cities – the muggings, the rapes, and the racial troubles – and we believe that our sort of organisation could help. The young people out of work with nothing to do but hang around street corners could be the backbone of the organisation. It's awful to realise that many people, especially old people, are frightened when they go to the supermarket to do their shopping. The fear is there, and we've got to do something about it."

2 *delight* (n) something which gives great pleasure 2 *grim* cruel, hard, causing fear 3 *dim* not bright 3 *light socket* (n) opening into which the light fits; G: Lampenfassung 4 *uncanny* G: unheimlich 5 *hollow* not solid, having an empty space inside 8 *belt* G: Gürtel 9 *bother* (v) cause trouble (to) 11 *dissuade* [dɪ'sweɪd] (v) prevent from doing sth (by giving reasons) 12 *rear carriage* [rɪə] (n) the last carriage in the train 14 *abuse* [ə'bjuːz] (v) say unkind, cruel or rude things to sb 16 *shrug it off* treat as not important 17 *throat* (n) G: Kehle 20/21 *pull sb's leg* make fun of sb (in a friendly way) 22 *urgent* G: dringend 22 *proof* G: Beweis 23 *spread out* [spred] (v) G: sich ausbreiten 27 *racial* ['reɪʃl] (adj) concerning people of different colours 29/30 *backbone* ['--] (n) *(fig.)* the main support

A Scotland Yard spokesman says: "We can only condemn people who take the law into their own hands. People should report crimes to us and not act as vigilantes. And simply the way these people dress in combat gear would provoke more violence here than it would stop."

Lisa Sliwa disagrees, "We're not vigilantes, we're a community group. And let me tell you – I've been to London, to Birmingham and to Manchester, and people want our help. You've got to protect innocent people, and teach them to defend themselves. If you give in easily to muggers, what you're really saying is that your possessions or your body are not worth defending. These criminals are not human beings, they're mutants. They place no value on their own lives. How then can they value yours?"

1 *condemn* [kən'dem] (v) express strong disapproval of; G: verurteilen 3 *vigilante* [ˌvɪdʒɪ'læntɪ] (n) (often *derog.*) member of a group of people forming an unofficial organisation to keep order 3 *combat gear* ['kɒmbæt gɪə] (n) equipment for fighting 7 *innocent* ['ɪnəsnt] not guilty of a crime or sin 8 *give in* (v) give way, allow oneself to be beaten 9 *possessions* [pə'zeʃnz] (n) personal property (ie., what one owns) 9 *worth* [wɜːθ] (adj) having a certain value 9/10 *defend* [-'-] (v) protect against attack 10 *mutant* ['mjuːtənt] (n) result of a genetic change (mutation) ie., having none of its parents' characteristics 10/11 *place no value (on)* G: keinen Wert auf etwas legen

Comprehension

1. Describe the origin and purpose of the 'Magnificent Thirteen'.
2. Compare the equipment of the Guardian Angels with that of the policeman.
3. Repeat in your own words Sliwa's explanation of the use of their special clothes.
4. Describe the procedure the Guardian Angels follow when the train stops.
5. Summarize the policeman's opinion of the Magnificents.
6. Try to explain the name "Muggers' Delight". Say what you know about Brooklyn.
7. Interpret the meaning and the consequences of the following two statements by Kato Lee: 'I dissuade him' (p. 209, l. 11) and 'You're dead' (p. 209, l. 18).
8. Explain why Lisa Sliwa has been to Europe.
9. Outline her argument about unemployed youngsters in Europe in your own words.
10. Apparently the British police are not altogether happy with the arrival of the Guardian Angels. Rephrase their argument.
11. Explain the difference between *vigilantes* and a *community group*.
12. Comment on Lisa's opinion of muggers especially in relation to her use of the word *mutant* for them.

Grammar: the use of the modals *would* and *should*

Compare these two sentences:

a) A Scotland Yard spokesman said: 'People *should* report crimes to us.'

b) There is quite a bit of violence on public transport. A group like the Guardian Angels *would* do a lot of good.

Now use *should* or *would* in the sentences below:
1. You ____ see that film. You ____ like it.
2. You ____ put on a sweater. It's cold outside.
3. I don't think you ____ like John. He's not a very nice person.
4. You work too hard. You ____ take a holiday. It ____ do you good.
5. The car didn't start this morning. We ____ have it serviced. ____ you take it to the garage tomorrow?
6. You ____ go and see your kids perform in the school play! They ____ be so proud.
7. She ____ see a doctor if she's not feeling well.
8. How much ____ I tip the waiter? – 'Oh, a pound ____ be enough'.

INFO BOX

CRIME ON PUBLIC TRANSPORT (1987)

Transport system	Police officers	Incidents*	Murders	Rapes
New York subway	4,200	100,000	12	34
London underground	400	19,000	1	4

* Incidents = pickpocketing, theft, assault, robbery, vehicle damage, indecent exposure etc.

(Adapted from *The Times* 27. 1. 1989 and *The Sunday Times* 29. 1. 1989)

Give examples of how the New York subway is more dangerous than the London underground.

Talking points

1. Form your own opinion about an organization like the Guardian Angels.
2. Explain why the forming of vigilante groups has become so popular in the USA.
3. "Vigilantism is not a solution to the problem of crime in our societies, but only a reflection of the 'urban wilderness' our big cities have become." – Discuss.
4. "The presence of groups like the Guardian Angels can reduce people's fears of being attacked." – Give your opinion.
5. Try to find the reasons for Scotland Yard's negative attitude towards the Guardian Angels' activities in Britain.
6. Consider the idea that an initiative like the 'Angels' could provide a meaningful task for unemployed youths.
7. Do you think a similar kind of patrolling could become necessary and/or popular in Germany? State the arguments for or against such a private crime control system in the area where you live.

Text 6.4

The Test

Angelica Gibbs

On the afternoon Marian took her second driver's test, Mrs Ericson went with her. "It's probably better to have someone a little older with you," Mrs Ericson said as Marian slipped into the driver's seat beside her. "Perhaps the last time your Cousin Bill made you nervous, talking too much on the way."

"Yes, Ma'am," Marian said in her soft unaccented voice. "They probably do like it better if a white person shows up with you."

"Oh, I don't think it's *that,*" Mrs Ericson began, and subsided after a glance at the girl's set profile. Marian drove the car slowly through the shady suburban streets. It was one of the first hot days in June, and when they reached the boulevard they found it crowded with cars headed for the beaches.

"Do you want me to drive?" Mrs Ericson asked. "I'll be glad to if you're feeling jumpy." Marian shook her head. Mrs Ericson watched her dark, competent hands and wondered for the thousandth time how the house had ever managed to get along without her, or how she had lived through those earlier years when her household had been presided over by a series of slat-ternly white girls who had considered housework demeaning and the care of children an added insult. "You drive beautifully, Marian," she said. "Now don't think of the last time. Anybody would slide on a steep hill on a wet day like that."

"It takes four mistakes to flunk you," Marian said. "I don't remember doing all the things the inspector marked down on my blank."

"People say that they only want you to slip them a little something," Mrs Ericson said doubtfully.

"No," Marian said. "That would only make it worse, Mrs Ericson, I know."

6 *show up with* (v) come along together with 7 *subside* [səb'saɪd] (v) stop talking 8 *glance* (n) a quick look 8 *shady* (adj) in shelter from sunlight (because of trees) 9 *suburban* [sə'bɜːbən] (adj) belonging to the outer parts of a town 10 *head for* (v) *(infml.)* go towards 13 *jumpy (infml.)* nervous 16 *preside over* [prɪ'zaɪd] (v) *(fml.)* be in charge of, lead 16/17 *slatternly* (adj) dirty and untidy (of women) 17 *demeaning* lowering, in the opinion of oneself or others 18 *insult* ['--] (n) G: Beleidigung 19 *steep* (adj) rising or falling quickly 21 *flunk* (v) *(infml.)* fail (especially an examination) 22 *blank* (n) empty sheet of paper (to be filled in) 23 *slip sb sth* give sb sth secretly, unnoticed 24 *doubtful* uncertain

The car turned right, at a traffic signal, into a side road and slid up to the curb at the rear of a short line of parked cars. The inspectors had not arrived yet.

"You have the papers?" Mrs Ericson asked. Marian took them out of her bag: her learner's permit, the car registration, and her birth certificate. They settled down to the dreary business of waiting.

"It will be marvelous to have someone dependable to drive the children to school every day," Mrs Ericson said.

Marian looked up from the list of driving requirements she had been studying. "It'll make things simpler at the house, won't it?" she said.

"Oh, Marian." Mrs Ericson exclaimed, "if I could only pay you half of what you're worth?"

"Now, Mrs Ericson," Marian said firmly. They looked at each other and smiled with affection.

Two cars with official insignia on their doors stopped across the street. The inspectors leaped out, very brisk and military in their neat uniforms. Marian's hands tightened on the wheel. "There's the one who flunked me last time," she whispered, pointing to a stocky, self-important man who had begun to shout directions at the driver at the head of the line. "Oh, Mrs Ericson."

"Now, Marian," Mrs Ericson said. They smiled at each other again, rather weakly.

The inspector who finally reached their car was not the stocky one but a genial, middle-aged man who grinned broadly as he thumbed over their papers. Mrs Ericson started to get out of the car. "Don't you want to come along?" the inspector asked. "Mandy and I don't mind company."

Mrs Ericson was bewildered for a moment. "No," she said, and stepped to the curb. "I might make Marian self-conscious. She's a fine driver, Inspector."

"Sure thing," the inspector said, winking at Mrs Ericson. He slid into the seat beside Marian. "Turn right at the corner, Mandy-Lou."

1 *slide* move slowly and smoothly 2 *curb* (n) *(AmE)* = kerb *(BrE):* the edge of the pavement 5 *permit* ['--] (n) an official written statement giving one the right to do sth 5 *registration* (n) paper with details of the car and the people who have owned it 6 *settle down to* give one's serious attention to 6 *dreary* ['drɪərɪ] dull, uninteresting 7 *dependable* [-'---] reliable, trustworthy 9 *requirement* (n) sth needed 14 *affection* [ə'fekʃn] (n) fondness 15 *insignia* [ɪn'sɪgnɪə] (n) here: symbols which represent the power of an official, eg. the crown of a king 16 *leap out* [li:p] jump out 16 *brisk* (adj) quick and active 16 *neat* [ni:t] (adj) tidy, orderly 17 *tighten* (v) become tight 17 *wheel* (n) the steering wheel 18 *stocky* (adj) thick, short and strong 24 *genial* ['dʒi:nɪəl] (adj) cheerful and kind, good-tempered 24 *thumb over* [θʌm] (v) go through, turning over with one's thumb 27 *bewildered* [bɪ'wɪldəd] confused 28 *self-conscious* [ˌ-'--] nervous and uncomfortable about oneself as seen by others 29 *wink at* (v) G: zwinkern

From the curb, Mrs Ericson watched the car move smoothly up the street.

The inspector made notations in a small black book. "Age?" he inquired presently, as they drove along.

"Twenty-seven."

He looked at Marian out of the corner of his eye. "Old enough to have quite a flock of pickaninnies, eh?"

Marian did not answer.

"Left at this corner," the inspector said, "and park between that truck and the green Buick."

The two cars were very close together, but Marian squeezed in between them without too much maneuvering. "Driven before, Mandy-Lou?" the inspector asked.

"Yes, sir. I had a license for three years in Pennsylvania."

"Why do you want to drive a car?"

"My employer needs me to take her children to and from school."

"Sure you don't really want to sneak out nights to meet some young blood?" the inspector asked. He laughed as Marian shook her head.

"Let's see you take a left at the corner and then turn around in the middle of the next block," the inspector said. He began to whistle "Swanee River." "Make you homesick?" he asked.

Marian put out her hand, swung around neatly in the street, and headed back in the direction from which they had come. "No," she said. "I was born in Scranton, Pennsylvania."

The inspector feigned astonishment. "You-all ain't Southern?" he said. "Well, dog my cats if I didn't think you-all came from down yondah."

"No, sir," Marian said.

"Turn onto Main Street and let's see how you-all does in heavier traffic."

They followed a line of cars along Main Street for several blocks until they came in sight of a concrete bridge which arched high over the railroad tracks.

"Read that sign at the end of the bridge," the inspector said.

"'Proceed with caution. Dangerous in slippery weather'," Marian said.

1 *smooth* ['smu:ð] even in movement, without sudden changes of speed 2 *notation* [-'--] written note 6 *flock* a large number 6 *pickaninny* (n) *(not polite)* a small child of a black-skinned race 8 *truck (AmE)* = lorry *(BrE)* 10 *squeeze in between* put (the car) in a small space between 11 *maneuvering (AmE)* [mə'nu:vrɪŋ] = manoeuvring *(BrE):* moving in different directions with skill 16 *sneak out* [sni:k] go out quietly and secretly 21 *swing* turn 24 *feign* [feɪn] (v) pretend 24 *astonishment* (n) great surprise, amazement 24 *you-all ain't (dial.)* = you aren't 25 *dog my cats (dial.)* exclamation of astonishment 25 *yondah* = yonder: (over) there 29 *arch* [ɑ:tʃ] (v) to form a curved shape 30 *tracks* (n) lines 32 *proceed* [-'-] (v) *(fml.)* go forward 32 *caution* (n) great care and attention

"You-all can read fine," the inspector exclaimed. "Where d'you learn to do that, Mandy?"

"I got my college degree last year," Marian said. Her voice was not quite steady.

As the car crept up the slope of the bridge the inspector burst out laughing. He laughed so hard he could scarcely give his next direction. "Stop here," he said, wiping his eyes, "then start 'er up again. Mandy got her degree, did she? Dog my cats!"

Marian pulled up beside the curb. She put the car in neutral, pulled on the emergency, waited a moment, and then put the car into gear again. Her face was set. As she released the brake her foot slipped off the clutch pedal and the engine stalled.

"Now Mistress Mandy," the inspector said, "remember your degree."

"*Damn* you!" Marian cried. She started the car with a jerk.

The inspector lost his joviality in an instant. "Return to the starting place, please," he said, and made four very black crosses at random in the squares on Marian's application blank.

Mrs Ericson was waiting at the curb where they had left her. As Marian stopped the car, the inspector jumped out and brushed past her, his face purple. "What happened?" Mrs Ericson asked and looked after him with alarm.

Marian stared down at the wheel and her lip trembled.

"Oh, Marian, *again*?" Mrs Ericson said.

Marian nodded. "In a sort of different way," she said, and slid over to the right-hand side of the car.

4 *steady* ['stedɪ] regular, not moving up and down 5 *creep* move very slowly 5 *slope* (n) here: the part where the bridge rises 6 *scarcely* ['skeəslɪ] (adv) hardly 9 *neutral* (n) G: Leerlauf 10 *emergency* the emergency brake *(AmE)* = hand-brake *(BrE)* 10 *put into gear* [gɪə] move the gear stick from neutral into a position which will engage the engine 11 *release* [rɪ'li:s] (v) let go of 11 *clutch pedal* G: Kupplungspedal 12 *stall* [stɔ:l] (v) stop (of engines) 14 *jerk* (n) a short quick strong movement 15 *joviality* [ˌdʒəʊvɪ'ælətɪ] (n) good humour 15 *in an instant* at once, immediately 16 *at random* without any plan or system 17 *application blank* the paper to be filled in as part of Marian's request for a driving licence 19 *brush past* go past touching someone lightly 20 *purple* ['pɜ:pl] (adj) a dark red colour 20/21 *with alarm* with sudden fear and anxiety 22 *tremble* (v) shake 24 *nod* (v) move one's head quickly up and down

Close reading

1. Comment on the following remarks; the first by Mrs Ericson (p. 212, l. 2): 'It's probably better to have someone a little older with you', the second by Marian (p. 212, ll. 5/6): 'They probably do like it better if a white person shows up with you."
2. Explain why Mrs Ericson "subsided after a glance at the girl's set profile" (p. 212, ll. 7/8).
3. Describe the relationship between Marian and Mrs Ericson, and point out the special reason why Marian was taking a driving test.

4. Try to read between the lines: What did Mrs Ericson and Marian say and what did they (probably) think about the reasons why Marian failed the first driving test?
5. Why did the inspector ask her "Driven before, Mandy-Lou?" (p. 214, l. 11)?
6. Give reasons for the inspector's repeated use of phrases like *Dog my cats* and *you-all* (which are taken from Black American English).
7. Explain why he whistled the song "Swanee River".
8. Consider why the inspector suddenly burst out laughing and how this led to Marian's mistake.
9. Describe the effect of Marian's outburst on the inspector's behaviour towards her.

The author's craft

1. Take notes individually of all the subtle and (later on in the story) open provocations made by the inspector. Point out why these provocations were unfair.
2. List Marian's reactions to the inspector's insinuations (G: *Anspielungen*) and show how they change as the test goes on.
3. Consider if there are stages in the story where the inspector's behaviour changes markedly.
4. Comment on the title of the story.

Talking points

1. Discuss the following statement made by Stanley Grayson, black Deputy Mayor of New York City: "No matter what I achieve as an individual, I will always be judged by what people see first, my color." – Find examples of what you would consider racial prejudice and discrimination.
2. "The creation of racial equality in the States can only be achieved by pressure from the top (that is, compulsion by the government), because most black and white individuals have given up integration as a goal in their personal lives." – Discuss.
3. "Yeah, I'm all for integration (of blacks, foreigners etc.), but not in my neighbourhood, please." – Comment on this attitude.

Written work

Choose one of the two following quotations to write an essay pointing out how racial prejudice and discrimination can affect a person's everyday life. Feel free to discuss situations and cases which you consider similar in a German context:

1. "White prejudice and discrimination keep the Negro low in standards of living, health, education, manners and morals. This, in its turn, gives support to white prejudice" (Gunnar Myrdal: *An American Dilemma*. 1944).
2. "The status of black Americans today can be characterized as a glass that is half full – if measured by progress since 1939 – or as a glass that is half empty – if measured by the persisting disparity between black and white Americans since the early 1970s" (G. D. Jaynes & R. M. Williams: *A Common Destiny*. 1989).

RACE RELATIONS IN THE US: BLACK PROGRESS HAS STALLED

1. The black and the white middle class (US average)

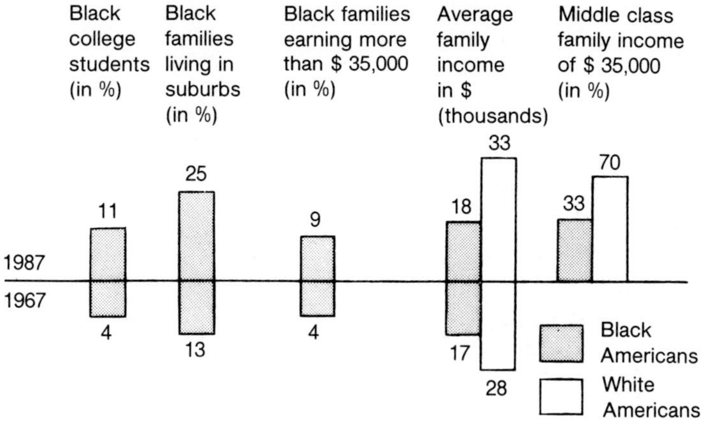

2. Birmingham, Alabama 25 years after the Civil Rights Act of 1964

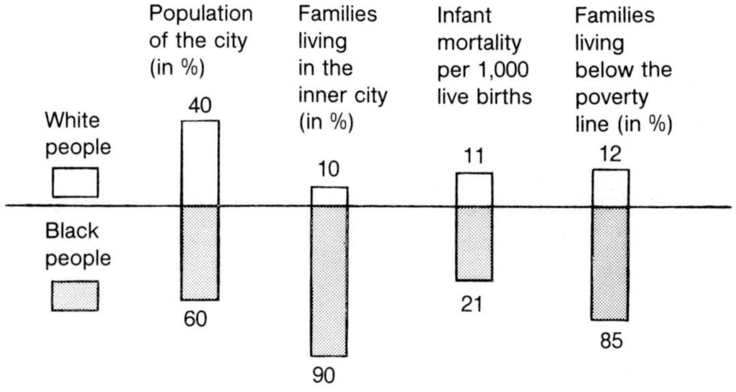

TASKS

1. Point out changes and non-changes for Black and White Americans between 1967 and 1987.
2. Name some of the differences in living conditions between black and white people in Birmingham, Alabama.

Text 6.5

✇ All God's Creatures

On the tape you will hear interviews with some British people giving their opinions about immigrants.
Go through the words and questions before you listen.

Annotations

flowery (adj) having flowers (on them)
nevertheless G: trotzdem
I don't care it doesn't matter to me
absorb [-'-] (v) take in
chat [tʃæt] (v) talk in a friendly way
penniless without any money
menial ['mi:nɪəl] (adj) not important or interesting (of work)
clerk [klɑ:k] (n) person employed in an office to do written work
blame (n) responsibility for sth bad
freeze sb out to prevent sb from being included
permission (n) act of allowing, agreement
germ [dʒɜ:m] (n) G: (Krankheits-)Keim
hard lines on them (infml.) bad luck for them
suffer from to experience sth unpleasant, especially an illness
disease [dɪ'zi:z] (n) illness
din (n) very loud noise
plead with [pli:d] (v) make continual and deeply felt requests to
depend on rely on
crowd together (v) put together in large numbers
assimilate [-'---] (v) become part of (a country, culture, etc.)
misgiving [ˌ-'--] (n) feeling of doubt and fear
large-scale in great numbers
fault [fɔ:lt] (n) mistake
separate ['seprɪt] (adj) different, divided, not joined
suspicion [sə'spɪʃn] (n) lack of trust and willingness to accept
disadvantage (n) a condition which makes one less successful than others; G: Nachteil
prejudice ['predʒʊdɪs] (n) G: Vorurteil
it's likely to be it is probably
sensitive to ['---] G: empfindlich gegen

Listening comprehension

Listening for understanding: multiple choice

Listen to the tape section by section and choose the best alternative:

PART I

1. *What can you say about Mrs Griffiths' opinions?*
   a) They are representative of many middle-aged people in Britain.
   b) Very few people in Birmingham hold these views.
   c) They are typical of most white people in Britain.
   d) We don't know exactly how many other people think in this way.

2. *What does Mrs Griffith think coloured people in Britain should do?*
   a) They should bring more money with them when they arrive.
   b) They should educate themselves to get better jobs.
   c) They should leave Britain and return to their native countries.
   d) They should tell other coloured people not to come to Britain.

PART II

3. *Why won't Eric Sharpley let his children play with the neighbours' children?*
   a) He's afraid his children will become ill.
   b) He doesn't want his children to learn bad habits.
   c) He's afraid they will damage his garden.
   d) He doesn't want them to catch a cold.
4. *What else does Mr Sharpley say about his neighbours?*
   a) They try to act like English people.
   b) They are very noisy.
   c) They depend on him for help.
   d) They are quite good musicians.

PARTS III & IV

5. *What is the biggest problem with Britain's immigrant population (according to Malcolm Jones)?*
   a) The immigrants are very poor.
   b) The authorities have introduced laws which forbid them to mix.
   c) The immigrants are frightened of the authorities.
   d) The immigrants live in separate communities, which makes it difficult for them to mix.
6. *What does Jenny Dunfield say about the children in her school?*
   a) Young children of different colours usually get on well together.
   b) Their parents help them to play happily together.
   c) Children often have prejudices before they start school.
   d) Very few coloured children speak with foreign accents any longer.

Check the details: right or wrong?

Listen to the tape again and decide whether the following statements are right or wrong. Correct the ones you consider wrong afterwards.

1. Mrs Griffiths' ideas are representative of those of other Britons.
2. She thinks coloureds are unwelcome because they can only do menial jobs.
3. Mr Sharpley thinks that coloured families are not clean.
4. He says coloured people in the neighbourhood are not prepared to make less noise.
5. Mr Jones says the biggest problem is one of overcrowding.
6. He says that the immigrants are suspicious of the British.
7. Miss Dunfield says children are not prejudiced against coloured immigrants.
8. She says that West Indians and Pakistanis are in fact English.

Talk about it

1. Listen carefully to parts I & II again and take notes to get the finer points of both speakers' arguments.
   a) *Lucy Griffiths*
   Is she consistent in her statements, or are there contradictions in what she is saying?
   b) *Eric Sharpley*
   – Find generalizations in his statement.
   – What kinds of opinion does he express?
2. "No one is entirely free of prejudice." – Discuss this statement and name some of the reasons which lie behind most kinds of prejudice.
3. "Social harmony can only be reached by way of *total integration* of the minorities into the cultural and behavioural patterns of the majority." –
   Discuss.
4. "Ethnic minorities are an *enrichment* to the social and cultural life of the majority. We must therefore accept differences in a multicultural society." –
   Discuss and compare with the previous statement.

Text 6.6

This Is British Telecom

John McClintock

It happened when they were walking home from school one afternoon in November. It was a Monday and it had been raining since early morning. That was why Jenny had taken the bus instead of cycling as usual.

The bus was full up downstairs so Jenny had splashed up the metal stairway to the top. The air was thick with cigarette smoke. Jenny tried not to breathe too deeply and sat down on the only seat that was free.

"Welcome to the gas chamber."

Tom Kelly grinned across the aisle at her from the seat opposite. The Kellys had moved into a semi just down the road at the start of the autumn term. Tom was an only child. He was a year older than Jenny, but he seemed younger. His school tie was decorated with the remains of his breakfast, his glasses sat crooked half-way down his nose, and his hair resembled a large haystack in a hurricane.

4 *splash* (v) here: move noisily with the rain running off one's clothes 8 *the aisle* [aɪl] a narrow passage between rows of seats 9 *semi (-detached house)* a house which is joined to another house by one shared wall 11 *remains* (n) the bits and pieces left over 12 *crooked* ['krʊkɪd] not straight 12 *resemble* [rɪ'zembl] (v) look like 13 *haystack* (n) G: Heuhaufen

They had talked all the way into town, and they went on talking when they met again on the bus going home. Tom Kelly could imitate most of the teachers in school. He was specially good at imitating the deep voice of the headmaster. "Kelly," he boomed, "you talk too much." And then it happened.

They had just got off the bus and were half-way across the zebra crossing when the milk van came round the corner towards them. The rain had almost stopped and there was a huge puddle between them and the far side of the road. Suddenly, instead of stopping, the van accelerated and tore into the roadside lake. As Tom said later, it was like being dropped into the middle of the Atlantic Ocean from a great height. "Come and see me when you've changed," he went on. "I saw who it was." And his blue eyes glittered behind the streaming glasses.

When Tom opened the front door half an hour later, he was holding the telephone directory in his hand. "Mum's gone shopping," he said. "We've got about twenty minutes." "What for?" Jenny wondered, but Tom didn't seem to hear. "His name's Harold White, he's a milkman, and he lives up the road," he went on quickly. "Now here's what we're going to do ..."

Harold White had just sat down to a nice cup of tea when the telephone rang. He hurried out into the hall and picked it up. "Hello," he grunted impatiently. A young woman's voice said, "This is British Telecom. Is that Mr. White, Mr. Harold White?"

"Yes, this is Harold White."

"We have an urgent call for you, Mr. White, from one of our engineers. Hold the line, please, and I'll connect you."

There was a short crackling sound and then a deep voice said, "Sorry to bother you, Mr. White, but we're working on your line at the moment and I'm having some difficulty in matching up the electric circuits."

"I see," said Mr. White doubtfully.

"Can I ask you," the voice boomed on, "*not* to answer the phone if it should ring in the next ten minutes. If you do, there is a very real danger that you will electrocute me. Do you understand?"

"Yes." Mr. White swallowed hard. "Yes, of course."

4 *boom* (v) make a deep hollow sound 8 *puddle* (n) a pool of water 9 *accelerate* [-'---] (v) go faster 9 *tear into* [teə] here: drive into with great force 10 *roadside* (adj) being situated at the side of the road 12 *glitter* (v) shine brightly with flashing points of light 20 *grunt* (v) make a short deep sound, like a pig 20/21 *impatient* G: ungeduldig 24 *urgent* ['ɜːdʒənt] (adj) G: dringend 26 *crackling sound* the noise of repeated short sharp sudden sounds 28 *match up* (v) join together (in pairs, groups) 29 *doubtful* ['daʊtfəl] uncertain 32 *electrocute* [-'---] (v) kill by passing electricity through the body 33 *swallow hard* G: kräftig schlucken

"Thank you for your cooperation," said the deep voice, and the line clicked and went dead.

Harold White put the phone down and wondered what was happening. It was all rather worrying. He had just sat down again and lifted the teacup to his lips when the telephone rang. "Brinng, brinng!" Hot tea splashed down Harold White's new slimline shirt. "Brinng, brinng! Brinng, brinng!" The telephone went on ringing. Harold White went on sitting in his armchair, his teacup half-empty, his eyes wide with wonder. "Brinng, brinng! Brinng, brinng!"

He let it ring for at least five minutes. It did not stop. In the end he could stand it no longer. He stumbled out to the hall, hesitated for a moment, then picked up the phone and put it to his ear. At the other end of the line Tom Kelly screamed in unbearable agony.

5 *splash down* here: spill down, G: herunterkleckern 6 *slimline* fashionable cut to show the figure 11 *stumble* (v) G: stolpern 11 *hesitate* ['---] (v) pause before doing sth 13 *unbearable* [ˌʌn'beərəbl] G: unerträglich 13 *agony* ['ægənɪ] terrible pain or suffering

Check your understanding

The main idea

Explain why the last line is the *punch line* of the story; that is, in what ways does it give meaning and surprise (or amusement) to the text as a whole?

Intensive reading

1. Use your own words to describe the setting of the story.
2. Summarize the additional information contained in the description of the upstairs of the bus.
3. Use your own words to describe Tom Kelly.
4. Retell the incident the car driver was guilty of.
5. Give a reason for the fact that Tom's eyes *glittered* (p. 221, l. 12).
6. Why do you think Harold White "grunted impatiently" (p. 221, l. 20).
7. Who is the young woman on the phone. Explain her role in Tom's plan.
8. Repeat the exchange between Mr White and the 'engineer' in your own words.
9. Sum up the events before Harold White finally answered the phone.

How it is said

Explain the meanings of the following words and phrases in the context of the story, and comment on the effects which the choice of these expressions has on building up the tension towards the final line:

a) use of the verb *happen* (stages in the story),
b) p. 220, l. 4: "Jenny had *splashed up* the metal stairway ..." (choice of verb),
c) p. 220, l. 7: "Welcome to the gas chamber" (kind of humour),
d) p. 220, l. 12/13: "his hair resembled a large haystack in a hurricane" (stylistic device),

e) p. 221, ll. 9/10: "the car ... *tore* into the roadside *lake*" (meaning of the verb and choice of noun),
f) p. 221, l. 10: "it was like being dropped into ..." (stylistic device),
g) p. 221, l. 30: "the voice *boomed* on" (more than one meaning),
h) p. 221, l. 33: "Mr White *swallowed* hard" (his feelings),
i) p. 222, l. 13: "Tom Kelly *screamed* in unbearable *agony*" (kind of sound and feeling).

Writing task

Continue the story for another 15 or 20 lines (around 150 words). Read out your endings to the class as a whole.

Grammar revision: the use of the gerund

Consider the following examples from the text:
a) p. 221, l. 1: ... and they went on *talking* when they met again on the bus going home.
b) p. 221, l. 3: He was good at *imitating* the voice of the headmaster.
There are certain verbs (or adjectives + prepositions) which are almost always followed by the gerund.
Now complete the following interview using the verbs given.
Example:
Interviewer (= Int): Do you *(mind/answer)* some questions, Tom?
→Do you mind *answering* some questions, Tom?

An Interview with Tom Kelly
Int: I wonder if you would *(consider/answer)* a few questions, Tom?
Tom: No, I *(not mind/talk)* to the press.
Int: Is it true that Mr White has *(stop/deliver)* milk to your house?
Tom: Yes, he *(stop/come)* here a couple of weeks ago.
Int: And he has *(give up/work)* in this area completely, hasn't he?
Tom: Well, he *(not enjoy/come)* here, does he?
Int: Do you *(mind/tell)* me why he *(dislike/bring)* milk to your house?
Tom: People say that he wants to *(avoid/meet)* me.
Int: But why should he not want to *(risk/see)* you?
Tom: I think someone has told him that I *(enjoy/play)* practical jokes or something.
Int: Do you *(deny/play)* practical jokes on Mr White?
Tom: Who? Me? I don't know what you mean. Can we *(finish/talk)* now? I *(not feel like/answer)* any more questions.

Talk about it

1. Did you find the story funny? If yes, was it *funny haha* (= amusing, causing laughter) or was it *funny peculiar* (= strange, weird)?
2. Do you find Tom's behaviour excusable, or should he be punished for what he did?
3. Tell stories of jokes played on people using the telephone.

Text 6.7

Tuning in

Has anybody told you about a really embarrassing experience, or have you ever had one yourself? Talk about the place and time, the chain of events and the outcome of the incident.

Jeffrey Archer (born 1940) has made his name both as a leading Conservative politician and as a best-selling author. His eight novels have sold 11 million copies in English and another 15 million copies in their translated versions in 20 languages. As a student at Oxford he was a well-known athlete and sprinted for Britain in international competitions in the mid-sixties. For one year (1985/86) he was Deputy Chairman of the Conservative Party, a post he had to resign from because he was involved in a much-publicized callgirl scandal.

Broken Routine

Jeffrey Archer

Septimus Horatio Cornwallis works as a claims adjuster at the head office of the Prudential Assurance Co Ltd in London. He lives in Sevenoaks with his wife, Norma, and his two children. He is a great follower of tradition and discipline, and a creature of habit . . .

PART I

Septimus rose every morning at seven-fifteen and donned one of his two pinhead patterned dark suits. He left his home at 47 Palmerston Drive at seven-fifty-five, having consumed his invariable breakfast of one soft-boiled egg, two pieces of toast, and two cups of tea. On arriving at Platform One of Sevenoaks station he would purchase a copy of the *Daily Express* before boarding the eight-twenty-seven to Cannon Street. During the journey Septimus would read his newspaper and smoke two cigarettes, arriving at Cannon Street at nine-seven. He would then walk to the office, and be sitting at his desk in his glass cubicle on the sixth floor, confronting the first claim to be adjusted by nine-thirty. He took his coffee break at eleven, allowing himself the luxury of two more cigarettes, when once again he would regale his colleagues with the imagined achievements of his children. At eleven-fifteen he returned to work.

1 *claims adjuster* person who examines the demands for sums of money made by customers of the insurance company   1 *prudential* [-'--] sensible and wise (especially in business matters)   3 *a creature of habit* person who does the same things at the same time every day   5 *don* (v) *(fml.)* put on   6 *patterned* G: gemustert   9 *purchase (fml.)* ['pɜːtʃɪs] (v) buy   10 *board* (v) get on to   16 *regale with* [rɪ'geɪl] (v) give enjoyment to   16 *achievement* [ə'tʃiːvmənt] G: Leistung

At one o'clock he would leave the Great Gothic Cathedral (one of his expressions) for one hour, which he passed at a pub called The Havelock where he would drink a half-pint of Carlsberg lager with a dash of lime, and eat the dish of the day. After he finished his lunch, he would once again smoke two cigarettes. At one-fifty-five he returned to the insurance records until the fifteen minute tea break at four o'clock which was another ritual occasion for two more cigarettes. On the dot of five-thirty, Septimus would pick up his umbrella and reinforced steel briefcase with the initials S. H. C. in silver on the side and leave, double locking his glass cubicle. As he walked through the typing pool, he would announce with a mechanical jauntiness "See you same time tomorrow, girls", hum a few bars from *The Sound of Music* in the descending lift, and then walk out into the torrent of office workers surging down High Holborn. He would stride purposefully towards Cannon Street station, umbrella tapping away on the pavement while he rubbed shoulders with bankers, shippers, oil men, and brokers, not discontent to think himself part of the great City of London.

Once he reached the station, Septimus would purchase a copy of the *Evening Standard* and a packet of ten Benson & Hedges cigarettes from Smith's bookstall, placing both on the top of his Prudential documents already in the briefcase. He would board the fourth carriage of the train on Platform Five at five-fifty, and secure his favoured window seat in a closed compartment facing the engine, next to the balding gentleman with the inevitable *Financial Times,* and opposite the smartly dressed secretary who read long romantic novels to somewhere beyond Sevenoaks. Before sitting down he would extract the *Evening Standard* and the new packet of Benson & Hedges from his briefcase, put them both on the armrest of his seat, and place the briefcase and his rolled umbrella on the rack above him. Once settled, he would open the packet of cigarettes and smoke the first of the two which were allocated

3 *dash of lime* just a little of the juice of a lime 3 *lime* G: Limone 4 *the dish of the day* the special meal for the day 5 *records* ['--] (n) written statements giving information about the past 7 *on the dot of* at exactly 8 *reinforced* [,--'-] strengthened (with added materials) 8 *briefcase* ['--] (n) a flat leather case which opens at the top, for carrying papers and books 10 *typing pool* (n) a group of secretaries who write out letters, papers, documents etc. on typewriters (*typewriter* = Schreibmaschine 10 *jauntiness* (n) the showing of self-satisfaction 11 *hum* (v) 'sing' music with the lips closed 11 *a few bars* some notes of music 12 *descending* [-'--] going down 12 *torrent* ['--] (n) *(fig.)* a violently rushing crowd of people 13 *surge* [sɜːdʒ] (v) move forward in waves 13 *stride* (v) walk with long steps 14 *tapping away* knocking lightly again and again 15 *rub shoulders with* mix with 15 *broker* (n) a person who does business for another, especially buying and selling foreign money and shares 15/16 *discontent* [,--'-] (adj) G: unzufrieden 20 *carriage* ['kærɪdʒ] (n) a railway passenger vehicle 21 *secure (fml.)* [-'-] (v) get, especially as the result of effort 21 *compartment* (n) one of the small rooms in a railway carriage 22 *inevitable* [ɪn'evɪtəbl] unavoidable 23 *smart* elegant, fashionable 24/25 *extract (fml.)* [-'-] (v) take out 27 *rack* (n) a shelf for luggage (over the seats) 28 *allocate* ['---] (v) set apart for a special purpose

for the journey while reading the *Evening Standard*. This would leave him eight to be smoked before catching the five-fifty the following evening.

As the train pulled into Sevenoaks station, he would mumble goodnight to his fellow passengers (the only word he ever spoke during the entire journey) and leave, making his way straight to the semi-detached at 47 Palmerston Drive, arriving at the front door a little before six-forty-five. Between six-forty-five and seven-thirty he would finish reading his paper or check over his children's homework with a tut-tut when he spotted a mistake, or a sigh when he couldn't fathom the new maths. At seven-thirty his "good lady" (another of his favoured expressions) would place on the kitchen table in front of him the *Woman's Own* dish of the day or his favourite dinner of three fish fingers, peas and chips. He would then say "If God had meant fish to have fingers, he would have given them hands," laugh, and cover the oblong fish with tomato sauce, consuming the meal to the accompaniment of his wife's recital of the day's events. At nine, he watched the real news on BBC 1 (he never watched ITV) and at ten-thirty he retired to bed.

This routine was adhered to year in year out with breaks only for holidays, for which Septimus naturally also had a routine. Alternate Christmases were spent with Norma's parents in Watford and the ones in between with Septimus's sister and brother-in-law in Epsom, while in the summer, their high spot of the year, the family took a package holiday for two weeks in the Olympic Hotel, Corfu.

Septimus not only liked his life-style, but was distressed if for any reason his routine met with the slightest interference. This humdrum existence seemed certain to last him from womb to tomb, for Septimus was not the stuff on which authors base two hundred thousand word sagas. Nevertheless there was one occasion when Septimus's routine was not merely interfered with, but frankly, shattered.

3 *mumble* (v) speak unclearly 4 *fellow passenger* someone with whom one is travelling 4 *entire* [-'--] whole 7/8 *check over* (v) go through, making sure there are no mistakes 8 *spot* (v) catch sight of 9 *fathom* ['fæðm] (v) here: understand 11 *Woman's Own dish* a meal described in the "*Woman's Own*" magazine 12 *fish fingers* G: Fischstäbchen 12 *peas* (n) G: Erbsen 13/14 *oblong* ['ɒblɒŋ] G: rechteckig 14 *accompaniment* [-'----] (n) G: Begleitung 15 *recital* [-'--] (n) here: account, report 16 *retire* (v) here: go away (to a quiet place) 17 *was adhered to* [əd'hɪərd] was kept to 18 *alternate* [ɔːl'tɜːnət] (adj) first one and then the other 21 *high spot* main event 21 *package holiday* a completely planned holiday at a fixed price arranged by a travel agency 23 *distressed* [-'-] upset 24 *interference* [ˌ--'--] (n) disturbance 24 *humdrum* ['--] without variety or change 25 *from womb to tomb* from the cradle to the grave, ie. all his life 25 *womb* [wuːm] G: Gebärmutter 26 *stuff* (n) material 26 *saga* ['sɑːgə] (n) a long story of brave and exciting action 27 *interfere with* disturb 28 *frankly* (adv) speaking honestly and plainly 28 *shattered* smashed to pieces

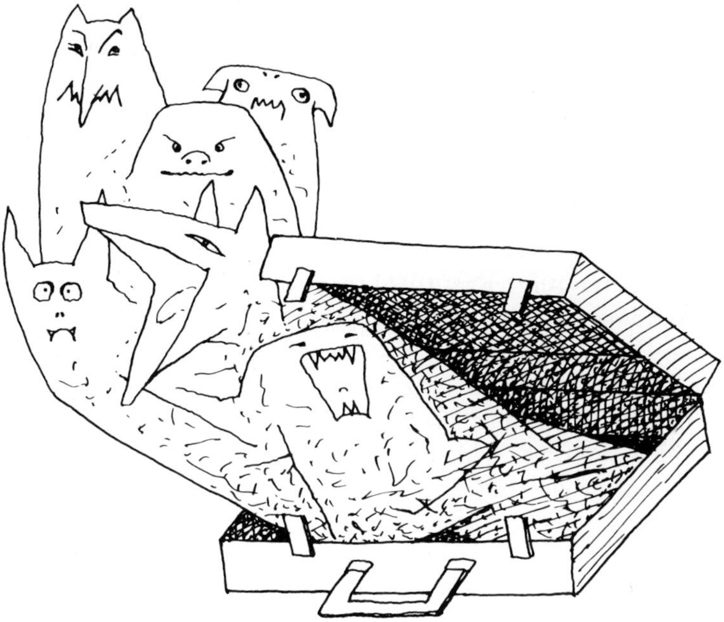

PART II

One evening at five-twenty-seven, when Septimus was closing the file on the last claim for the day, his immediate superior, the Deputy Manager, called him in for a consultation. Owing to this gross lack of consideration, Septimus did not manage to get away from the office until a few minutes after six. Although everyone had left the typing pool, he still saluted the empty desks and silent typewriters with the invariable, 'See you same time tomorrow, girls,' and hummed a few bars of *Edelweiss* to the descending lift.

As he stepped out of the Great Gothic Cathedral it started to rain. Septimus reluctantly undid his neatly rolled umbrella, and putting it up dashed through the puddles, hoping he would be in time to catch the six-thirty-two. On arrival at Cannon Street, he queued for his paper and cigarettes and put them in his briefcase before rushing on to Platform Five. To add to his annoyance, the loudspeaker was announcing with perfunctory apology that three trains had already been taken off that evening because of a go-slow.

1 *file* (n) G: Akte 2 *immediate superior* person of the next higher rank/position 3 *owing to* because of, due to 3 *lack of consideration* absence of attention to the thoughts and feelings of others 5 *salute (fml.)* [sə'luːt] (v) greet 9 *reluctant* G: zögernd 9 *dash* (v) rush 10 *puddle* (n) a pool of water 11 *queue* [kjuː] (v) join a line of people waiting for sth 13 *annoyance* [-'--] (n) irritation 13 *perfunctory* [-'---] done quickly and without thought, interest or care 13 *apology* [-'---] (n) the act of saying one is sorry for something 14 *go-slow* (n) refusal by workers to do any more than the very minimal amount of work

Septimus eventually fought his way through the dripping, bustling crowds to the sixth carriage of a train that was not scheduled on any timetable. He discovered that it was filled with people he had never seen before and, worse, almost every seat was already occupied. In fact, the only place he could find to sit was in the middle of the train with his back to the engine. He threw his briefcase and creased umbrella onto the rack above him and reluctantly squeezed himself into the seat, before looking around the carriage.

There was not a familiar face among the other six occupants. A woman with three children more than filled the seat opposite him, while an elderly man was sleeping soundly on his left. On the other side of him, leaning over and looking out of the window, was a young man of about twenty.

When Septimus first laid eyes on the boy, he couldn't believe what he saw. The youth was clad in a black leather jacket and skin-tight jeans and was whistling to himself. His dark, creamed hair was combed up at the front and down at the sides, while the only two colours of the young man's outfit that matched were his jacket and his fingernails.

But worst of all to one of Septimus's sensitive nature was the slogan printed in boot studs on the back of his jacket. 'Heil Hitler' it declared unashamedly over a white-painted Nazi sign and, as if that were not enough, below the swastika in gold shone the words: 'Up yours.' What was the country coming to? thought Septimus. They ought to bring back National Service for delinquents like that. Septimus himself had not been able to do National Service on account of his flat feet.

Septimus decided to ignore the creature, and picking up the packet of Benson & Hedges on the armrest by his side, lit one and began to read the *Evening Standard.* He then replaced the packet of cigarettes on the armrest, as he always did, knowing he would smoke one more before reaching Sevenoaks.

When the train eventually moved out of Cannon Street, the darkly clad youth turned towards Septimus and, glaring at him, picked up the packet of cigarettes, took one, lit it, and started to puff away. Septimus could not be-

1 *dripping* having drops of rain falling from their clothes 1 *bustling* ['bʌslɪŋ] having plenty of noise and movement 2 *schedule* ['ʃedjuːl] (v) put into a timetable 6 *creased* [kriːst] G: zerknittert 8 *familiar* [-'--] known 10 *soundly* (adv) deeply 13 *clad (lit.)* dressed 13 *skin-tight* fitting tightly against the body 14 *comb* [kəʊm] (v) G: kämmen 15 *outfit* ['--] (n) set of clothes 18 *boot studs* G: Nieten an den Schuhen 19 *unashamedly* [ˌ--'---] (adv) without shame 20 *swastika* ['swɒstɪkə] (n) G: Hakenkreuz 20 *Up yours (vulg.)* (used to express great dislike for a person) G: Leck mich ... 21/22 *National Service* the system of making all men serve in the armed forces for a period of time 22 *delinquent* [-'--] (n) person who tends to do socially unacceptable things and break the law 23 *on account of* because of 23 *flat feet* G: Plattfüße 30 *glare at* look angrily at

lieve what was happening. He was about to protest when he realised that none of his regulars was in the carriage to back him up. He considered the situation for a moment and decided that discretion was the better part of valour. (Yet another of the sayings of Septimus.)

When the train stopped at Petts Wood, Septimus put down the newspaper although he had scarcely read a word and, as he nearly always did, took his second cigarette. He lit it, inhaled, and was about to go back to the *Evening Standard* when the youth grabbed at the corner and they ended up with half the paper each. This time Septimus looked around the carriage for support. The children opposite started giggling, while their mother avoided looking at what was taking place, obviously not wanting to become involved; the old man on Septimus's left was now snoring.

Septimus was about to secure the packet of cigarettes by putting them in his pocket when the youth grabbed them, removed another and lit it, inhaled deeply, and then blew the smoke quite deliberately across Septimus's face before placing the cigarettes back on the armrest. Septimus's answering glare expressed as much malevolence as he was able to project through the grey haze. Grinding his teeth in fury, he returned to the *Evening Standard,* only to discover that he had ended up with situations vacant, used cars and sports sections, subjects in which he had absolutely no interest. His only compensation, however, was his certainty that sport was the only section the oik really wanted. Septimus was now, in any case, incapable of reading the paper, trembling as he was with rage.

His thoughts were now turning to revenge, and gradually a plan began to form in his mind with which he was confident the youth would be left in no doubt that virtue can sometimes be more than its own reward. (A variation on a saying of Septimus.) He smiled thinly and, breaking his routine, took a third cigarette and then replaced the packet on the armrest.

2 *regular* ['---] (n) here: a regular passenger 2 *consider* think about, give careful thought 4 *valour (fml.)* ['vælə] (n) courage, bravery 6 *scarcely* (adv) hardly; G: kaum 7 *inhale* [-'-] (v) breathe in (smoke) 8 *grab* (v) take hold of suddenly 9 *support* [-'-] (n) encouragement and help 10 *giggle* ['gɪgl] (v) laugh in a silly and uncontrolled way 11 *become involved* become connected with what is happening 12 *snore* (v) G: schnarchen 15 *deliberately* [-'----] (adv) intentionally 17 *malevolence* [mə'levələns] (n) the wish to do evil to others 17 *project* [-'-] (v) express (one's feelings) outwardly 18 *haze* (n) light smoke 18 *grind one's teeth* bite one's teeth very hard together 18 *fury* (n) great anger 19 *situations vacant* jobs available 21 *compensation* (n) a suitable payment for some loss 22 *oik* (n) *(slang)* [ɔɪk] G: Halbstarker 22 *incapable of* [-'---] unable to 23 *tremble* (v) shake 24 *gradual* ['---] happening slowly and by degrees 25 *confident* G: überzeugt, sicher 26 *virtue* ['--] (n) G: Tugend 26 *reward* [-'-] (n) G: Belohnung

The youth stubbed out his own cigarette and, as if taking up the challenge, picked up the packet, removed another one and lit it. Septimus was by no means beaten; he puffed his way quickly through his cigarette, stubbed it out, a quarter unsmoked, took a fourth and lit it immediately. The race was on for there were now only two cigarettes left. But Septimus, despite a great deal of puffing and coughing, managed to finish his fourth cigarette ahead of the youth. He leaned across the leather jacket and stubbed his cigarette out in the window ashtray.

The carriage was now filled with smoke, but the youth was still puffing as fast as he could, the children opposite were coughing and the woman was waving her arms around like a windmill. Septimus ignored her and kept his eyes on the packet of cigarettes while pretending to read about Arsenal's chances in the FA cup.

Septimus then recalled that Field Marshal Montgomery once said that surprise and timing are the weapons of victory. As the youth finished his fourth cigarette and was stubbing it out, the train pulled slowly into Sevenoaks station. The youth's hand was raised, but Septimus was quicker. He had anticipated the enemy's next move, and now seized the cigarette packet. He took out the ninth cigarette and, placing it between his lips, lit it slowly and inhaled as deeply as he could before blowing the smoke out straight into the face of the enemy. The youth stared up at him in dismay.

Septimus then removed the last cigarette from the packet and crumpled the tobacco into shreds between his first finger and thumb, allowing the little flakes to fall back into the empty packet. Then he closed the packet neatly and replaced the little gold box on the armrest. In the same movement he picked up from his vacant seat the sports section of the *Evening Standard,* tore the paper in half, in quarters, in eights and finally sixteenths, placing the little squares in a neat pile on the youth's lap.

The train came to a halt at Sevenoaks. A triumphant Septimus, having struck his blow for the silent majority, took down his umbrella and briefcase from the rack above him and turned to leave.

1 *stub out* to stop a cigarette burning by pressing down the end 1 *take up a challenge* ['tʃælɪndʒ] to accept an invitation to take part in a fight, match etc. 6 *coughing* ['kɒfɪŋ] G: Husten 8 *ashtray* ['--] (n) a small dish for the ashes of cigarettes 12/13 *Arsenal's chances in* the possibilities of Arsenal, a famous London football club, winning (the Football Association cup) 14 *Montgomery* British field marshal (1887–1976) of World War II 15 *weapons of victory* ['wepən] instruments with which to gain success 17/18 *anticipate* [-'---] (v) expect (something to happen, before it happens) 18 *seize* [si:z] (v) take hold of suddenly 21 *dismay* [-'-] strong feeling of fear and hopelessness 22/23 *crumple into shreds* break up into very small pieces 24 *flake* (n) small leaf-like piece (of tobacco) 28 *lap* (n) G: Schoß 30 *strike a blow for* do something important for

As he picked up his briefcase, it knocked the armrest in front of him and the lid sprang open. Everyone in the carriage stared at its contents. For there, on top of his Prudential documents, was a neatly folded copy of the *Evening Standard* and an unopened packet of ten Benson & Hedges cigarettes.

2 *lid* (n) the part of the briefcase which opens and closes 2 *stare at* look at with wide-open eyes, in wonder 2 *contents* ['--] (n) the things which are inside an object

Comprehension

Part I: Intensive Reading

1. After reading the first paragraph, describe Septimus' morning in your own words. Try to characterize it.
2. Comment on the descriptive remark on page 224, ll. 15/16: "once again he would regale his colleagues with the imagined achievements of his children."
3. Summarize Septimus' eating and drinking habits.
4. Describe the kind of "ritual occasion" mentioned on page 225, ll. 6/7.
5. Explain the phrase "mechanical jauntiness" on page 225, l. 10.
6. Interpret the figurative use of words such as *torrent* and *surge (down)* on page 225, ll. 12/13.
7. Describe the feeling Septimus has when he is walking to the station.
8. Decide whether Septimus is the only person with fixed habits amongst the commuters.
9. Comment on the choice of the verb *allocate* on page 225, l. 28.
10. Try to list the different occasions on which Septimus usually smokes.
11. Sum up the routine waiting for Septimus in his home after his return from work. Characterize his attitude to his specific kind of existence.
12. Explain the descriptive comment: "Septimus was not the stuff on which authors base 200,000 word sagas." (p. 226, ll. 25 f)

Part II: Extensive reading

1. Point out the first event which 'shattered' Septimus' beloved routine and identify its original cause.
2. Give a description of the young man sitting next to Septimus. What is Septimus' attitude towards him?
3. Explain why Septimus didn't protest when the youth took a cigarette.
4. Summarize the incident with the *Evening Standard* and name the feelings which boiled up in Septimus.
5. How did Septimus break his routine in order to take revenge on the young man?
6. Describe the other passengers' reactions to what was happening in the compartment.
7. If "surprise and timing ... are the weapons of victory" (p. 230, l. 14/15), how did Septimus show this to be true in the 'battle of cigarettes'?

Talking about the story

1. Describe the 'twist' at the end of the story.
2. Knowing what went wrong, re-interpret the behaviour of the two men.
3. Make individual notes on what makes the story amusing: the words and expressions, the style, or the characters. Discuss your notes in class.

Vocabulary: from noun to adjective

Form adjectives from the following nouns and use them in sentences of your own referring to the story:

1. fury	2. luxury	3. annoyance	4. consideration
5. reward	6. purpose	7. confidence	8. incapability
9. vacancy	10. challenge	11. deliberation	12. superstition

Grammar revision

Describing past habits: the use of would *and* used to

The story by Jeffrey Archer "Broken routine" contains many examples of the construction *would* + infinitive to describe a past habit:
p. 224, ll. 4ff: On arriving at Platform One he *would purchase* a copy of the "Daily Express" ... During the journey Septimus *would read* his newspaper ... etc.
This is mainly a characteristic of literary style. The modal *would* is a real past tense here. The more common, colloquial alternative to this structure is the construction with *used to:* I *used to* take the early train to London. What did you *use to* do regularly when you were a child; for example, after school, at weekends or during the holidays?

The use of the present perfect *vs.* simple past

Complete the following dialogue between the Deputy Manager (=DM) and the office boy (=Boy) choosing the simple past or the present perfect. Pay attention to the appropriate word order. – Example:
DM: (Have you seen) Mr Cornwallis today? – *(see)*
Boy: Yes sir, I (saw) him when he came in at 9.30 a.m. – *(see)*

DM: It's eleven-thirty now. ..... at his desk all morning? – *(be, he)*
Boy: No sir. He ..... there until the coffee-break. – *(be)*
DM: Do you know if he ..... his Daily Express yet? – *(read)*
Boy: Yes, I believe he ..... it on the train this morning. – *(read)*
DM: I'd like to have a look at it. ..... it on his desk, as he normally does? – *(leave, he)*
Boy: No sir, I ..... it there when I ..... to him at 10.30. He ..... it on the train today, I'm sure. – *(see, not; talk; leave)*
DM: ..... his coffee break already? – *(take, he)*
Boy: Yes sir. He ..... it at eleven, on the dot. – *(take)*
DM: Well, where ..... since 11 o'clock? – *(be, he)*
Boy: I'm not sure, sir. He ..... out into the corridor just a minute ago. – *(go)*
DM: Then I'll bet he ..... out for his usual smoke. – *(go)*
Boy: I don't think so, sir. Mr Cornwallis ..... smoking last week. – *(stop)*

Markers of politeness

The young man on the train would have had every reason to complain to Septimus about his behaviour (because he was not exactly polite). However, British people very seldom complain directly – if at all – as this seems rude. In fact, usually the important thing is to be polite at all costs. Consider, for example, the following situation in a train carriage:

Passenger A: '*Excuse me, I'm sorry* to bother you, but *do you mind if* I open the window?'

Passenger B: 'No, *not at all.*'
'*Please,* do.'
'No, *please,* go ahead.'

Which of the following expressions would you use in the situations below? You can also make up your own answers if they fit in. Act them out in pairs:

Excuse me . . .	*Please . . .*	*You're welcome.*
I'm sorry . . .	*Here you are . . .*	*Not at all.*
After you . . .	*Help yourself . . .*	*Do you mind if . . .?*
I'm afraid . . .	*Well, let me see . . .*	*I wonder if . . .*

1. You're having a party. Tom arrives first. You give him a coat-hanger. What do you say as you give it to him?
2. You've put lots of good things to eat and drink on a table. You want Tom to take anything he wants. What do you say to him?
3. More people arrive. You want them to take things to eat and drink. What do you say to them?
4. Sally asks if you have any old Beatles records. You go and get one from your bedroom and give it to her. What do you say as you give her the record?
5. Sally is delighted. "This is my favourite," she says, "thanks a million!" What do you say?
6. You and Pat go towards the toilet at the same time. You tell Pat that you will wait and that she can go first. What do you say?
7. Phil has a headache and asks you for a glass of water. You fetch a glass of water from the kitchen and give it to him. What do you say as you give him the water?
8. Phil puts a pill in his mouth and drinks some of the water. "Thanks a lot," he says. What do you answer?
9. The party's over, but Pat can't find her coat. You find it under another coat and give it to her. What do you say?
10. "Thank you," says Pat, "and thanks for a great time. I've really enjoyed myself." What do you say?

Put it in writing

Choose one of the two tasks:

1. The youth tells a friend about the train incident. Take his point of view in the narrative and continue the story *beyond* the ending chosen by Jeffrey Archer.
2. Septimus tells his wife about the incident on the train. Write the dialogue.

APPENDIX

Abbreviations, Labels and Symbols

adj. = adjective
adv. = adverb
AmE = (mainly) American English
bn = billion
BrE = (mainly) British English
cf. = confer; compare with, see
coll. = colloquial
conj. = conjunction
derog. = derogatory
dial. = dialect
eg. = exempli gratia; for example
esp. = especially
etc. = et cetera; and so on
fig. = figurative
fml. = formal
ie. = id est; that is
infml. = informal
interj. = interjection
l./ll. = line/lines
m = million
mph = miles per hour
n. = noun
NP = noun phrase
p./pp. = page/pages
pl. = plural
prep. = preposition
sb/s. o. = somebody/someone
sg. = singular
sth = something
v. = verb
vs. = versus
vulg. = vulgar
& and
[ ] phonetic transcription
- - syllable(s)
-'-- primary stress
ˌ--- secondary stress
★ unacceptable
→ transformed/changed to/ leading to

{ } choice of expressions
( ) optional expression
/ alternative expression

Glossary of Literary and Linguistic Terms

Note: Words printed in *italics* are terms which are also explained in this glossary.

action ['ækʃn]: a connected series of *events* started by the *characters*. In a *fictional* text, it normally has three phases: a beginning (introduction/*exposition*[1]), a middle part (rising action, *climax, turning point,* falling action) and an end *(solution)*.

alliteration [əˌlɪtə'reɪʃn]: the repetition of sounds, esp. consonants; usually in the main stressed syllable of words which are next to or close to each other, or at the beginning of neighbouring words. Eg. in text 1.10, l. 25: "*f*our little *f*ootball *f*ans"; cf. *assonance*.

antonym ['æntənɪm]: a word with the opposite meaning to another one in the same language; eg. *"good"* and *"bad"*, *"teach"* and *"learn"* etc.

argumentation [ˌ---'--]: *prose* dealing with ideas presenting an argument (= *thesis*) or a problem and developing it logically towards a conclusion. Personal comments, leading articles, interviews and letters to the editor are common examples of this *text type*.

assonance ['æsənəns]: the repetition of the same or similar vowel sounds within stressed syllables of neighbouring words; eg. text 1.1, l. 2: "We f*ou*nd my g*ow*n in an h*ou*r ...". – Cf. *alliteration*.

atmosphere ['ætməsfɪə]: the feeling or mood produced in a *fictional* text, setting free the reader's (or listener's) emotions. It can be tense, fearful, happy, peaceful, violent or gloomy etc. – Cf. *tone*.

blend: an invented word combining the meaning and form of two words; eg. *Chunnel* in text 3.7 is made up from *tunnel* and *Channel* (= portmanteau word).

caricature ['kærɪkətjʊə]: the exaggeration of certain features of a *character,* usually to ridicule or criticize. – Cf. *parody*.

cartoon [kɑː'tuːn]: a humorous drawing; a film using a series of such drawings.

character ['kærəktə]: a person in a *fictional* text as developed through what he (or she) does or says.

characterization [ˌkærəktəraɪ'zeɪʃn]: the way a *character* is presented in a literary work.

chart [tʃɑːt]: information drawn (and written) in the form of a picture in order to make it easier to understand. There are:

a) graphs b) bar charts c) pie charts

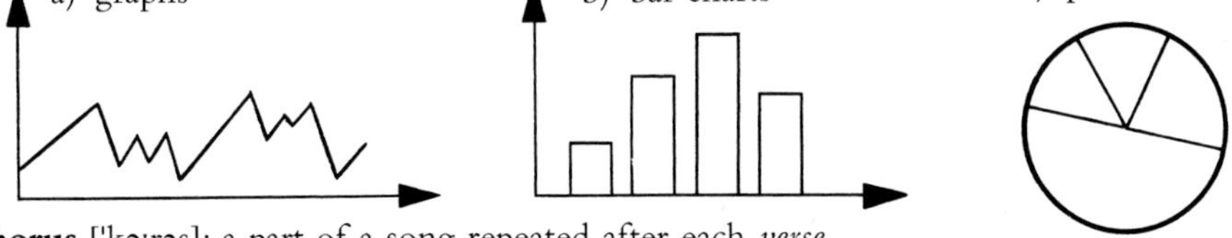

chorus ['kɔːrəs]: a part of a song repeated after each *verse*.

cliché ['kliːʃeɪ]: stereotyped idea or expression which has lost much of its meaning because of repeated use.

climax ['klaɪmæks]: the high point in a *plot,* when the *action* of a *fictional* text reaches its highest intensity. It follows the rising action and comes just before the *turning point*.

comment ['--]: a form of *argumentative prose* in which sb gives his personal judgement on a particular *topic,* mainly in order to convince a reader or listener.

conflict ['--]: tension between *characters* in a *fictional* text.

connotations [ˌ--'--]: the additional meaning(s), esp. the emotional one(s) suggested by a word.

contact language: when language is used primarily for its social function, ie. to establish or keep up contact between people (cf. *phatic communion*). Examples of this *text type* are the *small talk* of daily conversation, greetings, farewells, expressions of condolence etc.

description: *prose* which presents the outward appearance of objects, living beings, landscapes or processes, ie. what they look like. It is one of the major *text types.*

diagram ['daɪəgræm]: a drawing showing how sth works (adj.: diagrammatic).

didactic [daɪ'dæktɪk]: speech or writing that is meant to teach a lesson; cf. *fable, parable.*

drama: a piece of writing to be performed by actors on stage, in films or on television (=play for the theatre, radio or television).

emotive language [ɪ'məʊtɪv]: the use of words or expressions with certain *connotations;* ie. meanings which are linked up with certain feelings and emotions (usually the reader or listener is influenced emotionally in some way by this kind of language). Cf. *contact language.*

euphemism ['juːfɪmɪzm]: the use of a less direct word or name for something thought to be unpleasant. Cf. text 4.4: *"pass on"* is a euphemism for *"die".*

event: a happening; esp. an interesting, important or unusual one. – Cf. *state.*

exaggeration [-ˌ--'--]: make sth larger, worse, uglier, sillier etc. than it really is, often in order to produce laughter and humour (cf. *caricature, parody, grotesque*).

exposition[1] [ˌ--'--]: the introduction to a *story* or play giving information about the main *characters,* the *theme* and *setting* as well as first hints of the *atmosphere* or *tone.*

exposition[2] **(=explication):** sth is analysed and explained in a detailed and factual way. Common examples of this major *text type* are definitions (eg. in dictionaries), entries in reference books and expository essays.

fable ['feɪbl]: a short *story* containing a *moral.* The *characters* are often personified animals which stand for certain types of man (cf. *parable, personification*).

fiction ['fɪkʃn]: a group pf texts (=*genres*) in which the author creates his or her own reality. The world created by a fictional text makes up a contextual *setting* of its own. Cf. *non-fiction.*

figurative meaning ['fɪgjʊrətɪv]: a use of language which goes beyond the main or usual meaning of a word or phrase. The expression is then used in a new or different context (as compared with its normal use) and suggests a certain picture in the mind. Examples of figurative language (=figures of speech) are *metaphors, similes* (=comparisons) and *symbols.* – Cf. *literal meaning.*

flashback ['--]: a *scene* in a play, *story* or film that goes back in time to show what happened earlier.

foot: a unit of *rhythm,* with stressed and unstressed syllables in a *line* of *poetry;* cf. *metre.*

free verse: a form of *poetry* whose internal structure is created by *rhythm, repetition, alliteration* and *assonance* (but not by *rhyme* and *metre*).

genre ['ʒɑːŋrə]: a group or class of literary works (cf. *fictional* texts) characterized by a particular form, *style* and/or *topic.* Examples of genres are tragedy, comedy, satire, novel and *short story.*

grotesque [grəʊ'tesk]: a kind of *fictional* text which gives rise to both amusement and fear/horror at the same time (cf. *exaggeration, macabre, parody, caricature*).

image ['ɪmɪdʒ]: a picture created by a speaker or writer in people's minds; imagery appeals to the hearer's or listener's imagination; it produces an idea of something in a poetical form (cf. *metaphor, simile* and *symbol; figurative meaning*).

instruction: one of the major *text types* whose function it is to influence people's behaviour by instructing or directing them. Common examples are laws, rules and regulations but also manuals and guides. The language of advertising, politics (eg. speeches, propaganda) and religion (eg. sermons) is full of recommendations, persuasion and advice.

interior/inner monologue: a particular *mode of presentation* (ie. a scenic or detailed one) in which a *character's* thoughts and feelings are reproduced with as little intervention and comment by the narrator as possible. It is meant to reflect the course and rhythm of consciousness in a *character's* mind.

irony ['aɪərənɪ]: a use of language expressing the opposite of what is really meant, usually in order to be amusing or show light annoyance. The reader or listener is supposed to understand the 'real' meaning of the statement. – Cf. *sarcasm*.

line: a row of words in a *poem* which is usually structured into a certain number of *feet* (cf. *metre, stanza*).

literal meaning ['lɪtərəl]: the original meaning of a word or phrase; not the extended meaning one gets in *figurative* language use.

lyrics: the words of a song, esp. of modern pop songs.

macabre [mə'kɑːbrə]: sth causing fear or shock, esp. because it is related to death or the dead (cf. *grotesque*).

metaphor ['metəfə] or ['metəfɔː]: words and expressions used to make an implicit comparison; ie. one that is not introduced by *"as"* or *"like"* (cf. *simile*).

metre ['miːtə]: the regular order of stressed and unstressed syllables within the *line* of a *poem*, cf. *foot, rhythm, free verse*.

moral ['mɒrəl]: something that can be learnt from a text with a *didactic* function (cf. *fable, parable*). Morals (which can be explicit or implicit in a *story*) tell the reader how to behave or lead his (or her) own life.

narration [nə'reɪʃn] or **narrative** ['nærətɪv]: a major *text type* telling a *story* or giving a *report*.

narrator [nə'reɪtə]: a fictitious person who tells the *story* in a *narrative* text. Narrator and author are normally not identical.

non-fiction [ˌ-'--]: a group of texts in which the author or speaker *refers* to the people, objects and *events* of the world around us. The truth of these statements can (in principle) be checked upon by way of a comparison with the things and situations in the outside world. Cf. *fiction, text type*.

open ending: in a *fictional* text the opposite of a *solution*; ie. the *conflict* is not resolved and it is up to the reader or listener to draw his/her own conclusions (= interpretation).

parable ['pærəbl]: normally a short, simple *story* which teaches (explicitly or implicitly) a *moral* or religious lesson (cf. *didactic function*). Like the *fable* it is an allegorical text form; it presents people as types (cf. *character*) and makes a general statement (cf. *thesis*) about human behaviour.

parallelism ['pærəlelɪzm]: the repetition of the same or similar grammatical *patterns* in different clauses or sentences.

paraphrase ['pærəfreɪz]: using different words for sth written or said, esp. in order to be better understood.

parody ['pærədɪ]: a piece of writing which copies the form and *style* of a well-known (usually *fictional*) text but changes its *tone* and context. Its main purpose is to amuse the reader or audience.

pattern ['pætən]: a regularly repeated arrangement of sounds, words or *lines*.
personification [-,---'--]: representing sth that is without life (eg. objects, floods and earthquakes, abstract ideas etc.) but also plants and animals as a human being or as having human qualities.
phatic communion ['fætɪk kə'mjuːnjən]: a special use of language which stresses the social function of human interaction (cf. *contact language, emotive language*).
plot: the structure of the *action* in a *fictional* text, ie. the set of connected *events* on which a *story*, play or film is based. The incidents are arranged in a certain time sequence and are linked up by cause and effect. They also involve one or more *conflicts*. A plot is usually structured in the order: *exposition*[1], rising action, *climax, turning point*, falling action, *solution* or *open ending*.
poem: a *fictional* text arranged in *patterns* of *lines* and sound, often divided into *stanzas;* expressing some thought, feeling or human experience in imaginative language.
point of view: signifies the relationship between the *narrator* and the *story*. The way a story is told sets up a certain perspective in which the *setting, action, topic, events* and *characters* are presented to the reader. The most important difference is the one between first and third person point of view.
presentation: the speaker's or writer's choice between a more personal (= subjective presentation: influenced by his/her feelings and opinions) or an impersonal way of presenting information (= objective presentation: a detached, matter-of-fact account of a situation).
prose [prəʊz]: written language in its usual or 'ordinary' form (as opposed to *verse*[1]); ie. without units of *metre*.
protagonist [prəʊ'tægənɪst]: the central *character* in a *fictional* text (the hero or heroine).
pun [pʌn]: an amusing play on words using either a word with two meanings or words with the same sound but different meanings.

reference ['refrəns]: mentioning a person, an object or an idea.
report: a *non-fictional* text form giving an account of *events*, usually told in the past tense (cf. *narration*). It answers at least five WH-questions: *"who", "what", "where", "when"* and *"why";* often it also says sth about *"how"* and *"what for"*.
rhetorical question [rɪ'tɒrɪkl]: a question to which the speaker expects no answer (because it is obvious). It is asked only to get a specific effect; mainly to guide someone's thinking in a certain direction (cf. *instructive texts:* persuasion). – Example: Who cares?
rhyme: identity or similarity of sound between word endings, eg. end rhyme = repetition in sound at the end of *verse lines*.
rhythm ['rɪðəm]: a regular *pattern* of speech with variations of stressed and unstressed syllables (adj.: rhythmic).

sarcasm ['sɑːkæzm]: the aggressive use of language (by saying the opposite to what is felt) in order to be unkind or offensive (adj.: sarcastic). – Cf. *irony*.
scene [siːn]: part of an act in a *drama* characterized by the unity of time, place and *action* (cf. *character*).
setting: the context in time and place in which the *action* of a text takes place.
short story [,-'--]: a short *narrative* with a densely constructed *plot*, limited in both *theme* and *setting*, containing usually only a few *events* and *characters*.
simile ['sɪmɪlɪ]: an explicit comparison usually introduced by *"like"* or *"as"* (cf. *metaphor, figurative meaning*): eg. *"as slow as a slug"*.

slang: very informal language which is often used only among specific groups of people; slangy expressions should not be used in serious speech or writing (cf. *style*[2]).

small talk: light conversation on unimportant *topics* (cf. *contact language, phatic communion*).

solution: that part in a *fictional* text in which the *conflict* is resolved (cf. *plot, open ending*).

stage direction ['--,--]: the author's notes in a *drama* on how the play is to be performed, giving details about the *setting*, the *characters'* movements, gestures, ways of speaking etc.

stanza ['stænzə]: a group of *lines* in a *poem*.

state: a condition in which a person or thing is; especially their location, feeling or thinking (cf. *event*).

story: an account of *events*, real or imagined (cf. *fiction, narration, plot; non-fiction)*.

style[1]: the choice of words and expressions typical of an individual writer or speaker (eg. Shakespeare's style).

style[2]: the level of formality chosen in speaking or writing; eg. neutral style, formal style, colloquial style, informal style, *slang* etc.

stylistic device [dɪ'vaɪs]: phrases and expressions used to produce a particular effect in a text (cf. *style*).

summary: a short text giving the main points of another text without presenting the summary writer's own opinion of the original text.

suspense [sə'spens]: a feeling of tension and anxiety or of excitement and expectation caused by a state of uncertainty about the development of the *characters, conflict* and *plot* in a *fictional* text.

symbol ['sɪmbl]: sth that means more than what it names or describes (cf. *reference*); ie. a person, animal or object can also stand for some abstract idea (cf. *image, figurative meaning*). Example: *"Alcatraz"* in text 1.7 is a symbol of the American Indian's living conditions (adj.: symbolic).

synonym ['sɪnənɪm]: a word with the same (or nearly the same) meaning as another one in the same language (adj.: synonymous); eg. *"sad"* and *"unhappy", "ask"* and *"question"* (v) etc. – Cf. *antonym*.

table: a set of figures or facts arranged in rows and columns.

text type: a classification of texts (cf. *fiction, non-fiction*) on the basis of the main uses or functions of language as realized by a speaker or writer. The major text types are *argumentation, description, instruction, exposition*[2], *narration* and *phatic communion*.

theme [θi:m]: the central idea or *topic* in a *fictional* text.

thesis [θi:sɪs]: an opinion or statement backed up by reasoned *argument* (pl. *theses* [θi:zi:z]).

tone: the attitude of an author or speaker towards the *theme* and *character(s)* as well as to the audience or readers. It can be humorous or serious, optimistic or pessimistic, friendly or annoyed, arrogant or modest etc. – Cf. *atmosphere*.

topic ['--]: a subject in conversation or writing (adj.: topical).

turning point: in a *fictional* text the point after the *climax* when the *plot* begins to move in a different direction.

verse[1] [vɜ:s]: a *synonym* of *poetry* (cf. *prose*); especially writing arranged in regular *lines* (cf. *metre, rhyme*).

verse[2]: a set of *lines* which forms part of a *poem* (= *stanza*) or song (cf. *chorus, lyrics*).

Vocabulary for Text Analysis and Interpretation

Die nachstehend abgedruckte Sammlung von Wörtern und Ausdrücken soll ein Wegweiser für die Textanalyse und Textinterpretation sein. Sie versteht sich als Vorschlag und ist weit davon entfernt, vollständig zu sein. Die kursiv geschriebenen englischen Begriffe werden rechts auf deutsch erklärt.

TEXT STRUCTURE

The	text	is divided into ...	parts.	
	story	can be subdivided into ...	sections.	
	play	is *composed of* ...		(aufgebaut aus)
		contains ...	scenes.	(enthalten)
		consists of ...	acts.	(bestehen aus)
		has ...	*paragraphs.*	(Absatz)

The	main	elements	of ... are ...	
		points		
	essential	*passages*		(Textstelle)

Possible *headings* for these	sections	are ...	(Überschriften)
	scenes		

The	first	part	*constitutes* ...	(bilden)
	last	scene	*presents* ...	(vortragen)
		sentence	*conveys* ...	(vermitteln)
		line	gives us ...	

In the	opening	paragraph	the author ...
	final	chapter	

Note also: extract, monologue, dialogue, complex sentence (Satzgefüge), main clause (Hauptsatz), dependent clause (Nebensatz), utterance (Äußerung).

THEMES & TOPICS

The	text	*deals with* ...	(behandeln)
	scene	is about/*concerns* ...	(betreffen)
	extract	*presents/conveys*	(vermitteln)
		describes/*portrays* ...	(ausmalen/schildern)
		gives a description of ...	
		gives an *account* of	(Darstellung)

The	general	idea	expressed in the text	is ...	
	main	*concept*	of the text	are ...	(allgemeine Vorstellung)
	central	*notion*	put forward here		(Idee, Vorstellung)
	essential	*issue*			(Frage)

The	theme	of the	text	is ...	
	topics		paragraph	are ...	(Themen)
	main points		story		
	key issues				(Schlüsselfragen)

The	issue	is	how/when/what to ...
	question		whether ...

The	*common*	opinion	is that ...	(allgemeine)
A	popular	*view*		(Ansicht)
One	general	belief		
		assumption		(Annahme)

Note also: problem, subject (Thema), dilemma, detail; important, minor (kleiner, weniger bedeutend); to clarify (klären), to explain, to consider (überlegen, in Betracht/ Erwägung ziehen), to state (darlegen), reveal (enthüllen), highlight (hervorheben).

AUTHOR

The	author	deals/*is concerned* with ...	(sich befassen)
	writer	discusses ...	
	speaker	speaks/talks about ...	
		explains how ...	
		asks/*raises/poses* the question ...	(aufwerfen, stellen)
		(mis)interprets ...	

The author gives	an exact	analysis	of ...
	a precise	definition	

The author	gives	a subjective	interpretation of ...	
	presents	his personal	opinion of ...	(vortragen)

The author	thinks/believes	that ...
	seems to think/believe	

The author	gives his opinion of/on the	problem	of ...	
writer		question		
	expresses his (point of) view *concerning* ...			(betreffs)
	holds the *view* that ...			(Ansicht)
	advances the idea that ...			(vortragen)
	presents the *thesis*/hypothesis that ...			(These)
	supports the view/*claim*/opinion that ...			(unterstützen, Behauptung)
	engages in a discussion of ...			
	throws (some interesting) *light on* ...			(beleuchten)
	comments on why ...			

The author	presents	an argument	for ...	
	puts forward	the arguments	against ...	(vorbringen)
		the pros and cons of		

The author	uses *rejects*	the following arguments ... the argument that ...		(zurückweisen)

The author	gives *provides*	*evidence*	in support of ... for/against ...	(Beweise) (bereitstellen)

The author	comes to draws	the *conclusion* that ...	(Schluss)

The author's	line of argument argumentation way of looking at the *matter*/problem *train of thought* arguments/reasons	is are	(not) convincing. questionable. wrong/right. (il)logical.	 (Sache) (Gedankengang)

The author's	opinion conclusions position	is are	based on ... (not) acceptable ... (un)*reasonable* (well) *reasoned*	because ... (vernünftig) (durchdacht)

Note also: objective, subjective, fair, (im)personal, impartial, factual; to argue, to assert (behaupten), to assume (annehmen), to challenge (anfechten), to claim (behaupten), to convince (überzeugen), to defend (verteidigen), to demand (fordern), to doubt (bezweifeln), to imagine (sich vorstellen), to impress (beeindrucken), to influence, to insist on (bestehen auf), to judge (urteilen), to maintain (behaupten, vertreten), to object (widersprechen), to persuade (überreden), to pretend (vorgeben), to promise (versprechen), to provoke, to question (in Frage stellen), to reason (vernünftig denken), to suppose (sich vorstellen, annehmen), to think, to understand.

ACTION & PLOT

The text	tells the story gives a *report*	of ...	 (Bericht)

The plot/*action* of the story is set in ... (Handlungsverlauf)
The story *takes place* in ... (stattfinden)

The	events of the story incident	*happen* *occur*	at the time of	(geschehen)

The	context *setting*	of the	story plot	is ...	 (Schauplatz)

The *course*/phases/stages of the action ... (Verlauf)

The	main constituent	elements of the *plot* are ...	(Handlung)

The	*climax*	is reached	when …	(Höhepunkt)
	turning point	comes		(Wendepunkt)

The story	ends in a		catastrophe …
	has	an open	ending …
		a surprise	

Note also: conflict, dilemma, solution, suspense, scenery (Landschaft, Gegend), surroundings (Umgebung), narrator (Erzähler), unity of time and place (Einheit von Zeit und Ort der Handlung).

ATMOSPHERE

An atmosphere of danger/*gloom*/happiness/	(düstere Stimmung)
peace/*tension*/fear etc.	(Anspannung)

The atmosphere of the	text	is	sad.
	play		tense.
	passage		shown by/in …

The scene *is dominated* by …	(wird beherrscht)

The	feeling	the reader gets	is one of …	
	impression	we get		(Eindruck)

The author pays	little	attention to	detail …
	great		the local colour of …

The description of … is *lively*/detailed/accurate etc.	(lebendig)
It's a first-hand/*ghastly/faithful* etc. description of …	(schrecklich, wahrheitsgetreu)

CHARACTER & CHARACTERIZATION

BEHAVIOUR

The hero's	behaviour/actions …
	way of talking/behaving …

The main protagonist's behaviour is polite/*nasty*/eccentric	(gemein)
impudent/irresponsible	(unverschämt)
etc.	

[Character] A	behaves well/badly/*rudely* etc.	(grob)
	shows good/bad/*pleasant* etc. behaviour	(angenehm)

Personally I	*feel*	*sympathy*	to(wards) A	(mit jem. mitfühlen)
		sympathetic		(verständnisvoll)

I	have no	sympathy with	A's *views* ...	(Ansichten)
		understanding of	*aims* ...	(Ziele)

I	feel unable	to	criticize	A for his behaviour	
	have no right		*blame*	(because) ...	(Schuld geben)

Note also: experience (Erfahrung), background, environment (Umgebung), social conditions (Bedingungen), development, role, attitude (Einstellung), motive, purpose (Zweck), goal (Ziel), effect (Wirkung).

FEATURES (Merkmale)

The author	*mentions*	the	features	of A	(erwähnen)
	describes	following	character-istics		
	points out				

A	realistic	description	of a	character ...	
	detailed	characterization		person ...	
	rough				(grob)

The	hero	is	described	as ...
	character		presented	

The author	characterizes A as ...	
	compares A to/with ...	(vergleichen)

The following characteristics are	typical	aspects	of	
	prominent	qualities		(hervorstechend)
	distinctive	features		(unterscheidend)
	noticeable			

Note also: outward appearance (äussere Erscheinung), intellect.

TRAITS

The	basic	*traits* of A's	character	are ...	(Charakterzüge)
	essential		personality		

One of A's most *striking* characteristics/traits is ... (auffallend)
A stands in clear contrast to B (in that) ...

A's	behaviour	is	completely different from	B's (in that) ...
	character		similar to	

Note also: balanced, calm (ruhig), clever, friendly, good-natured, intelligent, moderate (massvoll, gemässigt), patient, sensitive (empfindsam, einfühlend), sensible (vernünftig), tolerant etc.; aggressive, brutal, bad-tempered (übellaunig), cruel, impulsive, irritable (reizbar), obstinate (starrsinnig), ruthless (rücksichtslos), self-centred, stubborn (stur), stupid, violent (gewalttätig).

MORALITY

to feel guilty/*innocent*	– to feel sorry for sb	(unschuldig)
to show *mercy* / *repentance*	– to hold sb responsible for sth	(Mitleid) (Buße)
to have a guilty/troubled/tortured *conscience*		(Gewissen)

STYLE

The	author writer speaker	uses/*employs* makes use of *chooses/selects*	literary formal colloquial slang	words ... expressions ... phrases ... language ...	(verwenden) (auswählen)

The	phrases *terms* *images* stylistic devices	used chosen employed	by the author	*refer to* ... describe ... stand for ... *emphasize* ... *underline* ...	(sich beziehen auf) (Ausdruck) (Bild) (betonen) (unterstreichen)

The author's	use choice	of	language expressions imagery	is ...

Note also: to express, to state (vortragen, darlegen), to name (benennen), to signify (bedeuten, erkennen lassen), to clarify, to highlight, to point to, to connote, to compare (vergleichen); careful, clear, correct, deliberate (absichtlich), exact, humorous, matter-of-fact (sachlich, nüchtern), narrow, precise, serious, subjective, witty, wrong.

APPRECIATION (Würdigung)

PERSONAL COMMENT

I wish to make it (very) clear that ...
The first point to mention ...
To *back up* my opinion/position ... (unterstützen)

One	*reasonable* argument convincing *reason* interesting interpretation	would could might	be ...	(vernünftig) (Grund)

The author is	completely utterly	wrong	to believe that ... when he says/states ...

Another way of looking at the problem/*matter* is ... (Sache)
What is really at issue here is (that) ...
The real *issue* is whether (Frage)
There still *remains* the problem of ... (bleiben)

The question, however, is not ... but ...
To conclude .../In conclusion .../My *conclusion* is .../ (Schluß)
One can conclude from ... that

GIVING EVIDENCE (mit Textstellen belegen)

As *proof*/support/evidence we can refer to ... (Beweis)
All the *evidence* shows that ... (Beweismaterial)
For further evidence I would like to *refer to* ... (verweisen)
As noted earlier .../As was said *above* .../ (weiter oben)
As was indicated before ...
It says in the text ... (es heißt)
Looking at line ... on page ...
Take as a *telling* example the image in/on ... (aufschlußreich)
We can/Let us take an example from page ...
To *quote* a telling example/expression from ... (zitieren)
Reading between the lines ...
What is *implied* here is ... (impliziert)
– to refer to/referring to/with reference to ... (mit Bezug auf)
– as regards/with regard to/regarding ... (bezüglich)
– in relation to/to be related to ... (in bezug auf)
– concerning/as far as X is concerned/as to ... (betreffs)

Note also: according to (zufolge, nach); in response to (als Antwort, auf etwas hin); speaking/talking of ...; bearing in mind ... (unter Berücksichtigung); having said this ...; apart from this (abgesehen davon); in this/that respect (in dieser Hinsicht), in other respects.

Phrases to Be Used in Discussions

Da sich die einzelnen Mitteilungsabsichten zum Teil überschneiden, ist es nicht verwunderlich, daß gelegentlich die gleichen Ausdrücke für unterschiedliche Redeabsichten benutzt werden.

OPINIONS

ASKING FOR AN OPINION

Do you believe (that) ...?
How do you feel about ...?
What's your opinion of ...?
How do/did you find ..., then?
What do you think of/about ...?

EXPRESSING AN OPINION

(Personally,) I (don't) feel/believe (that) ...
My (own) view/My (personal) opinion is that ...
In my view/opinion ...
As/The way I see it ...
It seems to me that ...
I'm *convinced* that ... (überzeugt)
From my point of view (I think) ...
Wouldn't you say (that) ...?
Don't you think (so) ...?
To my mind ...

GIVING REASONS

Well, you see ...
I think (so) ... because ...
The thing/reason is ...
Well, the point is ...

REFUSING TO BELIEVE SOMETHING

How can you expect me to believe/accept ...?
This can't be true ...
This is hard to believe ...

DEFENDING YOUR POSITION

You've got to *admit* that ... (zugeben)
That's not what I said. I said ...
Can't you understand that ...?
Look, I can *prove* it. (beweisen)

ADMITTING YOU WERE WRONG

I *suppose* you're right. (hier: wohl, vermutlich)
You've convinced me.
I must admit, I hadn't *considered* that. (bedenken)
I must have misunderstood you.
Perhaps I was wrong.
Perhaps it was wrong of me to say/think ...

AGREEING AND DISAGREEING WITH AN OPINION

AGREEMENT

Right/Correct/Exactly!
I'd go along with that.
That's what/how I feel too.
That's exactly/precisely what I think.

That's just what I was thinking.
I couldn't agree more.
That's a good point.

HALF-AGREEING

I see what you mean but ...
I see your point but ...
Yes, but on the other hand ...
That may (well) be the *case* but (Fall)
Yes, perhaps/in a way but (don't you think) ...?
Possibly/Maybe but ...

DISAGREEMENT

Neutral usage
I don't/can't agree (I'm afraid).
I don't think so/that's right.
I can't/wouldn't *go along* with you there. (zustimmen)
Surely that's not the point.
I have to *contradict* you on that point. (widersprechen)
That argument just doesn't stand up.

Polite usage
You may be right, *all the same* ... (und dennoch)
I'm not (so) sure I (quite) agree with you ...

Informal usage
You can't be serious.
You must be joking!
You can't really mean that.
You don't really believe that yourself, do you?
Rubbish!/Nonsense!

ASKING AND ANSWERING QUESTIONS

INTERRUPTING

Sorry to interrupt but (I didn't quite get that.)
May I interrupt you for a moment?
Just a moment, please ...
By the way .../That reminds me ... [to change the subject]

SAYING THAT YOU CANNOT FOLLOW

I'm sorry I didn't catch that.
I didn't get you/your point, I'm afraid.
I'm not sure I understood you.
I'm afraid I don't (quite) understand what you mean (by) ...
Sorry, do you mean .../did you say (that) ...?

ASKING FOR CLARIFICATION (Klarstellung)

I beg your pardon, could you repeat it/say that again (please)?
Could you say a little more about ..., please.
Would you mind explaining ...? (würde es Dir etwas ausmachen)

HESITATING (zögern)

Phrases to gain time to think and to organize one's thoughts:

er	in fact	as a matter of fact
well	I mean	how shall I put it?
you see	mind you	well, let me see/think for a moment
you know	sort/kind of	if you really must know
actually	the thing is	that's a good question
		I thought you'd ask me that

SAYING THAT YOU CANNOT FIND THE RIGHT WORD

I can't remember what it is/what they are (called).
You know the kind of thing/person I mean, I'm sure.
I don't quite know how to put it.
Do you/Does one of you *happen to* know ...? (zufällig)

ASKING AWKWARD QUESTIONS (peinlich)

This may sound a stupid question but I'd like to know ...
Perhaps I shouldn't really ask this (but) ...
You don't have to answer this if you don't want to (but) ...
I hope you don't mind me/my asking this but ...

GIVING CLARIFICATION

Yes, that's (exactly) what I mean.
Yes, that's what I wanted to say.
The point (I'm trying to make) is (that) ...
I thought it was quite clear that ...
No, I don't believe I said so/that.

EVADING CERTAIN QUESTIONS (vermeiden)

I don't follow you, I'm afraid.
You don't really expect me to answer that question, do you?
I'd rather not answer that, if you don't mind.

SAYING THAT YOU DO NOT KNOW THE ANSWER

I have no idea, I'm afraid.
I'm terribly sorry, (but) I really don't know.
I must admit, I don't know (the answer to that).
I can't answer that one.
I (really) haven't *the faintest/least* idea. (hier: die leiseste, geringste)
How should I know? (informal usage)

DEGREES OF CERTAINTY (Gewißheit)

Definitely/Certainly/Absolutely!
I am absolutely sure/certain (that) ...
There is no *doubt* about it. (Zweifel)
There is no doubt *in my mind* that ... (meiner Meinung nach)
You can take my word for it.

I'm positive.
I'm quite sure (that) ...
I'm *fairly/pretty* certain (that) ... (ziemlich)

Well, perhaps/maybe/possibly (that) ...
Well, it's possible that ...
It could/might be ...
There might be ...

I doubt it.
I have my doubts.
It's doubtful.
I'm not at all convinced.

I'm not (absolutely/really) sure/certain (that) ...
I can't say for certain ...
I wouldn't like to say for sure ...

I couldn't say if ...
You never know (, of course,).

DEGREES OF PROBABILITY (Wahrscheinlichkeit)

There is no doubt (that) ...
There can't be any doubt (that) ...

In all probability ...
Yes, almost certainly/definitely.

I'm pretty sure (that) ...
There's a (very) good chance that ...

I expect ...
The chances are ...

Perhaps ...

No, probably not.

Actually, I don't think so.

It's highly unlikely (that) ...

There is not much chance of ...
There is very little chance of ...
There is only a small chance of ...

Believe me, it (just) doesn't/won't/can't ...
There's absolutely no chance of ...

Acknowledgements

Texts

Y. Yevtushenko: "Lies", from *Selected Poems,* translated by Robin Millner-Gulland and Peter Levi, S. J. (Penguin Books 1962), © Robin Milner-Gulland and Peter Levi, 1962. 1.1 Jacqueline Jules: "Mother of the Bride", *Cosmopolitan,* September 1988. 1.2 Sue Townsend: from *The Secret Diary of Adrian Mole Aged 13 3/4,* © Methuen London 1982. 1.3 The Beatles: "She's Leaving Home", (John Lennon/Paul McCartney) © 1967 by Northern Songs Ltd., London. 1.4 "In Mortal Danger", © *The Observer,* London 1983. 1.5 Milton Kaplan: "Feels like Spring", from *Dreams,* John Schaffner Associates Inc., New York. 1.6 "Getting Out", from *Cults in America. Programmed for Paradise,* by Willa Appel. © 1983 by Willa Appel. Reprinted by permission of Henry Holt and Company, Inc. New York. 1.7 "Proclamation", Excerpts reprinted from *Newsletter,* San Francisco, Nov. 1969, a printed paper sent out by the Indians on Alcatraz. 1.8 "Hispanic Americans": compiled from an interview by the authors. 1.9 "A West Ham Football Fan", *Cross Section 2,* © Liber Läromedal, Malmö, Sweden 1986. 1.10 Peter Kett; "Hooliganism", from *Story-Second Book,* Jackson & Pepper Ltd., London. 2.1 Miroslav Holub: "The Door", from *Selected Poems,* translated by Ian Milner and George Theiner (Penguin Books, 1967), © Miroslav Holub, 1967; Translation © Penguin Books 1967. 2.2 Joan Baez: "What Would You Do If?", from *Daybreak,* Dial Press Ltd., New York. 2.3 Willis Hall: "Killing an Enemy", from *The Long and the Short and the Tall,* © Lemon Unna & Durbridge Ltd., London 1958. 2.4 "Services for Peace", compiled from various sources by the authors. 2.5 "Friends of the Earth", reprinted by permission of *Friends of the Earth.* 2.6 Edwin Brock: "Song of the Battery Hen", © Unwin Hyman Ltd., London. 2.7 D. Bolton: "Incident on the Underground", from *Scope 2,* © Almquist & Wiksell, Solna, Sweden. 2.8 William March: "The Untouchable", from *99 Fables,* Charles Scribner's Sons, New York. 2.9 Toeckey Jones: "The Meeting", from *Go Well, Stay Well,* © The Bodley Head, London 1979. 2.10 George Vukelich: "The Turtle", source unknown. 3.1 "Computers of the '90s", from *Newsweek,* © October 24, 1988, Newsweek, Inc. All rights reserved. Reprinted by permission. 3.2 "Autoguide": compiled from an interview by the authors. 3.3 "Hello, This Is Your Future Calling": compiled from various sources by the authors. 3.4 "The Medical Consequences of Nuclear Weapons": compiled from an interview by the authors. 3.5 "A New Life", from *Flashpoint,* © Corona Publishers, Malmö, Sweden. 3.6 "We've Always Been a Close-Knit Family", © Ewan MacNaughton Associates, Tonbridge, Kent. 3.7 "The Chunnel", compiled from various sources by the authors. 3.8 David Filkin: "Genetic Engineering", reproduced from *Tomorrow's World Today* by David Filkin with the permission of BBC Enterprises Ltd. 3.9 William F. Nolan: "And Miles to Go Before I Sleep", from *A Science Fiction Reader,* Kirbey McCauley Ltd., New York. 4.1 "Claire and Mike", from *Overall Resursbok,* © Esselte Studium, Stockholm, Sweden. 4.2 "A Perfect Pronounciation?", from *Lingua,* Lingua Publishers Sweden 1973 © John McClintock. 4.3 David Crystal: "Why Do We Use Language?" from *The Encyclopedia of Language,* © Cambridge University Press, 1987. 4.4 Monty Python: "The Dead Parrot", Monty Press, New York. 4.5 "The Couch Potatoes", from *Flashpoint,* © Corona Publishers, Malmö, Sweden. 4.6 Roald Dahl, "Never, Never, Never Let Them Near a Television Set!", from *Charlie and the Chocolate Factory,* © Unwin Hyman Ltd., London 1967. 4.7 "The Perfect Match", *Scholastic Scope Magazines,* November 5, 1970, New York. 4.8 Kurt Vonnegut: "EPICAC", from *Welcome to the Monkey House,* © Jonathan Cape, London. 5.1 Sue Townsend: from *The Secret Diary of Adrian Mole Aged 13 3/4,* © Methuen London 1982. 5.2 "Not Enough Homework?": compiled from interviews by the authors. 5.3 "Opting out of College": compiled from an interview by the authors. 5.4 Margaret Drabble: "Elders and Betters?", © *The Observer* October 9, 1977, London. 5.5 "The Teacher and the Pupil", compiled from an interview by the authors. 5.6 Sally Pearce: "Worlds Apart: The Teenagers of Two Very Different English Towns" 5.7 "There Shouldn't Be a Difference", compiled from an interview by the authors. 5.8 John McClintock: "Next Time", © John McClintock. 5.9 Henry Slesar: "Examination Day", H. M. H. Publishing Inc., New York. 6.1 "Sweet Sixteen", from *Cross Section,* © Liber Läromedel, Malmö, Sweden 1986. 6.2 Keith Dewhurst: "Last Bus", © Keith Dewhurst, by permission of London Management. 6.3 "Riding the New York Subway", from *Cross Section,* © Liber Läromedel, Malmö, Sweden 1986. 6.4 Angelica Gibbs: "The Test", from *The World's Best Stories,* The New Yorker Magazine, Inc., 1968. 6.5 "All God's Creatures": compiled from an interview by the authors. 6.6 John McClintock: "This is British Telecom", © John McClintock. 6.7 Jeffrey Archer: "Broken Routine" from *A Quiver Full of Arrows,* © Hodder and Stoughton Ltd., Sevenoaks, Kent.

Illustrations

p. 16 John Patrick Byrne; p. 18 Ullstein Bilderdienst; p. 23 Thomas Müller, Göttingen; p. 39 Pressens Bild AG; p. 44/45 Julia Walch, Bad Soden; p. 47 Rodin, Grande main crispée avec figure implorante; p. 48 Charles M. Schulz, Hodder Fawcett Ltd; p. 62 Friends of the Earth; p. 67 Reprinted by permission of Faber and Faber Ltd from 'What on earth ...?' edited by Judith Nicholls, illustration by Alan Baker; p. 70 Barry Fantoni; p. 71 *The Times* 8. 2. 1989; p. 82 Thomas Müller, Göttingen; p. 92 above: *The Times* 12. 4. 1988, below: *The Guardian* 14. 4. 1988; p. 93 Thomas Müller, Göttingen; p. 97 *Observer Magazine*; p. 107/108 Thomas Müller, Göttingen; p. 111 DIE ZEIT, 21. 4. 1989; p. 121 *The Guardian Weekly,* 28. 5. 1989; p. 125 *The Guardian,* 8. 6. 1989; p. 128 Gary Larson, © 1990 by Universal Press Syndicate reprinted by permission of Editors Press Service, Inc.; p. 137 James Thurber, Hamish Hamilton Ltd.; p. 138 Times Newspapers Ltd.; p. 143 Auth, © 1979 by Universal Press Syndicate, reprinted by permission of Editors Press Service, Inc.; p. 147 TIME, 1. 5. 1989; p. 155 Thomas Müller, Göttingen; p. 163 Gary Larson, © 1990 by Universal Press Syndicate, reprinted by permission of Editors Press Service, Inc.; p. 170 *Sunday Times*; p. 180 Erich Rauschenbach, Cartoon-Caricature-Contor; p. 186 Les Gibbard, London; p. 189 Joachim Zwick, Gießen; p. 196 Thomas Müller, Göttingen; p. 200 Gary Larson, © 1990 by Universal Press Syndicate, reprinted by permission of Editors Press Service, Inc.; p. 208 TIME, 21. 8. 1989; p. 216 Joachim Zwick, Gießen; p. 227 Thomas Müller, Göttingen.

The editor and publishers are grateful to the authors, publishers and others who have given permission for the use of copyright material identified in the text. It has not been possible to identify the sources of all the material used and in such cases the publishers would welcome information from copyright owners.

987 654 321